THE POLITICS OF
GOVERNMENT GROWTH

LIBRARY OF POLITICS AND SOCIETY
General Editor Michael Hurst

*Church Embattled: Religious Controversy
in Mid-Victorian England* by M. A. Crowther

THE POLITICS OF GOVERNMENT GROWTH
Early Victorian Attitudes
Toward State Intervention,
1833–1848

William C. Lubenow

DAVID & CHARLES
ARCHON BOOKS 1971

This edition first published in 1971 in
Great Britain by David & Charles (Pub-
lishers) Limited, Newton Abbot, Devon
and in the United States of America by
Archon Books, Hamden, Connecticut
07514

ISBN 0 7153 5159 1 (*Great Britain*)
ISBN 0–208–01227–3 (*United States*)

Set in eleven on twelve point Imprint
and printed in Great Britain
by Latimer Trend & Company Limited Plymouth

TO MY MOTHER
AND THE MEMORY OF
MY FATHER

Contents

7

Foreword

MUCH HAS been written concerning the modifications in British government in the nineteenth century which G. M. Young called 'the emergence of a new State philosophy' and which O. O. G. M. MacDonagh calls 'the nineteenth-century revolution in government'.[1] As a result of this interest, the interpretation of Victorian politics found in Albert Venn Dicey's *Law and Public Opinion in England* (1905) has been revised. The early Victorian period is no longer seen as an age of laissez-faire and the growth of the central government is now generally recognised by the students of Victorian politics. Yet while Dicey's interpretation is dead, its ghost continues to animate much of the discussion of Victorian administrative history, and his categories of discussion, with a special emphasis upon a polarised tension between 'individualism' and 'collectivism', are retained.

Dicey's ghost is a troubling intellectual phenomenon for two reasons. My reading of parliamentary debates and political pamphlets suggests that the expressions 'individualism' and 'collectivism' were not used in the discussions over government growth in the 1830s and 1840s. Moreover, the *Oxford English Dictionary* dates the first use of those expressions to the 1880s. More important, however, the continued use of Dicey's categories indicates that the historiography of Victorian government growth has imposed a conceptual framework upon early and mid-nineteenth-century politics that, whatever its values for understanding the late Victorian period, is inadequate for the analysis of political issues earlier in the century. For example, in the 1830s and 1840s, industrial and corporation management was frequently perceived in terms other than that of an individualistic ethic. In the controversy over railway regulation, railways were not conceived as the empires of individuals riding roughshod over the rest of humanity. They were taken to be analogues to the turnpike trust and canal companies already in existence. Railways were regarded as local associations possessing delegated authority to make improvements.[2] They were understood to have both a public as well as a private character. Railway companies derived their authority from parliament and conferred benefits upon the public at large rather than to just the narrow circle of railway directors and shareholders.

Moreover, though the central government came to play an increasing role in the nineteenth century, it is not appropriate to say that the structure of government was transformed during the 1830s and 1840s from an 'individualistic' to a 'collectivistic' system. Since the new poor law, the railway acts of the 1840s, the factory acts, and the Public Health Act did not provide for the nationalisation of public services or of the means of production and distribution it is difficult to see how they can be considered 'collectivist' measures. In each case, as this study seeks to show, instead of focusing power in a highly centralised system, a considerable sphere of action was left to local and corporate authorities. The administrative system in the 1850s, to use language familiar to readers of Jeremy Bentham's *Constitutional Code*, more closely resembled a 'federative' than it did a 'simple' structure of government. Power continued to be distributed among a range of authorities rather than tightly centralised in a single authority.

This study, benefiting from the extensive prosopographical, psephological, and sociological research into the structures of Victorian politics over the past several years, rejects the easy formulations of government growth provided by misleading conceptualisations such as 'individualism', 'collectivism', and 'laissez-faire'. Rather than seeing administrative reform in the 1830s and 1840s as the creation of a 'welfare state', this essay views the issue of government growth in the terms emerging from Gash's, Hanham's, and D. C. Moore's reappraisal of nineteenth-century British politics. Building upon the recent research on the character of Victorian politics and administrative history, the issues involved in the controversy over government growth are re-examined and reinterpreted, while being placed in the context of early Victorian political discourse. To put the matter another way, this study, as an essay in popular political culture, examines the context of early

Victorian political opinion and attitude and seeks to show that
government growth was less informed by novel values than it was
by traditional assumptions. Rather than resurrecting old and
outworn controversies for antiquarian purposes, an attempt is
made to examine attitudes towards the role and function of
government on the level of political practice for the purpose of
formulating and testing generalisations concerning the nature of
and attitudes towards government growth and state intervention
in early Victorian Britain.

The most important sources used for this book include the
parliamentary debates as published by Hansard, the reports of the
Select Committees of the House of Commons and the Royal
Commissions concerned with social issues. To a somewhat lesser
extent the division lists of the House of Commons and the private
papers of eminent Victorian politicians provided valuable information and insights into the issues discussed. In addition, I have
found the ephemeral political pamphlet literature and contemporary periodicals and newspapers from the second quarter of the
nineteenth century an invaluable mine of information. These
latter materials are not merely of incidental importance. Political
pamphlets and periodical materials provide a kind of mirror and
measuring stick against which political discussion was reflected
and evaluated. Far from being just an additional source of data,
these materials were themselves part of the matrix of Victorian
political debate. The casual reader might be struck by the quantity
of examples used to support the generalisations formulated in this
study. However, since many of these materials have not been
subjected to systematic analysis, and since this book suggests a
departure from the usual interpretation of these issues, it seemed
wise to provide several relevant examples.

The scope of this study is the period from the passing of the
Factory Act in 1833 to the passing of the Public Health Act (1848).
These fifteen years, the age of Chartism, the Anti-Corn Law
League, the Hungry Forties, and the Irish Famine, seemed appropriate for study because they were a period of intense social
conflict as well as extensive government growth. Four of the most
famous cases of government growth in the first half of the nineteenth century are examined. Each case represents the efforts of
the Government to come to grips with the fundamental social and

economic problems created by industrial development and social dislocation. The new poor law attempted to deal with the problem of pauperism. The Public Health Act sought to provide the governmental machinery for dealing with the sanitary problems occasioned by increased urbanisation and urban disease. The railway acts were directed to the problem of economic monopoly, and the factory acts dealt with the hours and conditions of child labour in the factories. Other cases, such as the work of the Committee of the Privy Council on Education or the administrative machinery to provide assistance for famine-stricken Ireland, might have been chosen. They were not ignored because they were considered unimportant: rather, I have left them to another occasion because they raise problems quite different from those to be considered here. Since the character of this study is analytical rather than narrative, these cases will be considered topically rather than chronologically.

Based on these four case studies, this book seeks to test three generalisations concerning early Victorian government growth. First, that rather than establishing a welfare state through collectivistic legislation, the nineteenth-century revolution in government consisted of modifications in the administrative structure in which new structural forms were blended with the old in a kind of Victorian compromise which provided for a co-operative arrangement of central and local administrative forms. Second, that the opposition to these measures was based less upon laissez-faire theories emphasising a natural social and economic order than upon historical and legal assumptions and values which stressed concepts of English history, Common Law, and the English constitution. When economic arguments were used, they were most often directed to a concern for cheap government and a strong, healthy economy. Third, that the nineteenth-century revolution in government was encouraged and stimulated not by Benthamite theories of government but by social and demographic pressures manifest in the Blue Books of the parliamentary investigations, which stood as an implicit criticism of existing conditions and provided an explicit witness for the necessity of reform.

I must thank many people for their help in the preparation of this book. Dr William O. Aydelotte supervised my research while I was preparing an early version of this study as a PhD dissertation at the University of Iowa. Since then he has been generous with his advice and encouragement. Dr Rosalie L. Colie provided gracious help in the form of conversations which, while they were directed to quite different issues, stimulated and illuminated my work. In addition she gave generously of her time by reading an earlier draft of this book and gave valuable stylistic and substantive suggestions. Taking precious time from his own research, Dr David Roberts read the dissertation draft and provided invaluable suggestions for its improvement. Dr Laurence Lafore gave me the benefits of his reading of Victorian politics in several valuable conversations. Mr Michael Hurst has been very helpful in the preparation of this manuscript for publication and Mrs Pamela Thomas has been both kind and patient in the final stages of research and writing.

I wish to acknowledge the gracious permission of Her Majesty Queen Elizabeth II to make use of the letters of Sir Robert Peel to Queen Victoria preserved in the Royal Archives at Windsor Castle, a microfilm positive of which is located in the library of the University of Iowa. I also wish to thank Sir Fergus Graham, Bart, KBE, for his permission to use the papers of his great-grandfather, a microfilm positive of which is located at the Newberry Library, Chicago, Illinois. Dr Lawrence Towner and Mr James Wells, the Director and Associate Director of the Newberry Library, have been most helpful on those occasions when I have had the good fortune to work in their fine library. In addition, I must thank the Trustees of the Newberry Library for the generous gift of a grant-in-aid during the summer of 1969 which greatly facilitated the last stages of my research.

Finally I wish to thank the staffs of the library of the University of Iowa, the Newberry Library, and the Princeton University library for their time and efforts. The following people deserve my thanks for their patient kindnesses: Mr James Graham, Mr James Hamilton, Mrs Christine Lubenow, Mr Robert Omick, Mr Thomas Schlereth, and the members of the Central College Research Council. I must conclude these acknowledgements with the formal statement that, even after all this help, advice, and kindness, the defects remaining are my responsibility alone.

W. C. L.

Notes to the Foreword will be found on page 189.

Chapter 1 GOVERNMENT GROWTH IN EARLY VICTORIAN ENGLAND
The Context, 1833–1848

Session after session we are amplifying the province of the Legislature, and asserting its moral prerogatives. Parliament aspires to be the *pater patriae*, and is laying aside the policeman, the gaoler, and the executioner, in exchange for the more kindly and dignified functions of the father, the schoolmaster, and the friend.

The Times (4 May 1847)

I

IN 1832, the great reform year, the central agencies of the British government concerned with domestic affairs were small by Continental standards. Where the French Minister of the Interior had a staff of 200,000 subordinates dispersed throughout the country, the staff of the British Home Secretary consisted of only twenty-nine men. Between 1833 and 1848 the British system of domestic administration was significantly modified. In response to the massive social, economic, and demographic changes which posed significant threats to the social and political security of the country, central commissions were created to aid in the government of several aspects of the national life. Those included pauper relief, public health, railways, the factory system, prisons, education, mining, and emigration. Professor David Roberts has identified sixteen distinct and discrete central agencies created for such purposes in the second quarter of the nineteenth century.[1]

These modifications in the British administrative structure involved not only a quantitative proliferation of central agencies but important qualitative changes as well, the most important of which was the addition of central inspection to the system of social administration. Indeed, in Professor Roberts's view, inspection was the chief feature of the early Victorian administrative state.[2] The problems of government in the first half of the nineteenth century, as Dr Kitson Clark has indicated, demanded a systematic collection of facts and statistics. As a consequence, Edwin Chadwick, Leonard Horner, William Farr, James Kay-Shuttleworth, Sir John Simon, and a host of others participated in social investigations which produced a vast amount of demographic and environmental information relating to life and labour in a society being transformed by industrial pressures.[3] These changes in the British administrative structure were of great political significance for they provided one of the means for shaping and disciplining the formative social forces of the early Victorian period. Combining with the growth of the permanent civil service, these modifications made their contribution to the creation of the modern structure of the British state, with its government by experts and delegated authority.[4]

A preliminary perspective is required if the nineteenth-century revolution in government is to be perceived in terms of early Victorian thought and action. This perspective can, perhaps, best be obtained by understanding Victorian administrative modification in three contexts: the structural context of local and national government; the context of the philanthropic ideal; and the context of attitude and opinion in early Victorian Britain.

II

Before 1833, English local government consisted of approximately 15,500 parishes, each with autonomous responsibility for the management of poor relief, the maintenance of highways, and the policing of the countryside. In addition, 5,000 Crown-appointed justices of the peace were charged with the administration of justice and the management of jails and asylums. Finally, 200 boroughs chartered by the Crown were administered by bailiffs, mayors, and aldermen. Courts leet, courts barons, courts sewers, and approximately 1,800 special authorities provided by parliament for the establishment of special poor-relief authorities, turnpike trusts, and local improvement commissions were superimposed on this structure.[5]

Sydney and Beatrice Webb characterised the years between the Glorious Revolution and the Municipal Corporations Act (1835) as a period of local independence in which Crown and parliament were largely indifferent to the concerns and work of local administrative bodies. For the Webbs, this was a period in which the justices of the peace indulged themselves in absolute independence from central control and authority. In their view, the anarchy and autonomy of the local authorities in the eighteenth century precluded anything which could be considered a 'system' of local government. Such government as there was consisted of 'a confused network of local customs and the Common Law, of canon law and royal decrees or charters, interspersed with occasional and unsystematic parliamentary statutes'.[6]

The industrial revolution eroded whatever merit existed in the structure of local government in the eighteenth century. The growth of population centres and the great increase of pauperism, crime, and sedition undercut the traditions of local government, which were enshrined in custom, Common Law, and Tudor-Stuart legislation.[7] Undermined by new social pressures and inherent political corruption, the institutions of local government became incapacitated and distrusted. In an address to the Health of Towns Association, Hugh Fortescue Fortescue, Viscount Ebrington said:

> . . . the corporations had ceased to represent the wants and feelings of the citizens, and therefore had ceased to be trusted by them. They had become a self-elected clique, with interests in many cases opposed to those of the community, instead of being a popular body trusted and looked up to by their fellow citizens. They had been for years in many respects untrustworthy, and therefore they were not trusted; and being trusted no longer they became untrustworthy, in others.[8]

Between 1833 and 1836 new political values were applied to the structure of local government.[9] These new principles were contained in the Poor Law Amendment Act (1834), which created a new system of local government areas for the administration of poor relief; the Municipal Corporations Act (1835); and the Act for Registering Births, Deaths, and Marriages (1836), which created the Office of the Registrar-General for the systematic collection of social statistics. The Municipal Corporations Act was

B

especially important, since it ended the oligarchical government of the towns which fell under its provisions by providing for the election of town councillors by the rate-paying householders. The town councillors were authorised by this Act to elect mayors and aldermen. Further, the Act enabled local officials to take over the elementary functions of local government, including the control of the constabulary force and lighting, as well as the power to make bylaws for the curtailment of nuisances. The new principles of local government were also expressed in new statutory authorities, which provided for the creation of *ad hoc* local boards for the construction and maintenance of sewers, turnpikes, paving, and lighting.

In spite of these measures local government was not systematised or rationalised in the 1830s. The Municipal Corporations Act applied to only 178 chartered boroughs. Non-chartered boroughs could adopt the provisions of the Act only by a complicated procedure. The creation of new statutory authorities did nothing to simplify the structure of local government, which remained a confused and tangled overlapping of authorities and institutions in the continual process of growth and decay. As the Webbs pointed out, in the 1840s as in the 1690s there was nothing systematic or coherent about English local government.[10]

The central administration of Britain before 1833 employed but 21,305 civilian officials, the largest number of them working in the revenue departments. Of these, the largest was the Board of Customs with 9,459 employees, and the second largest was the Board of Excise with 6,377 employees. The military departments employed 1,740 civilian officials. Other departments of the central government were small indeed: the departments for external affairs employed only 106, and the departments for internal affairs only 101. The central bureaucracy for the management of the Crown properties consisted of eleven men.[11]

Yet, the small size of the central administration should not lead one to assume that government never interfered in the jurisdictions of the local authorities. Perhaps the recent interest in the nineteenth-century revolution in government has diverted attention from those functions of the central government which had traditionally impinged upon the country as a whole. Parliament was the chief source of this continuing interventionism. Since the seventeenth century the sovereignty of Parliament had been regarded as total and absolute. As Coke put it:

Of the power and jurisdiction of the Parliament, for making of laws in proceeding by bill, it is so transcendent and absolute, as it cannot be confined either for persons or causes within any bounds. Of this Court it is truly said: *Si antiquitatem spectes, est vetustissma, si dignitatem, est honoratissma, si jurisdictionem, est capacissima.*[12]

Most local authorities obtained their authority from parliamentary statute and none could contravene one. Parliament, as Professor Roberts has indicated, could establish any judicial or administrative authority it wished and could legislate on any matter. Indeed, since the Elizabethan period parliament had passed all manner of social and economic legislation.[13] The central government also touched on the life of the country in other ways. The justices of the peace were selected by the Crown and sworn in by the lord chancellor. The Board of Excise, although poorly organised and recruited by patronage, affected the life of the average Englishman directly. The same might be said of the Board of Customs and the Post Office Department. In addition, even before 1833, commissions for penitentiaries, metropolitan lunatic asylums, metropolitan turnpike roads, and temporary commissions of inquiry for the poor law, the factory system, and municipal corporations were already attached to the Home Office.

The second context in which the nineteenth-century revolution in government should be appreciated is the continuing philanthropic tradition. The growth of the central government between 1833 and 1848 did not mean that public authorities superseded private agents in the attempt to alleviate the sufferings occasioned by economic, social, and technological transformations. Private philanthropy continued to be important all through the century. Beatrice Webb said that the elimination of private charity was one of the more significant changes which had occurred in her own lifetime.[14] As Professor Owen has suggested, Victorian philanthropy went a long way and attained significant victories in the relief of social tensions in the nineteenth century. Private charity was a 'principal weapon of the nation during the age of intermittent crisis'.[15]

Two examples may serve to show the way in which continuing

private philanthropy paralleled the growth of government in the early Victorian period. On 7 May 1842 Sir Robert Peel met with Sir James Graham, his Home Secretary, and the Archbishop of Canterbury to discuss working-class poverty in the neighbourhood of Paisley and in some of the manufacturing towns of Lancashire. As Peel noted, the local funds for pauper relief were nearly exhausted and the local magistrates warned of fearsome consequences if those funds became completely depleted. Peel, Graham, and the Archbishop did not determine upon a programme of state action to meet the pressing needs of the working classes in those areas. Rather, they called for an effort to stimulate private benevolence and charity. As Peel put it in a letter to Queen Victoria:

> Under these circumstances it appeared to Sir Robert Peel and Sir James Graham that the occasion would be a very fitting one (if your Majesty could be pleased to sanction it) for the issue of a Queen's Letter inviting Charitable contributions for the relief of the sufferers in the several Churches and Chapels of the Country —This was done on a former occasion in the case of distress in Ireland and also in the case of distress in the manufacturing districts of Great Britain. Independently of the actual relief which would be afforded by such contributions—the moral effect of a demonstration of a general sympathy with the distressed—and of approval of their peacable [sic] conduct and submission to the laws might be very advantageous.[16]

On 6 February 1846, after the failure of the Irish potato crop, Sir James Graham, in a letter to the Lord Lieutenant of Ireland, explained his views on the use of public monies for the relief of the stricken population. He recognised that a case had been made for government intervention by those who argued that the government must step in and fill the place of those Irish landowners who were either unwilling or unable to provide for the relief of their tenants and neighbours. Nevertheless, Graham 'directed that except in cases of the last extremity Public Money should not be granted unless the Gift were met by an equal Subscription from the Neighbourhood'.[17] Thus, Graham required that private philanthropy should determine the extent of public assistance: public assistance was not to take the place of charity.

The continuance of private philanthropy testifies to the persistence of aristocratic values and traditions of *noblesse oblige* in the nineteenth century. As a consequence, frequently discussion of government growth was framed in the language of upper-class responsibility and paternalism. *The Times*, as the prescript at the head of this chapter indicates, saw parliament as a *pater patriae* with the benevolent characteristics of a father, teacher, and friend rather than the harsher qualities of the policeman, jailer, and executioner. The report of the Health of Towns Committee in 1840 pointed out the obligation of the 'Government and the more opulent classes' to care for the needs of the industrious classes of the community.[18] In 1841, Lord Normanby, in a debate on the health of towns issue, appealed to the peerage's 'high character', 'kindness of feeling', and the habit of charity which they traditionally practised in their own regions but which now must be extended to society as a whole.[19] Sir John Simon, the medical officer of the City of London, insisted that the poorer classes had insufficient power to initiate model-dwellings projects. Therefore, he turned to the wealthier classes and suggested they give the working classes the benefit of their 'patronage and succour' in this matter or else turn the project over to the Common Council of the City.[20] In 1847, *Fraser's Magazine* referred to an adequate sanitary measure as an aspect of 'benevolent and paternal government'.[21] On 10 May 1844, *The Times* put the matter this way:

> Let the Government and the institutions of the country cease to be gracious and beneficial. Let the people see a gorgeous structure of ranks and dignitaries, which only contrasts with their own degradation. Let there be gold and glitter, but no universal light and warmth. . . . There can be one only consequence. You are vitiating and destroying the very soil wherein all this grandeur is planted, and whence it derives its beauty. The affections of the people cannot long survive. That ancient dream of a sacred and gracious Government will shortly pass away. Soon the aristocratical institutions of the Country will stand alone, naked and helpless, in an uncongenial region, and become a fiction of antiquity.

In these ways, the tradition of paternalistic philanthropy played an important role in the shaping of men's understanding of government growth in early Victorian England.

This is not to say that the philanthropic tradition was uniformly accepted and admired. John Stuart Mill was aware that the incidence of philanthropy had increased during the 1840s. In his view, philanthropy was both inadequate and superficial. Mill believed that its growth was fostered by the anti-poor-law movement in the north of England; the sanitary condition of the towns, which was the subject of Chadwick's famous Sanitary Report; the condition of the working classes in the mines and factories as revealed in the reports of the Royal Commissions; and the speculations of Carlyle and the Puseyites. These philanthropists, according to Mill, were motivated by a concern to avoid revolution and 'the desire to take the popularis [sic] aura out of the sails of the Anti-Corn Law League'.[22] An article in the *Westminster Review* considered charity a 'vulgar, shallow, and aristocratic' misconception, which informed all the ameliorative measures of the powerful and mighty. The *Westminster Review* demanded the removal of social problems, not just relief from them. It demanded justice rather than concessions. The same article stated: 'We are weary of this cuckoo-cry—always *charity, never justice*, always the *open purse*, never the equal measure'.[23]

The third context in which government growth should be viewed is the twisted and complicated pattern of thought and opinion in early Victorian Britain. Certainly classical political economy constituted a broad and thoughtful body of intelligent opinion. The work of the classical economists raised all the major issues of economic policy of the age. Yet, while recent scholarship has taught us not to expect complete opposition to government growth from them, one is surprised to find they spoke neither to common purpose nor to common effect with regard to these issues. As Mark Blaug has observed, there was no specific theory of economic policy in Ricardian economics. As a consequence one finds a wide range of attitudes towards state intervention in the writings of the economists. Edward Kittrell has been only the most recent scholar to show that laissez-faire was never a dogmatic formulation in classical political economy, but was always subject to the practical test of utility.[24]

Abstract theories, for example, apparently were of little immediate usefulness in the shaping of the policy positions of Nassau Senior. Senior favoured the Poor Law Amendment Act while, at the same time, opposing the Ten Hours Bill. As his *Letter to Lord*

Howick (1831) shows, Senior believed the problem of Irish poverty
could be solved neither by time nor free trade. Pauperism, in his
view, was a vast social problem which required vigilant central
supervision for the continuing correction and adjustment of the
poor-law administration. Indeed, once such intervention was
judged expedient, the continuing action of the government was
less its right than its duty.[25]

The case of the poor law reflects ideological uncertainty in other
ways. In the first edition of his *Essay on the History of the English
Government and Constitution* (1821), Lord John Russell recommended a Malthusian remedy—the elimination of relief—as the
only effectual theoretical solution to the problem of the poor laws.
In the second edition, published only two years later, the Malthusian corrective was omitted and replaced by a more pragmati-
cally limited proposal. Russell observed: 'The poor laws must be
pruned, not rooted up; the knife, and not the axe, must be used'.[26]
Similarly, Lord Brougham, in his speech on the poor laws in the
House of Lords, praised Malthus as the contributor of a major
addition to the science of political philosophy, but alluded to
English history, the findings of the Royal Commission, and the
practical experience of politicians in finding a solution to the
problem of the poor laws.[27]

Laissez-faire theories were also of little guidance in the attempts
of the economists to find a consistent policy position concerning
the relationship of the state to the burgeoning railway system.
Even the most inveterate champions of free trade could apparently
accept state intervention so long as the normal market mechanisms
failed to cope with the problems of monopoly and excessive
speculation.[28] The Political Economy Club, to take but one important body of economic thought, after a discussion of public
control over the railways in 1842, agreed unanimously that they
should be placed under the custody of the state.[29] John Stuart Mill
held laissez-faire to be the general rule in economic policy matters.
However, even as a general rule, laissez-faire was not adequate as
a guiding principle when considering the relationship of the
government to roads, canals, and railways. Railways, in Mill's
view, were 'practical monopolies'. As such, the state should either
preserve for itself a 'reversionary property' in these ventures, or
'retain, and freely exercise, the right of fixing a maximum of

fares and charges, and from time to time varying that maximum'.[30]

The discussion of the factory question was also characterised by uncertainty and inconsistency among intelligent opinion. James Ramsay McCulloch favoured and praised Lord Ashley's Ten Hours Bill in 1833. George Poulett Scrope, while viewing the government bill of 1833 with disfavour, believed it was 'necessitated by the circumstances of the times'. Colonel Robert Torrens represents a peculiarly ambiguous case: he supported the Ten Hours measure in 1833 but opposed it in 1844. Nevertheless, as his *Letter to Lord Ashley* (1844) shows, Torrens rejected the maxim of laissez-faire but opposed Ashley's bill after considering the more practical matters of wage levels, the health of industry, and the threat of foreign competition. Nassau Senior based his objection to the ten hours bill on similar considerations.[31]

If one fails to find consistent attitudes towards government growth in the writing of the economists, one is even more pressed to identify coherent patterns of opinion in the intelligent public at large. In reading Hansard, the mass of pamphlet literature, and the quarterlies one can only be struck by the differences of opinion with regard to the role of the state. One can only conclude, the frequent generalisations about Victorian optimism to the contrary, that Victorian England possessed little confident certainty when it came to the issues involved in the role of the government, the character of administration, and the responses to the problems of industrialisation. Party attitudes and loyalties, as Professor Gash has indicated, provided no basis for agreement on these matters.[32] The proceedings of the House of Commons reveal, as W. L. Burn wisely suggests, that a member of parliament might support government growth on one measure of policy, but might just as easily oppose it on the next.[33] These attitudinal self-contradictions were not at all uncommon. Even a national institution with the stature of *The Times* opposed government growth in the form of the new poor law, but supported it in the form of the Public Health Act. George Cornwall Lewis, the Liberal statesman, who was the son of a Poor Law Commissioner and a Poor Law Commissioner himself, as well as a patient and careful participant in the discussion of interventionist issues, recognised the uncertainty characterising the discussion of these measures:

Interferences with the freedom of labour and capital, which one party consider as fraught with ruin to the prosperity of the country, are regarded by the other as ranking amongst the first duties of a Christian and humane legislature. On most subjects the divergence of opinion between opposite political parties is rather one of *degree* than *principle*. But with respect to legislation for the working classes, there is a thorough anarchy of opinion;— maxims, which some people regard as forming the very corner-stone of the existing order of society, are by others utterly repudiated, as fit only for savages and heathens.

The discussion of legislation for the working classes, as Lewis observed it, was void of common principles and common assumption; it was 'unconnected and multifarious'.[34]

While the attitudinal pattern of Victorian Britain presents important difficulties and ambiguities, it is neither beyond analysis nor comprehension. Recent research has gone a long way towards a description of the fundamental assumptions which governed constituency politics in the periods following the great nineteenth-century reform bills. Valuable insights have been obtained by examinations of the poll books of contested elections, as well as the use of technically sophisticated methods to tap a previously untouched treasury of voting data in the divisions lists of the House of Commons.[35] Taken together, these researches have done much to indicate and illuminate the essential continuities and discontinuities of Victorian political life. With regard to the subject of early Victorian government growth, the British political community was divided between two overlapping models of political behaviour containing the assumptions and implications underlying two very different conceptions of politics and public policy.

The first of these models stresses essential political continuities, and consequently places primary emphasis on the concept of a natural social order based upon custom, tradition, and the sanctity of historic political and social institutions. In accord with these assumptions, state action in the early nineteenth century was sharply governed and limited by localist and traditionalist pre-dispositions. The early Victorian administrative system consisted of a combination of central and local authorities which provided central supervision while allowing for improved local administration. Just as important, the debate over government growth was often conducted in the language of the Common Law tradition, political custom, constitutional practice, and historical precedent. In turn, political and social concepts such as the 'ancient Saxon constitution' and 'local self-government' were idealised within this historical and legal context. The organic model of politics based upon custom and tradition was used by men of all political affiliations. Conservatives, such as Oastler, Disraeli, and Sibthorp, as well as Reformers like John Walter and Radicals like Thomas Wakley and G. F. Muntz used analogies drawn from English history.

As one might expect, some of the more important intellectual sources for this organic model of politics were provided by the mass of historical writings produced in the first half of the nineteenth century, including synoptic accounts of English history by Sharon Turner, John Lingard, Henry Hallam, and Thomas Babington Macaulay; the attempt to recover and preserve the documents of the English past by the Record Commission, the Camden Society, and the Aelfric, Surtees, Shakespeare, and Parker Societies; and a major revival of Anglo-Saxon studies by John Mitchell Kemble, Sir Francis Palgrave, Benjamin Thorpe and Joseph Bosworth.[36] This body of historical literature contained a number of themes which were reiterated in the state-intervention controversy. These themes included a veneration for an heroic English past, a reverent confidence in the relevance of Anglo-Saxon law, the certainty of progressive improvement, and an insistence upon the tradition of English limited government.

The second pattern of political behaviour evident in the debate over government growth can best be described as an exercise in incrementalist politics.[37] To emphasise an incrementalist concept of politics suggests that early Victorian government growth was neither a result of a carefully prepared blueprint for political change nor a consequence of a comprehensive and exhaustive policy analysis. Rather, government growth, as a part of normal political life, was a matter of selecting from viable political alternatives that differed from each other only in small degrees. Consequently, from this point of view, the political values at stake were not the absolute values of 'laissez-faire', 'local self-government', or 'Anglo-Saxon freedom'. The question was not whether the state should intervene or not. Instead, for those who viewed government growth in incrementalist terms, the values at issue were the marginal values of the manner and the extent of state intervention. Government growth was characterised by a certain indefiniteness. Instead of a programme for administrative reform designed to produce a collectivist utopia, state intervention consisted of a series of legislative actions which produced modifications in the existing administrative structure. In addition, incrementalist government growth was characterised by a probing quality. As new administrative and political experience produced new information about desirable objectives, the very goals of public policy shifted. Experience derived from continuing administrative and political activity was a major element in incrementalist government intervention. The language and argument of government growth based upon incrementalist assumptions was derived from the major repositories of administrative and political experience: the records of the Registrar-General, the reports of the Poor Law Commissioners, and the Blue Books of parliamentary investigations. While those who prefer a more omniscient and directive kind of policy formulation have cavilled at incrementalist politics, it has, as Professor Popper notes, the advantage of producing information about environmental problems and government responses which might not be known in any other way.[38]

Participants in the Victorian debate on state intervention, aware they were dealing with incrementalist issues, had a variety of responses. Joshua Toulmin Smith, an extremely articulate critic of government growth, denounced it, stating: 'we are losing sight daily, more and more, of *principles* and are allowing ourselves to be made the dupes of presumptuous *empiricism*'.[39] On the other hand, George Cornwall Lewis was obviously favouring social amelioration by an incremental process when he urged the creation of a new 'form of society resembling the present, with its evils diminished, and its characteristic excellences increased and diffused'. Lewis, in describing those who held similar views to his own, said:

> They do not disguise from themselves the uncertainty and risk which attend all political and social reformations. They are aware of the blindness even of the most keensighted, when the future is

concerned. They admit that society advances by groping its way in the dark, like miners exploring a vein. But they can discover no other mode of social progress, and they believe that experience, the only light, points steadily in this direction.[40]

Macaulay not only approved of the politics of incrementalism, he characterised the politics of caring 'nothing for symmetry and much of convenience' as the major theme in the work of parliaments from the age of King John to that of Queen Victoria.[41] Government growth following an incremental process of legislative behaviour may have been objectionable to some, but proponents as well as opponents of state intervention accepted its reality. As such, incrementalism constituted one of the major modes of political discussion in the consideration of early Victorian public policy.

The organic model of political discussion and its incrementalist counterpart were not mutually exclusive; at times they overlapped. For example, George Cornwall Lewis, for all his talk of society 'groping its way', included a comparative analysis of working-class history in his elucidation of the problems of social legislation.[42] Similarly, Lord Brougham's analysis of the poor law on the floor of the House of Lords contained, in addition to a discussion of the general principles at issue and the evidences of the Royal Commission, an appraisal of the history of the Elizabethan poor law and an idealisation of the life of the independent yeoman and master-servant relationships before the establishment of the allowance system.[43]

All of this suggests that, while the context of attitude and opinion concerning government growth was rich and complex, there was a complicated but clear pattern consisting of two alternative ways of viewing the problems of politics and society: (i) an organic model resting on historical and legal presuppositions, and (ii) an incrementalist model based upon a concern for political and administrative experience. These alternative perspectives, based on quite different assumptions, quite naturally posed different political and social priorities. Together they formed the cross-axes of the intellectual matrix within which the discussion of government growth occurred.

III

The context within which government growth and state intervention occurred was one of tension and conflict. Traditional institutions and values, exposed to the severe tests of industrial development and population shifts, were challenged by new social realities expressed in the increasing poor-rates and statistics revealing the conditions of life in the towns and labour in the factories. This tension reveals the first efforts of a nation, in the process of modernisation, to deal with major social crises. The result, as the following case studies of interventionist legislation seek to show, was an administrative system sired by the pressures of environmental change, but born in the womb of localist ideals, a continuing emphasis on private philanthropy, and traditional values.

Notes to Chapter 1 will be found on pages 189-92.

Chapter 2 CENTRAL AND LOCAL GOVERNMENT I
The Victorian Poor Law, 1834-1847

We have ever sought to exercise our powers in such a manner as to avoid all unnecessary interferences with the Boards of Guardians and other local authorities; and we have abstained carefully from doing anything which might extinguish the spirit of local independence and self-government which, when guided by an enlightened discretion, we consider the characteristic excellence of the English people. Whatever irritation which may have been caused in some places by the measures necessary for the first introduction of the law, we are satisfied that all our proceedings will, if impartially examined, be found to have been dictated by the spirit which we have just described.

*Report of the Poor Law Commissioners
to the Most Noble Marquis of Normanby*

I

POVERTY IS not the creature of an industrial society and attempts to deal with it predate the development of English industry. The Elizabethan poor law touched on the entire social and economic structure of the English state. The orphaned, the aged, the enfeebled, the unemployed, the underpaid, all came within its purview. It has been estimated that in the early nineteenth century one-fifth of the total national expenditure was disbursed under this legislation.[1] The Elizabethan poor law, furthermore, authorised parish overseers of the poor, appointed by the justices of the peace, to assess a poor-rate for the purpose of providing relief for the sick and aged and work for the unemployed. The only means for curbing the incompetence of the overseers was supervision by members of the vestry and the justices of the peace. This is not to say there were no attempts to provide national supervision. The two centuries after 1601 was a period in which there was an increased tendency towards greater executive authority through the Privy Council. In January 1631, Charles I appointed a Royal Commission which directed the justices of the peace to investigate the operation of the poor law and to levy penalties for maladministration on the part of the local authorities. However, as de Schweinitz has pointed out, localism was the chief characteristic of the administration of the old poor law.[2] Neighbours administered relief to neighbours; parishes were largely autonomous; parliamentary statutes were more frequently ignored than observed. 'There has never been a more literal demonstration of home rule.'[3]

An important innovation in the administration of the poor law was made by the magistrates of Berkshire, at Speenhamland, in 1795. That innovation was the introduction of the allowance system. Confronted with inflation and increasing hardship the Speenhamland magistrates did not fix local wages, which they had the legal authority to do. Rather, they supplemented wages of agricultural workers out of the local rates. That allowance was to be based on the cost of bread and the size of the family seeking relief. The Speenhamland solution was soon implemented in other counties. As Professor Briggs observed: 'in time "Speenhamland" became a shorthand expression for rural pauperisation'.[4]

The old poor law was censured on the ground that the parish was too small a unit for administration. The settlement laws of 1662 were criticised because they made birth or established residence a condition for the receipt of relief. Large towns, it was argued, were less able to cope with the problem of migrating poor than were the rural villages. It was recognised that social conflict, even in the traditional village, was a likely consequence of the social strains produced by poverty. Cobbett and Hunt demanded more relief in the name of the 'rights of the poor'. Owen and Attwood demanded useful work for the poor. Malthus demanded the cessation of relief altogether. The old poor law was also criticised on the ground that there was a basic inequality in the assessment of rates to provide poor relief. Since the increase of England's wealth after 1760 was chiefly in the manufacturing sector of the economy, and with the location of that wealth in the growing manufacturing centres, those communities with the highest poor-rates were not always the best able to pay.[5]

By 1832 the complex structure for the administration of the poor law, which was composed of 15,000 autonomous parishes 'affected everybody, pleased few, and was understood by nobody'.[6] A Royal Commission[7] was established to investigate the question of the poor-rate, which had increased from £1,500,000 in 1775 to £8,000,000 in 1818 and was still £7,000,000 in 1832 in spite of the fact that in the preceding decade the price of bread had declined by one-third.[8] The Royal Commission met for two years collecting evidence to demonstrate the expense and ineffectiveness of the old poor-law administration. Edwin Chadwick and Nassau Senior collaborated in writing its report,[9] which led to the formulation of the Poor Law Amendment Act (1834).

The bill for the amendment of the poor law originated with Lord Brougham and Lord Althorp, the latter the Chancellor of the Exchequer and leader of the Whigs in the House of Commons. However, before the bill was sent on to parliament it was subjected to a minute examination by a committee of the cabinet consisting of the Duke of Richmond, Lord Ripon, Sir James Graham, Lord Althorp, Lord Melbourne, and Lord John Russell.[10] The bill passed into law on 14 August 1834 after extensive debate and a series of divisions which demonstrated the overwhelming support of parliament. After eight years of controversy[11] Sir Robert Peel's government, once again, brought the new poor law before the House of Commons for renewal. Again, it received overwhelming approval. In the Webbs' considered judgement this must be regarded 'as a decisive ratification, not only of the act of 1834, but also of the general policy and the administration of the [poor law] Commissioners'.[12] In 1844 the poor law again came before parliament for minor modifications. Finally, in May of 1847, after an investigation into the scandal of bone-crushing at Andover, Sir George Grey, Lord John Russell's Home Secretary, introduced the bill that became law as the Poor Law Board Act. Under this legislation the functions of the Poor Law Commissioners were transferred to a poor-law board consisting of the Lord President of the Council, the Lord Privy Seal, the Home Secretary, and the Chancellor of the Exchequer *ex officio*, with a president eligible to sit in parliament.

The traditional interpretations of Victorian poor-law legislation have, almost without exception, emphasised its novel character. The Webbs described it as 'revolutionary legislation' giving 'a dogmatically uniform direction to English Poor Law policy'.[13] Sir William Hart regarded the new poor law as 'a practical application of Benthamite theories' which intended to 'set up almost autocratic authority in the Poor Law Commissioners with the widest powers of controlling poor law authorities in the minutest details of their work'.[14] What follows is a re-examination of early Victorian poor-law legislation and the controversies which surrounded it. The poor-law legislation of the 1830s and 1840s, as this book reveals, did not call for the complete and absolute assumption of administrative authority by the central Poor Law Board. Indeed, administrative authority remained localised. The chief criticism raised against the new poor law was that it was a despotic and unconstitutional violation of the English tradition of government. Proponents of this legislation denied the charge and viewed the new poor law as a practical and humane means for coping with a profound social problem.

II

The fundamental concern of the poor-law reformers in the 1830s was to return English paupers to a condition of economic and moral independence by eliminating the practices associated with the allowance system of the old poor law. Consequently, the twin principles guiding poor-law reform were 'the workhouse test' and 'less eligibility'. According to these principles, relief was to be granted, on a basis relatively unfavourable to independent labouring conditions, only in workhouses. The point of these considerations, of course, was to increase incentives among those seeking relief from the poor-rate by encouraging them to find their place on the open labour market. However, the Royal Commission recognised that the issues with which it was dealing were larger than the rising poor-rate and the provision of relief to the pauperised. Aware that their correctives must touch the lives and habits of those prone to pauperism, the Commissioners believed poor-law reform would provide a means 'for elevating the intellectual and moral condition of the poorer classes'.[15]

C

While no one seriously quarrelled with the typically Victorian social values of industriousness and self-reliance for the working classes, the methods for achieving those values aroused severe controversy within and without the houses of parliament. The governmental structure recommended by the Royal Commission and put into effect by the legislation of 1834 was an especial source of criticism. That government structure placed a central bureaucratic authority in a special position of responsibility with regard to matters of poor relief—matters previously under the responsibility of parochial authorities alone. However, the governmental structure of the reformed poor law had a unique double character. On the one hand, the poor-law reformers called for the creation of a central poor-law board to *supervise* the operation of the new poor law. On the other hand, reformed local authorities, acting within their local jurisdictions, were to carry on the *administration* of the poor law. The general formula adopted in early Victorian poor-law legislation, therefore, was local administration under central supervision.

The primary function of the central poor-law board was to supervise the administration of pauper relief and, thereby, gradually eliminate unsatisfactory practices by the local authorities. Central authority, as the report of the Royal Commission noted, was essential in order to provide uniform administration in a system consisting of 'upwards of 15,000 unskilled and (practically) irresponsible authorities, liable to be biased by sinister interests'.[16] The Royal Commission, however, and this point should be especially emphasised, did not intend the central poor-law board to enforce an absolute uniformity upon local administration. It recognised the compelling importance of certain local conditions and requirements and, therefore, suggested the necessity of squaring uniformity with those special conditions. Legislation reforming the poor laws, as the Royal Commissioners' report indicated, should ensure

> . . . that those modes of administering relief which have been tried wholly or partially, and have produced beneficial effects in some districts, be introduced, *with modifications according to local circumstances*, and carried into complete execution in all.[17]

One of the best means for accomplishing this object, as the report noted, was for the central agency to serve as a 'depository of comprehensive information *to guide local officers*' who had but limited knowledge and experience.[18]

The Poor Law Amendment Act authorised the central poor-law commissioners to make inquiries into the administration of the relief system. To that end they were empowered to administer oaths, to examine persons under oath, and to require such persons to produce local records dealing with the relief of the poor. In addition, and in keeping with the recommendations of the Royal Commission, the poor-law commissioners were authorised to make, issue, and alter the 'Rules, Orders, and Regulations' necessary for the direction and the management of the poor, for the government of the workhouses, and for the appointment of local officers. In addition, they were empowered to formulate specific regulations regarding the extent and period of outdoor relief for able-bodied persons and their families in a particular parish or union. They were, however, prohibited from giving a special dispensation to special cases concerning only individuals.[19]

The poor-law legislation of 1844 extended the sphere within which the commissioners could establish regulations. One such provision enabled the central board to prescribe the duties of masters to whom poor children might be apprenticed. It also came within the purview of the commissioners to require statements from all property holders giving account of their rents, property and income for the purpose of rating and the adjustment of rates.[20]

The poor-law commissioners were given the power, by the Poor Law Amendment Act, to appoint and, if necessary, recall as many as nine assistant commissioners as well as any number of secretaries, clerks, messengers and officers deemed necessary. The commissioners could delegate any of their powers to the assistant commissioners for the purpose of implementing the act. When the new poor law was renewed in 1842, the commissioners were given the additional power to delegate authority for special investigations to doctors, barristers, members of the Royal College of Surgeons, architects or surveyors. Such special delegated authority was to extend for only thirty days.[21]

The Royal Commissioners, in 1834, took pains to demonstrate the expense of poor relief under the highly decentralised system of parochial management. They, therefore, suggested the central authority should have the power to create convenient 'unions' or consolidations of parishes for the construction and management of workhouses. Parishes, they recommended further, should be incorporated into unions for purposes of appointing and paying permanent officers to administer pauper relief. The power to effect this recommendation was enacted in the Poor Law Amendment Act of 1834. The legislation of 1844 carried this further. By the act of that year, the central board was authorised to amalgamate parishes and unions for the purpose of auditing accounts, for providing school districts for poor children under sixteen years of age, and for providing and managing asylums for the temporary relief of the 'destitute harmless poor not charged with any offense'.[22] The amalgamation of parishes into poor-law unions was an especially important economic device, for through this means it was possible to recruit and finance a corps of professionally competent administrators. This was an administrative ideal which the central poor-law board would struggle to preserve in opposition to the resistance of ratepayers in poor and backward regions as well as other critics of the new poor law who opposed bureaucratic extension.[23]

The report of the Royal Commission, in attempting to deal with the problem of the embezzlement and peculation of poor-relief funds by the parish authorities, suggested the central board should be empowered to act as public prosecutor in such cases. Further, the poor-law commissioners should be authorised to 'take measures for the general adoption of a complete, clear, and as far as may be practicable, uniform system of accounts'.[24] The act of 1834, however, went only so far as to require the central commissioners to 'direct the Overseers or Guardians' of the parishes and unions to appoint officers for the purpose of auditing accounts. Nevertheless, the commissioners were empowered to relieve auditors from their duties just as they could relieve other paid officers of the unions.[25] The inability of the central board to appoint auditors was criticised on a number of occasions.[26] As a consequence, a select committee, reporting in 1838, recommended that the central board should have the power to appoint district auditors for poor-relief accounts. In 1844, poor-law legislation enabled the commissioners to appoint men who served as auditors on district poor-law school boards as auditors for the entire district.[27]

These innovations and extensions of central authority constituted a significant re-ordering of the power structure in the
administration of poor relief. However, this is but half the story.
Significant limitations were placed upon the authority and jurisdiction of the central board. It was not a permanently established
organ of the government; commissioners and assistant commissioners were limited to five-year terms. Moreover, the poor-
law act itself had to be renewed every five years. All general rules
issued by the central board were to be submitted to a 'Principal
Secretary of State' who, with the consent of the Privy Council,
could disallow such of them as he saw fit. No rule or order of the
commissioners could go into effect until forty days had elapsed and
each year the central board was required to submit a report of its
proceedings to the Home Secretary.[28] One class of parishes was
specifically excluded from the reorganisations detailed in the
legislation of 1834: those whose administrations had been established by the Act of 22 George III, c 83, usually known as Gilbert's
act. The central board, however, was authorised to issue rules for
the relief of the poor in such parishes.[29]

The report of the Royal Commission did not call for the central
authorities to take over the administration of poor-relief. The
function of the central board was, as we have seen, to guide and
assist local authorities so that their management of poor-relief
conformed to the intention of parliament. Aside from this, the
Royal Commission recommended that the management, collection of rates, and the entire supervision of expenditure for the
relief of the poor was to be in the hands of officers 'appointed
immediately by the ratepayers'.[30] By the legislation of 1834, the
central board was authorised to determine the number, duties, and
qualifications of local poor-law guardians. However, the guardians
were to be elected by the ratepayers and property owners of the
union. Once elected, the guardians were to have all 'Government
and Control' for the 'ordering, giving, and directing of all relief
to the poor'. The direct election of such local authorities constituted an important change in the structure of local government.
This did not, however, undermine their independence of the
central authorities. In the first place, guardians were very frequently chosen from those families that had always dominated the
local power structure—the landed gentry. In the second place, the

act of 1834 specifically provided the central board with the authority to alter the 'Mode of Appointment, Removal, and Period of Service' of the guardians only with the consent of a majority of the ratepayers and owners of property of a parish or union. Furthermore, the guardians, not the central board, were authorised to appoint the necessary paid officers for the administration of the poor law in each union.[31] The Royal Commission had emphasised the necessity of keeping this function in the hands of the local authorities. They felt it would be beyond the powers of the central board to recruit sufficient numbers of well qualified persons, that this would occupy too much of their time and energy, and that this 'patronage, though really a painful incumbrance to them, would be a source of public jealousy'.[32]

The Poor Law Amendment Act, while calling for the selection of a new variety of local administrators in the form of elected guardians, did not eliminate the traditional county officials from the administration of the poor law. The justices of the peace continued to sit on local poor-law boards as *ex officio* guardians with the authority to inspect workhouses, to 'disallow as illegal' all relief issued contrary to the regulations of the central board or the act of 1834, and with instructions to summon violators of regulations laid down by the central board before any other two justices. In addition, they were empowered to supervise the living and working conditions of apprentices bound under the provisions of the poor-law act. Furthermore, any two justices could dispense relief outside the workhouse to the aged and infirm.[33] While the initial importance of these magistrates was great because of their local prestige and influence, they gradually, as Professor McCord's discussions of the implementation of the Victorian poor law suggests, took an increasingly restricted part in the detailed administration of relief in the unions.[34]

The authority of local administrative agencies was also guaranteed by certain clauses of the poor-law act which required the consent of those bodies before the regulations of the central poor-law board could be applied. For example, the poor-law commissioners could neither alter the size nor dissolve a poor-law union without the consent of the guardians. The agreement of the guardians was required before a union of parishes could be considered a single parish for the administrative purposes of determining settlement and rating. The central board might direct the guardians of a union to purchase land and build workhouses, but only with the consent in writing of a majority of the guardians or the consent of a majority of the ratepayers and property owners entitled to vote.[35]

The continued administrative autonomy of the local poor-law authorities is also suggested by the fact that they were empowered to depart from or delay the implementation of regulations established by the central board when they considered such a step expedient. Such a delay was effective for only thirty days, and required an immediate report to the commissioners. Yet, guardians were specifically required by the poor-law act to depart from established regulations in case of emergencies. In 1838 a select committee recommended that the assistant commissioners remind the local authorities of their 'duty to relieve cases of sudden and urgent necessity'.[36]

In retrospect, from the vantage point of the twentieth century, the Poor Law Amendment Act appears highly significant as a measure altering the relationships between central and local government. To be sure, the establishment of the central poor-law board constituted a major instance of the growth of the central government in early Victorian England. Yet, as this examination of the new poor law indicates, reformed, elected, and local poor-law authorities maintained both administrative power as well as considerable independence from the central board. Moreover, as contemporary observers recognised, the Victorian poor law played a significant part in the process whereby the structure of local government was reconstructed in the nineteenth century. In 1835 Nassau Senior wrote to George Villiers:

. . . our domestic revolution is going on in the most peaceful and prosperous way possible. The Poor Law Act is covering England and Wales with a network of small aristocracies, in which the guardians elected by owners and rate-payers are succeeding to the power and influence of the magistrates. . . . At the same time all the old corporations are overturned, and new ones are to be elected during the course of next year. All sorts of local ambitions are everywhere at work; never, in short, was any country more thoroughly dug up, trenched, and manured than ours will have been during the last and the ensuing year.[37]

As Senior's letter indicates, the effect of the legislation of 1834 on the structures of local government was as important as the changed relationships between those structures and central authorities. Perhaps the most important conclusion to draw from this analysis of the poor-law act is that the reorganisation of the system of pauper relief in early Victorian England constituted a juxtaposition of central and local forms. These structural changes imposed a new tone upon the system for the relief of the poor. The new system was perhaps not more rationalised or simplified than the old, but professional bureaucratic values were extended into a society which had still not outgrown the social controls indigenous to an essentially landed society where the landed estate and social status still comprised the most legitimate and valid justification for political and administrative authority. It is the injection of these bureaucratic values which seems the most novel feature of the Poor Law Amendment Act.

These poor-law provisions were the subject of intense debate at regular intervals in the House of Commons between 1834 and mid-century. The opponents of the Victorian poor law were violently vocal. The strident tones of Richard Oastler and the Tory-Radicals outside parliament were matched by passionate opposition inside. Yet, it is important to state that Thomas Slingsby Duncombe (Radical Reformer: Finsbury) was incorrect when he claimed ninety-nine out of every one hundred members of the House of Commons opposed the Poor Law Amendment Act.[38] As the most cursory glance at the division lists suggests, the measure which *The Times*, on 11 December 1847, criticised as a 'bad measure badly administrated', received the approval of the House of Commons by overwhelming majorities in the 1830s and 1840s. In May 1834, the second reading of the Poor Law Amendment Act was carried by a vote of 299 to 20. It received 260 ayes to 61 nays on the second reading when it came before the House of Commons for renewal in 1842. In 1847, on the occasion of the reconstitution of the central board, the poor-law bill passed its second reading by a vote of 218 to 42.[39]

An examination of the division list for the second reading of the poor-law bill in 1842[40] indicates that no political group had a monopoly on support or opposition to the measure. Indeed, the bill received, almost without exception, massive support from all political groups in the House of Commons.[41] Further, it is clear that the poor law was not a party issue since it did not separate Liberals from Conservatives but, rather, divided both parties internally. Indeed, partisan support and opposition to the measure was nearly identical: 83 per cent of the Conservatives and 76 per cent of the Liberals supported it, while 16 per cent of the Conservatives and 23 per cent of the Liberals opposed it. This point is confirmed in discussions of the issue, for contemporary participants in the controversy over the new poor law emphasised its non-partisan character. Samuel Roberts, who opposed the measure, conceived of it as an issue which was above political concerns:

> Let it, however, be constantly kept in mind by all, that this is no *party*, no *political* question. . . . Every disinterested man, who fears GOD, who honours the KING, who cares for the POOR, must, I conceive, join hand and heart with those of all sects and parties, in legally and peaceably opposing the continuance of a measure which, if persisted in, must inevitably lead to the most lamentable circumstances.[42]

The view of most political observers, many of them harsh critics of the legislation of 1834, was that the new poor law, as a crucial instrument for national policy which was important for the country as a whole, should not be dealt with in the normal arena of partisan conflict and political debate.[43]

Traditionally this massive support has been viewed as a response to the new poor law as a corrective to the problem of the rapidly increasing poor-rates. Consequently, the poor law is sometimes seen as 'part of a body of class legislation based on selfishness and class interest'.[44] However, it is a major problem to determine the class in whose interest this legislation was intended. It is improbable the reformed House of Commons, dominated by the landed interest, should contrive a measure intended 'to suit the pockets and prejudices of the "middling classes" '.[45] The new poor law, more likely, was intended to appeal to a wide range of class and economic interests. Indeed, Professor Henriques indicates that the political success of the poor-law reformers was due to the anxieties of the gentry in the southern counties after the risings of 1830. Therefore, where some social interests could support poor-law reform as a method of reducing rates, others could support it as a means of social discipline.[46] Moreover, the debates in parliament confirm the view that the new poor law was not put forward on behalf of a single narrow class interest. Instead, the issues were generalised, not specified, and formulated in terms of the country's economic and social health, rather than the economic security of the landowners or the 'middling classes'. On introducing poor-law reform in the House of Commons, Lord Althorp maintained that the old poor law was 'fraught with the most destructive consequences for the *whole community*'. John Richards (Whig: Knaresborough) believed the poor-law bill would benefit the poor as well as the propertied classes, and Robert Aglionby Slaney (Reformer: Shrewsbury) welcomed it as a measure preventing the ruin of the entire country's property.[47]

III

The reformed poor law raised a storm of controversy in the 1830s and 1840s. Contemporary observers identified a wide range of criticisms of the new legislation. In their report to Lord Normanby, the poor-law commissioners suggested much poor-law opposition arose from the challenge of the new act to important local interests and, as such, constituted a significant departure from the habits, traditions, and customs of the country.[48] George Cornwall Lewis, while not denying the importance of material interests in human motivation, attributed much poor-law criticism to those prejudices which are 'nine times out of ten, quite as strong as the interest of money, and very often far stronger'.[49] Nassau Senior believed the opponents of reform were either men governed by political motives and influenced by newspaper opinion, or anarchists who recognised that the new poor law was conducive to social tranquillity. Senior knew what the division lists confirm: men of all political tendencies opposed the act of 1834. As Senior put it:

> The ultra-Tories hate the law, as democratic, the ultra-Radicals and Chartists as aristocratic; and both these parties detest it as Whig.[50]

These observations suggest that, while the numerical opposition to reform in the House of Commons was small, criticisms of the new poor law were extremely diverse, touching on what might be interpreted as the major uncertainties in the country at large. These uncertainties are perhaps best revealed in the attitudes of members of parliament caught in the ambiguous position of criticising the old poor law but also opposing the particular legislation of 1834. Many of these men believed the allowance system of poor relief constituted a social and economic problem requiring reform, but opposed the new poor law because it suggested abrupt and radical changes in the political and social structure.[51] For example, Sir Samuel Whalley (Reformer: Marylebone) believed the function of the legislature was merely to abolish all provisions for outdoor relief or supplements from the rates for wages. He, therefore, approved of the restrictive principles which stood behind the bill of 1834, but opposed the concept of government growth explicit in those clauses of the legislation calling for the creation of poor-law commissioners, assistant commissioners, and a central poor-law board. Others, like Henry Phillpots, Bishop of Exeter, hoped it might be possible to return to the essential principles of the Elizabethan poor law 'with such checks as may and ought to be provided against the repetition of those abuses under that system which were made the plea for the present law'.[52] George Poulett Scrope (Reformer: Stroud), to take a final example, also provides a relevant case in point. He recognised the importance of a central authority for ensuring uniform administration of poor relief. In fact, Scrope believed the main difficulties in the old poor law were a result of the allowance system and 'the want of some central control over the local administrators of the law'. Yet, Scrope had reservations about the poor-law bill in 1834, for he feared the consolidation of power in the hands of a central board of poor-law commissioners.[53]

The critics of the new poor law generally focused their attack on the issue of the central board and the supervision of poor relief by the Poor Law Commission. Hence, these objections constituted an attack on government growth (what the critics termed 'centralisation'). At the heart of this was a criticism of the central poor-law board as a despotic and unconstitutional agency whose efforts were damaging to the body politic. However, the attack on the new poor law was more generalised, for the amendment act was perceived by its critics as legislation containing latent and active tendencies which were destructive for both society and politics. In their objections to the new poor law, these critics drew on two kinds of arguments. First, they defended the efficacy of the instruments and agencies of parochial government. Second, critics of the Victorian poor law used both historical and constitutional arguments in an attempt to justify the arrangements existing before 1834. This opposition to government growth in the poor law, it should be emphasised, was not based upon a concept of laissez-faire, with its mechanistic assumptions regarding the operation of the economic and social order, but was founded on an opposition to the destruction of traditional institutions. That is to say, the criteria for a durable and stable social and political order were not drawn from a view of the world posited on a fixed and unchanging universe governed by fixed and unchanging social laws. Critics of government growth found their criteria for good government in the natural order of custom and tradition sanctioned by historical precedent and practice. As a consequence, as the controversy over the new poor law shows, opposition to government growth often took the form of an idealisation of the English past.

The criticism of government growth in the new poor law was not, therefore, based upon a carefully worked out theory of government. Frequently it spoke less to the intellect than the emotions, since opposition to 'centralisation' consisted of a kind of social prejudice reinforced by habits and customs generations old. These predispositions favouring local government based upon customary and traditional arguments were shared by men of all political affiliations. In the case of the poor law, Conservatives like Sibthorp and Newdegate were the political bedfellows of Reformers and Radicals such as Fielden, Muntz, and John Walter. Furthermore, because of the emotional content of this position, criticisms of the new poor law were sometimes held with dogmatic tenacity. For Colonel Charles Delaet Waldo Sibthorp (Conservative: Lincoln), 'there was not a clause, not a sentence, not a line, not a word of it, which could meet with his approbation'. John Fielden (Radical Reformer: Oldham) also opposed the measure in its totality. 'He had always voted for the total repeal of the bill,'

Fielden observed in 1842; 'he was not one of the modifiers of whom there were so many now in the House.'[54]

Certainly the most persistently recurrent theme cutting through the criticisms of the new poor law emphasised the unconstitutionality as well as the despotic character of power vested in the central board of poor-law commissioners. This was the point of Samuel Roberts's characterisation of the central board as the 'GREAT BASHAW, POPE, TYRANT and Woglog having its palace in London'.[55] Most critics of the new poor law viewed the authority with which the central board was vested as an arrogation of power from legitimate parochial agencies. Hence, Peter Borthwick (Conservative: Evesham) believed the poor-law commissioners, because of their power to make regulations regarding pauper relief, had become the administrators of all forms of local law. For William Sharman Crawford (Liberal: Rochdale), the central board upset and violated all the 'grand principles' of the constitution making 'nonentities' of existing representative bodies. As Sharman Crawford put it:

> It not only destroyed all local boards of guardians, but it struck at the root of all representation. If this bill passed, representation would be a humbug.

Similarly, Thomas Wakley (Radical Reformer: Finsbury) resented the new poor law as a violation of local government, claiming 'it took from the rate payers the power of managing their own poor, and transferred it to the commissioners sitting in Somerset-house'.[56]

The allegation of despotism and unconstitutionality in the new poor law was supported by a variety of arguments. Perhaps the response of *The Times* can be taken as typical. On 1 March 1847, *The Times* released another part of its continuing barrage against the poor law by charging that the central board existed in violation of the moral axiom at the root of the English constitution: 'Power is not made for men'. *The Times* went further, however, and compared the central board unfavourably with the Court of Star Chamber which, at the very least, had the greatest and most responsible men in the country as its members. The Poor Law Commission, on the other hand, was too easily corrupted into an instrument of 'ministerial tyranny and intrigue' liable to perform any act of 'political darkness'. Critics such as this were not inclined to be appeased when, in 1847, Lord John Russell's administration prepared to reconstitute the central board by providing it with a president sitting in parliament. Such an action did not remove the constitutional objections of men like George Bankes (Conservative: Dorsetshire) who believed such changes would only provide the poor-law commissioners with a 'higher dignity and honour than ever' by declaring them competent to hold seats in parliament.[57]

Not content to focus their criticisms on the central board alone, the opponents of the new poor law extended their objections in an attack upon what they considered its destructive tendencies for the entire social and political order. Hence, they attributed the increase of crime, the problem of public order in the hungry forties, growing class tensions and antagonisms, and threats to the property of the ruling classes to the new poor law.[58] The Rev Henry Johnson Marshall, the curate of Kensing in Kent, succinctly summarised the socially destructive tendencies he believed implicit in the new poor law:

> . . . it militates against the principles of religion, and breaks down the sanction of morality; it destroys the home and wounds the feelings of the poor,—it takes from him every inducement to labour for himself and his family, and tends to excite sedition against the State, and to encourage depredation upon property; it supplies false motives for action; it punishes distress, and makes no distinction between vice and virtue; it exposes the weak to injury, the innocent to the snares of the seducers, and to accomplish this it breaks down the constitution of the empire, and raises an arbitrary despotism between the poor and their natural protectors. . . .[59]

William Howitt, the poet, and Joseph Rayner Stephens, the defrocked Wesleyan Methodist minister, viewed the new poor law, and especially the regulations established by the central board for separating the sexes in workhouses, as an instrument for promoting social alienation and disintegration. This, from their perspective, constituted a threat not only to hearth and home, but to all forms of domestic security.[60]

In addition to these threats to the social structure, critics of the new poor law perceived it as a threat to political order. *The Times*,

on 26 January 1844, warned against wounding the honest feelings
and insulting the ancient prejudices of the English lest the parliament pave the way for the rise of democrats, agitators, and
'sectarian railers' who would use the rancour and vengefulness
generated by the new poor law for the 'most sordid and dangerous
ends'. Increased expenditure and corruption, which were viewed
as complements to government growth, were also considered
destructive flaws by the opponents of the new poor law. As early
as 1834 some critics, such as George Robinson (Reformer: Wor-
cester), predicted that the new legislation would not reduce the
rates. As new facilities for pauper relief were created, such as new
workhouses in newly formed unions, poor-rates could not help but
increase. Robinson was unaware of the potential economies which
a rationalised poor-law administration might provide. Poulett
Scrope had quite a different point of view, for he believed the
principle of economy implicit in the new poor law was a false one.
By forcing an entire family to seek relief in a workhouse, Scrope
reasoned, greater expenses would be required than if they received
temporary outdoor relief, because workhouse relief would prevent
such families from seeking permanent employment and they
would remain a burden on the union for a longer time. General
Johnson's (Liberal: Oldham) perspective on expenditure was
rooted in his objection to government growth, for, in 1842, he
complained of the increasing poor-rates which resulted from
the 'enormous salaries' paid to the poor-law commissioners and
their officers. Colonel Sibthorp, as one would expect, readily
concurred in a criticism of the heavy expenses supporting a
system 'which he deprecated as arbitrary, despotic, and wholly
useless'.[61]

The critics of the new poor law identified the danger of political
corruption with government growth. As a consequence, John
Walter (Reformer: Berkshire), the owner of *The Times*, opposed
the new poor law, not only because of the despotism of the central
board and increased expenditures, but because it created a fresh
source of patronage 'immeasurable in its effect and extent'.[62]
Samuel Roberts viewed the problem of political 'jobbery' in moral
terms. The Poor Law Commission, from Roberts's point of view,
would be used as a source of jobs for a class of degenerates whose
salaries could not keep pace with the price of their vices. As

Roberts put it in his pamphlet *England's Glory: or, The Good Old Poor Laws*:

> They will be the hangers on, perhaps the bastards of *great* men, who love to dally with little ladies. Such and more will often be the men who are to compel Englishmen to oppress the poor.[63]

Colonel Sibthorp, Edward Buller (Whig: Staffordshire) and George Bankes, on the other hand, regarded the issue of patronage in exclusively political terms. Sibthorp believed the bill reconstituting the central board in 1847 was 'pumped up to create patronage, and to satisfy the longing expectancy' of friends of the new Liberal Government. Where Buller expected the Crown to benefit from 'jobbery', Bankes feared the advantage would accrue to party.[64]

Unconstitutional despotism, increasing expenditure, political corruption, as well as crime and social disintegration, in the minds of the opponents of the new poor law, resulted from the erosion of parochial government. They maintained that the social and political values of local government were essential for the order, harmony, and well-working of society. For Conservatives such as Sibthorp, Newdegate, and Ferrand as well as for Liberals such as Walter, Fielden, and Whalley, the local order was a 'natural' order of parish and parish priest, of county and the justice of the peace. As such, the local order stood in striking contrast to the 'unnatural' and artificial poor-law union, central board and inspecting assistant commissioners. Because of its political and social importance the local order was neither to be taken lightly or rejected easily.

The new poor law, therefore, was taken as an attack on all forms of local government. Critics of the legislation of 1834 valued parochial management of pauper relief because it was based on traditional norms and provided social cohesion and stability. Further, in the discussion over the Victorian poor law, themes emphasising the importance of local government were combined with an insistence upon the values of upper-class responsibility.[65] For example, John Walter contrasted the advantages of relief by neighbours, who provide 'all those little occasional helps which might soothe . . . distress', with the new faces and 'severe custody' of the assistant commissioners and elected guardians, who were unfamiliar with the natural arrangements and social habits of earlier times. Poulett Scrope insisted the security of the poor rested in a system of relief by justices of the peace who, familiar with local conditions and customs, could best minister to them. In 1842, John Stuart Wortley (Conservative: Yorkshire), to take one final example, argued that the efficiency produced by 'centralisation' was purchased at the excessive price of the destruction of the 'habits of self-government'. He called for a return to political forms in which the 'natural established functionaries' would take up the responsibilities placed upon them by their place in society. For opponents of the new poor law like Lord Kenyon, the concern for uniformity in the new legislation would frustrate the 'spirit of improvement' at work in certain parishes.[66] Opposition to the poor law of 1834, then, was based in large measure on a confidence in what was called 'local self-government'. Behind this political value lay a whole range of assumptions and attitudes which stressed the importance of parish government as the only means for stimulating improvements and maintaining social cohesion through agencies sanctioned by custom and tradition.

Since custom and tradition were frequently cited in the opposition to the Poor Law Amendment Act, it is not unexpected that the rhetorical content of such opposition should consist of historical allusions and references. Many of these historical assumptions were merely generalised idealisations of the English past. For some, such as George Robinson and John Richards, the poor-law legislation consisted of innovations, 'hitherto unknown to the history of the country', which violated the controls over poor relief that the people of England had held for centuries. Colonel DeLacy Evans (Radical Reformer: Westminster), Richard Godson (Reformer: Kidderminster), and Thomas Wakley perceived the powers granted to the poor-law commissioners as novelties without precedent in England's constitutional history.[67] Other instances of historical argumentation were set forth more precisely and in greater detail. Perhaps the best as well as the most comprehensive attempts to use historical arguments in political controversy can be found in the work of the publicist Joshua Toulmin Smith.[68] While Toulmin Smith supported his political position by precise allusion to a disparate corpus of legal and antiquarian sources, others utilised similar notions in a far more informal way.

D

The argument against the new poor law using historical assumptions is neatly illustrated by the following passage from an anonymous article in *Fraser's Magazine*:

> Alfred's system, that under which England flourished so long and free, and by which the Saxon race were reared up in that hardy spirit of self-dependence which has enboldened them to march forth the conquerors of the world, the Saxon system was to multiply the centers of government, so that the energies of all were brought into play.[69]

Here, clearly presented, are political concepts and notions of parochial government supported by historical images and symbols. Here one can discern the idealisation of local government forms which, for the critics of the new poor law, produced political independence and the racial strength required to found empires.

As a corollary to this general idealisation of the English past, the new poor law critics idealised a specific English institution: the Elizabethan poor law. Some, such as Poulett Scrope, conceived of the Elizabethan poor law as the 'ancient, legal, authorised security' guaranteeing to the poor their right to relief. Peter Borthwick, however, pushed this a step further, maintaining that the right of the poor to relief was known from the earliest ages and specified precisely in the Book of Leviticus. The Elizabethan poor law, he said, merely 'acknowledged' the right to relief.[70] It should be noted here, if only in parenthesis, that the 'right to relief' as expressed by the critics of the new poor law was not conceived as a natural right in the tradition of seventeenth- and eighteenth-century political theory. Rather, it was defined as a historical right with a basis in the customs and traditions of parochial government. The Bishop of Exeter, for example, described the Elizabethan poor law as 'the Magna Carta of the poor'.[71] Others, such as Toulmin Smith, viewed the old poor law as an autonomous system with a moralising effect: it enabled all citizens to develop their faculties and, in turn, imposed social duties and responsibilities.[72] Still other opponents of the legislation of 1834 characterised the old poor law as a 'God-like' institution established by the greatest statesmen of Elizabethan England.[73] Whatever their particular views on the Elizabethan poor law, many of those who idealised it were agreed that it had been effective social legislation producing economic productivity and comfort as well as social peace and harmony. As Samuel Roberts put it:

> During more than two hundred prosperous years England was peaceable and happy under the *Divine Old Poor Law*. During the existence of the new one, every parish has been in a state of perpetual confusion.[74]

The attitudes of Benjamin Disraeli and the Tory-Radicals towards the new poor law suggest some interesting illustrations and variations on the themes examined above. Certainly one of the major emphases in Disraeli's romantic Toryism, as Robert Blake observes, was opposition to the centralisation of political power.[75] In 1839, 1841, and again in 1847 Disraeli made important speeches against the new poor law on the floor of the House of Commons, indicating his continued admiration for the parochial basis of local government. For Disraeli, the new poor law, and especially the union of parishes under regulations established by the central board, constituted nothing less than a 'total revolution' in the ancient parochial jurisdiction of England. Parish organisation, he maintained, was older than the political organisation of the country and had a closer affinity with the lives and feelings of the lower classes. As a consequence, the parish authorities were both competent to deal with the problem of poverty as well as in accord with the constitutional principle that 'self-reformation should accompany self-government'.[76] Indeed, the great achievements of the English people, Disraeli further asserted, were derived from the local character of government.[77] Therefore, Disraeli did not oppose the new poor law because it increased the power of the executive authority (indeed, he paraphrased Dunning in reverse, saying 'the power of the Crown has diminished, is diminishing and ought to be increased'), but because it 'outraged the manners of the people', and destroyed the parochial constitution of the country for mere 'sordid' and pecuniary considerations.[78]

While Disraeli carefully distinguished between the parliamentary constitution and the parochial constitution of the country, he made no claim for the complete independence of parochial institutions from the authority of parliament. He recognised that attempts to carry on the business of the country without the 'palpable interference' of parliament had always proved a failure.

However, government growth was desirable only in so far as it touched on matters of a 'merely material character'. Since Disraeli classed neither poor relief nor education under that heading, he excluded them from the sphere of a central authority. For government to deal with these matters meant a weakening of social institutions and the destruction of feelings of social obligation and duty. Disraeli believed the radical changes brought about by the implementation of the new poor law required some kind of authority to supervise poor relief. However, as this discussion of Disraeli's attitudes towards the legislation of 1834 indicates, he disapproved of such supervisory power if vested in a central agency. As a consequence, Disraeli proposed the concept of a local controlling authority. Rather than sitting in London the agency supervising the administration of poor relief should reside in the chief city of the district or county to be dominated by local figures of social and political importance. The guiding assumption behind Disraeli's admiration for parochial government is found in his notion that 'it was *more natural* that the population of a county should be under the control of the chief persons of the county'.[79] As these views suggest, Disraeli, like most other critics of the new poor law, was captivated by ideas of parochial self-government idealised in terms of English history, custom, and tradition.

The attitudes of the Yorkshire Tory-Radicals—Richard Oastler, Joseph Rayner Stephens, William Busfeild Ferrand (Conservative: Knaresborough), and Michael Thomas Sadler—suggest similar, if more extreme, ideological tendencies. The four mottoes at the head of each issue of Oastler's *Fleet Papers* are, at least so far as such a creed can be neatly formulated, the best statement of Tory-Radicalism:

> The Altar, The Throne, and the Cottage
> Property has its Duties as well as its Rights
> The Husbandman that laboureth must be the first partaker of its fruits
> He shall judge the poor of the people. He shall save the children of the needy, and shall break in pieces the oppressor.

These social ideals are, essentially, the ideals of a pre-industrial culture in which the political structure is dominated by upper-class leadership and in which social tensions are resolved by upper-class paternalism. Holding these archaic views, the Tory-Radicals rejected all things 'modern', from the materialism of the industrial system to free trade and the new poor law. The opposition of the Tory-Radicals to the new poor law, therefore, should be seen as a function of political and social attitudes which were, fundamentally, reactionary and which cut them off from the new conservatism of Sir Robert Peel as well as the mainstream of political life.

Oastler did not believe the problems of the working classes, of poverty and unemployment, were simply results of dislocations in a rapidly developing economy. For him, the cause of contemporary disorder was nothing less than a departure 'from the mind and will of God as revealed in His most Holy Word'. Oastler identified the holy order, the natural order, the prosperous order, and the peaceful order with the traditional order. The bogy against which Oastler fulminated was nothing less than wrong-thinking 'enlightened liberalism'. It was that which produced 'the fallacy of free trade', which in turn severed the social nexus that had linked labourer and aristocrat. It was free trade which imbued the aristocracy with the notion that 'the labourers have no right to live upon and out of the soil' and provided the basis of the new poor law.[80]

Oastler contrasted his Toryism with the new conservatism which had become permeated with 'enlightened liberalism'. He said he remained a Tory because the new conservatism, 'the labyrinth of expediency', was a dangerous course leading to either anarchy or despotism. While Oastler's Toryism is difficult to define in terms of precise political programmes, the spirit of it appears summarised in the expression 'the Throne, The Altar, and the Cottage'. To him, this meant the preservation of the prosperity and happiness of every class of society by maintaining those institutions 'in their original beauty, simplicity, and integrity'. Michael Sadler believed the country could be saved from disaster only if the slogan 'the Throne, the Altar, and the Cottage' was implemented in political practice.[81] However, this kind of political programme, and here lies its chief difficulty, is impossible to translate into legislative action. The political sentiments of the Tory Radicals spoke to men's moral sense and to men's emotions, having less impact in shaping specific policy recommendations.

In a Marxian sense, the humanitarian theme in Tory Radicalism has a reactionary quality about it. Oastler, Stephens, and Ferrand did not address themselves to the problems of urban poverty in the new industrial system. Oastler believed that while manufacture and commerce were well enough 'in their place' England was characteristically an agricultural country. The Tory Radicals were concerned with the problems of that working class which was closest to the agricultural sector. When Oastler called for the protection of 'native industry and skill' he meant those labourers on the margins of the economy—the handloom workers and the agricultural labourers.[82] The humanitarianism of Tory Radicalism was, therefore, a defence of a *lumpenproletariat* forced out of the labour market by technological change. Indeed, Oastler and Ferrand regarded the new poor law as part of a conspiracy which struck at the roots of traditional English society. The new poor law, as Oastler argued in his *Letter to Lord Normanby* (1840), was the result of a compact between the landowners and the factory masters to alienate impoverished agricultural labourers and their children from the soil and into the 'jaws of the factory monster'. In the House of Commons Ferrand linked James Kay-Shuttleworth and Edwin Chadwick to the conspiracy to 'absorb the population of the south into the north'.[83] For these Tory Radicals the new poor law and the factory system were related parts of the same threat to a traditional society which they wished to preserve.

The very name 'Tory Radicalism' is a paradox. Their concern, as Tories, for a particular order led them to attack an existing order. The oratory of Stephens, the pamphleteering of Oastler, and the parliamentary activity of Ferrand were directed against a system they regarded as subversive, tyrannical, and unnatural. But all they had to replace that system was the slogan of 'Throne, Altar, and Cottage'. Their demands for the 'rights of the poor' was a campaign for something that, given the economic realities of the 1840s, could not exist. Hence, the attitudes of the Tory Radicals were increasingly articulated in a rhetoric of demagogic values. The *People's Magazine* quoted Joseph Rayner Stephens as saying:

> The Poor Law cannot be amended. It is an evil tree and must be plucked up by the roots and burnt. Nothing must be left behind. From first to last it is a law of fear and death. It has plagued the poor till their lives are so embittered, that they would rather die than live.[84]

W. B. Ferrand, similarly, appealing to both Christian principles and the ancient constitution, declared 'under the banner of that constitution, come weal or come woe, I will fight the battle of the people'.[85] In a very real sense, therefore, these Tories were driven to their radicalism because their political objectives were not politically viable and, as a consequence, could not be converted into legislative enactments. Their political creed was not merely concerned with the preservation of landed society in its traditional institutional manifestations—the crown, the church, and the House of Lords. It included the desire to preserve a style of social life based upon the ordered harmony of Throne, Altar, and Cottage. These idealised social forms, however, had never existed and could never exist in the new industrialised society experiencing its birth pangs. To the extent that the political options of the Tory Radicals rested upon idealisations of pre-industrial society they were removed from both the pragmatic conservatism of Sir Robert Peel as well as the opportunistic conservatism of Benjamin Disraeli.

The critics of the new poor law, for all their vociferous objections to the legislation of 1834, were caught in a curious dilemma. While opposing government growth, most opponents of the new poor law, like its advocates, accepted the criticisms of the allowance system, believing it perpetuated vice and indolence. This dilemma was expressed neatly in a letter to *The Times* on 21 May 1842 when it asked 'is there no *via media*, no middle path, between tyrant centralisation and a recurrence to the maladministration of the Poor Laws' which existed after 1795? Consequently their positive recommendations for providing pauper relief went no further than suggesting a return to self-government by parochial authorities. For example, Poulett Scrope, Peter Borthwick, and William Lutley Sclater suggested the administration of the poor law should be modified to allow the guardians greater discretion in dispensing outdoor relief and A. B. Cochrane (Conservative: Bridport) believed the function of parliament was to diffuse 'a warm spirit of charity' through all levels of society.[86] For these critics, government growth was not merely a jurisdictional issue. They perceived the intervention of the central government as a threat to traditional values as well as traditional social forms. Thus, as the critics of the new poor law conceived it, the choice was not between the legislation of 1834 or the old poor law with its abuses. The choice was between the new poor law and the Elizabethan poor law in the pristine state in which it had existed before 1795. Opposing both government growth and maladministration of pauper relief, the opponents of the new poor law demanded the restoration of ancient social and political forms dominated and actuated by paternalistic and philanthropic values operating independently of central bureaucratic interference.

IV

The advocates of poor-law reform, in contrast to their critics, eschewed the language of tradition and custom and based their position on what they considered pressing political and social requirements. The poor-law reformers neither ignored constitutional and historical arguments nor were their statements free of such references (see p 28). However, the central thrust of their rhetoric was derived from the facts and pressures revealed in the investigation of pauper relief conducted by the Royal Commission. As a consequence, the language of the poor-law reformers, fitting the incrementalist perspective, was one of political pragmatism based on a sense of political and administrative experience.

In defence of the poor law of 1834 its advocates responded to two allegations raised by their opponents: while rejecting charges of administrative despotism and unconstitutionality they also opposed the notion that the new system posed an inhuman and cruel threat to the defenceless and unfortunate. In the view of the poor-law reformers, the bill of 1834 was based on experience rather than abstract theories. Consequently, it consisted of the kind of prudent, cautious innovation which would provide structural flexibility allowing for both the application of uniform rules for the administration of poor relief as well as the opportunity for dealing with emergency cases on the basis of their own merits and circumstances.

The debates on the new poor law indicate that its proponents, from the very outset, stressed the notion that the legislation of 1834 was a product of political experience and practical knowledge rather than theory or economic dogma. When it was introduced in 1834, Lord Brougham indicated that the new poor law was recommended by Nassau Senior, whose chief qualifications consisted of his practical knowledge, for he was 'a Magistrate and no theorist'. Lord Althorp was aware the new system did not square completely with the strict principles of political economy, yet, as he pointed out, successful legislation required parliament to take advantage of administrative experience and utilise what were recognised as successful social experiments. Charles James Blomfield, the Bishop of London, assumed a correspondence of principle and practical experience when he suggested the amendment bill was consistent with both humanity and economic principles because the Royal Commission 'recommended nothing but what had stood the test of experience, and which had been tried in large and important parishes'. The argument from experience was used throughout the poor-law controversy. In 1847, when the poor-law board was reconstituted, Sir George Grey, Russell's Home Secretary, recommended a change in the relationship of the central board to parliament because experience, the sole guide in such matters, had demonstrated existing structural relationships to be less than satisfactory.[87] The fact that the poor-law reformers emphasised experience rather than principle in their defence of the new poor law was one of the issues most disturbing to their critics. The concern for practical experience was regarded as the kind of 'presumptuous empiricism' which opponents of the new poor law found reprehensible and which seemed to give proof of the poverty and barrenness of the poor-law reformers' arguments.

If administrative and political experience was one keynote of poor-law reform, an emphasis on prudent and cautious innovation was another.[88] On the one hand, careful innovation was required to produce administrative effectiveness. Sir James Graham, however, Peel's Home Secretary, recognised the difficulties of attempting to provide legislation which would address itself to the problems of poor relief with both effectiveness and prudence when he observed in 1842:

> . . . if by specific enactment you endeavour to provide for all cases, you will omit some, your law will be defective, and injustice will be done; if your enactment be vague and indefinite, it will be inefficient and be evaded. . . .[89]

On the other hand, advocates of poor-law reform insisted on cautious change so that no more than the required amount of power would be vested in the hands of a central bureaucratic authority. Lord Althorp, for example, insisted the object and intention of the Government was to give the central board only so much power as was necessary for its effective action.[90] This evidence, therefore, suggests the poor-law reformers were caught in a curious dilemma. While they wished to improve the efficiency and effectiveness of the poor-relief administration, they, like the critics of the new poor law, were chary of centralised authority and wished to delegate power to the central poor-law board only with circumspect caution.

The system of poor-law administration, as the discussion of the legislation of 1834 has shown, was calculated to accommodate the requirements of experience, administrative caution, and effectiveness. It took the form of local administration, conducted by guardians elected by the ratepayers and magistrates chosen by the Crown, and a central supervising authority appointed by the Crown. This system, combining centralism and localism, was advocated persistently by the proponents of the new poor law in the 1830s and 1840s. Lord Althorp, in 1834, conceived of the poor-law commission as an agency for controlling the administration of poor relief without administering the law itself. The poor-law commissioners, appreciating the essential duality of the system within which they had to work, understood that poor relief in England was characterised by neither the total centralisation of administration present in some continental countries nor the de-centralised structure of English poor relief which had been dominated solely by parochial authorities. As Sir George Grey put it in 1847, the administrative system contained in the new poor law was one 'of combining local administration with a general superintending and central authority'.[91]

The poor-law reformers, aware of the limited character of central authority in the legislation of 1834, rejected allegations of unconstitutionality and administrative despotism in a number of ways. In the first place, and this shows their continued respect for traditional institutions, they were careful to insist upon a role for the justices of the peace in the new system of poor relief. Even the most severe critics of parochial government were aware of the importance of retaining some of the traditional mechanisms of social control. Robert Slaney, whose consistent support for the central board extended over two decades, believed the magistrates should retain some discretionary authority to issue outdoor relief. Neither Edward Stillingfleet Cayley (Whig: Yorkshire) nor Nassau Senior regarded the establishment of a central supervisory agency as inconsistent with the authority and jurisdiction of the local magistrates. In Senior's view the amending legislation merely altered the character of the magistrates' authority. From officers with limited jurisdiction justices of the peace could become, because of their social prestige, the most influential members of boards of guardians. The new poor law converted them from judges into administrators.[92] This suggests that the poor-law reformers, far from being blind innovators insistent upon instituting complete bureaucratic centralisation, were concerned to establish new administrative forms and procedures in the context of conventional social and political forms.

The proponents of the new poor law also responded to charges of illegality and administrative despotism by indicating the legal and practical checks which operated upon the central board. Lord Althorp, for example, while agreeing it was to have considerable discretionary authority, insisted the central board was still subject to the scrutiny of the executive government and parliament each year when the salaries of the poor-law commissioners were moved in a bill of supply. Edward Cayley, in 1834, pointed out that the Government had no intention of allowing the poor-law commissioners to possess powers which were either beyond or contrary to the law, and J. A. Roebuck, in the debate on the reconstitution of the central board in 1847, insisted any new legislation should contain within it adequate safeguards and protections against the abuse of administrative authority.[93] Indeed, Edwin Chadwick, the poor-law commissioners, and other proponents of poor-law reform believed the most significant manifestations of administrative despotism had occurred under the parochial system dominated by local oligarchies. As the commissioners put it in their report of 1840:

> The old administration of the Poor Law *was* characterized by repeated arbitrary departures from the law, established by the systematic practice of parish officers and magistrates, over large

districts of [the] country. . . . The Poor Law Commissioners . . .
have sought to confine an abusive and lax administration within
the strict limits of the law.[94]

Consequently, the advocates of poor-law reform conceived of the
legislation of 1834 as a means for limiting the arbitrary and capri-
cious administration of poor relief by the parochial authorities.
Still another kind of response to the charge of administrative
despotism stressed the precedents for a poor-relief system combining central supervision and local administration. William
Ewart (Radical Reformer: Liverpool) pointed out that since
benefit societies profited from a system of management in which
general regulations were issued from a central board, other forms
of social organisation, such as a system of poor relief, would do
well to imitate them.[95] In 1840 the poor-law commissioners
answered the charge that they operated on the unconstitutional
principles of centralised administration and extraordinary legislation by identifying the large number of national agencies (the
army, navy, post office; the boards of customs, excise, stamps and
taxes; as well as the equity, ecclesiastical and admiralty courts)
which were permanently located in London. With regard to the
issue of extraordinary or subordinate powers of legislation, the
commissioners held the view that their authority was not unusual
since similar powers were held by the Treasury and Revenue
Boards, by the Lords Commissioners of the Admiralty, and the
justices of the peace in municipal matters.[96] The new poor law,
some went so far as to suggest, did not constitute a fundamental
break with the tradition of the Elizabethan poor law. Lord
Brougham believed drastic and arbitrary powers had been placed
in the hands of men who were 'self-elected, unknown, of no
weight, and of narrow mind', men who, in short, were likely to
abuse these powers, by the many expediential local poor-law acts.
The function of the new poor law was, therefore, to re-establish
responsible poor-law administration. As Brougham put it, the
object of the central board was to 'bring things back to their former
state, to put them on the right track, to reform them'. Lord
Althorp was in substantial agreement with this conception of the
new poor law as a device for eliminating the allowance system and
bringing the administration of the law back to what it had been
originally.[97]

Instead of viewing the new poor law as a measure containing despotically unconstitutional provisions, the poor-law reformers considered central supervision combined with local administration as an efficient mechanism, conceived in pragmatic terms, for solving the problems of poor relief. The central board, according to the poor-law commissioners, was a useful intermediary body, standing between parliament and the public, aiding the effective promulgation of the law by explaining and elucidating the intention of the legislature.[98] Seen in this light, the system of central supervision and local administration was believed to have at least four advantages: it could provide uniform procedures for the administration of poor relief, it was the means for reforming corrupt and inefficient local authorities, it could provide the means for administrative flexibility, and, finally, it could establish the basis for humane poor relief.

The chief advantage of a system containing both central supervision and local administration, as conceived by the poor-law reformers, was its ability to establish national uniform standards for relieving the poor in place of the chaotic variations which existed under the parochial system. Voluntary adoption of uniform standards, as the testimony solicited by Edwin Chadwick shows, was impossible to obtain. Althorp, drawing on his own experience as a magistrate, was pessimistic about the possibility of preventing justices of the peace from following misguided policies without firmly established uniform guidelines.[99] The poor-law reformers, therefore, conceived of the central poor-law board as the appropriate instrument for instituting national uniformity. William Dougal Christie (Liberal: Weymouth) believed a central board was necessary 'for the purpose of aiding, guiding, and controlling, local authorities'. The poor-law commissioners, Chadwick held, were qualified for this task because they possessed 'the widest experience and the most complete knowledge' concerning matters of pauper relief. As the commissioners themselves conceived it, their task was to maintain the new system of poor relief and strengthen the local authorities 'in the performance of their duties when they are unable to stand alone against the heavy pressure to which they are subject'.[100]

The poor-law reformers believed that a second advantage of poor relief through central supervision and local administration, and this coincides with their concern for national uniformity, would be the reformation of corrupt parochial institutions and authorities. Chadwick dismissed the talk of local self-government being the glory of Englishmen as just so much 'despicable rant'.[101] Indeed, the Royal Commission to investigate the old poor law collected evidence revealing considerable dissatisfaction with the structure and operation of local government. Working-class emigrants, for example, writing to friends back home, indicated little discontent with the 'general government' of England. Nevertheless, their letters contained 'felicitations that they are no longer under local control or parochial management'. Other testimony criticised the discretionary powers which had been placed in 'irresponsible' local institutions under the old poor law and recommended that they should be transferred to some kind of public authority.[102] The power structure of parishes, Chadwick concluded, was dominated by a small clique, often of the worst public character, who were 'directly or indirectly interested in profuse expenditure'. Therefore, in Chadwick's view, parochial institutions were nothing more than oligarchical 'job-ocracies' in which 'juntas of a dozen or two of individuals, composed of pot-house clubs . . . distribute among each other the parochial funds'.[103] Other advocates of the new poor law were less severe in their criticisms of local government. Lord Althorp, for example, believed local officials to have the most immediate knowledge of a social problem, yet, even he recognised that the parish authorities were subject to the most direct pressures and intimidations. The recognition of these weaknesses in the existing parochial institutions did not mean the advocates of the new poor law were eager or even willing to dispense with local administration of poor relief. Poor-law reformers, like Colonel Robert Torrens (who 'Entertains Whig principles, inclining, in some particulars, to Radicalism': Bolton), believed a good system of local government should be regarded as 'the perfection of all government'. Even the poor-law commissioners had no desire to eliminate the spirit of local independence so long as it was informed by 'enlightened discretion'. Holding to a relatively traditional position concerning the relationship between local and central authority, the poor-law commissioners, along with the critics of the new poor law, regarded the spirit of self-government as 'the characteristic excellence of the English people'.[104] As a consequence, central supervision was conceived of as a means for reforming local administration, guaranteeing its continued strength and vigour.

Central supervision and local administration, and this was a third advantage the poor-law reformers perceived in the legislation of 1834, could also provide the kind of administrative flexibility required to meet the needs of local peculiarities and special cases. The central board, with its discretionary power to make regulations, was conceived as the instrument for making this kind of administrative flexibility possible. As Lord Brougham noted, a single rule for the administration of poor relief laid down in statute law would necessarily be arbitrary in operation. Therefore, a central board 'with ample and unconfined power' should exist 'in order that the rules for its exercise may not paralyse its movement'. Such a central board vested with discretionary authority, as Lord Althorp observed, was the appropriate means for the effective yet gradual reform of the old poor law. While reducing the local poor-rates, there would be less danger of diminishing pauper relief below the subsistence level. The flexibility of the new poor law was a feature which received continued admiration from the proponents of poor-law reform. Sir James Graham, in 1842, characterised the Victorian poor law as a 'plastic system' which was able to adapt itself to the varying circumstances of each community. In 1844, in the debate on the modifications in the poor law, Graham specified some ways in which this flexibility was effective. Just as the poor-law commissioners could tighten the requirements for relief in some poor-law unions he observed, so they could also relax or modify the requirements for relief in other unions which might be under special or emergency conditions.[105]

The fourth advantage of central supervision and local administration, as the poor-law reformers conceived it, lay in its ability to provide poor relief on a humane basis. This was their response to the charge that the new poor law, with the restrictive provisions of less eligibility and the separation of the sexes in the workhouses, was cruel and ruthless. The advocates of poor-law reform tried to have the best of all possible worlds. By making their values—the habits of forethought, frugality, and independence—the goals of poor relief obtained through uniform standards, they claimed they were bringing poverty under social and political control. By citing the flexibility provided under a system of central supervision and local administration, they claimed the new poor law was humane in both conception and operation. As a consequence, Sir James Graham declared, with what was probably a good deal of sincerity, that the new poor law was formulated in the charitable and humanitarian spirit of Christianity because it provided relief for the needy and sick in their time of suffering. The aged and enfeebled, he argued, when confronted with restrictive regulations of the central board, had an unconditional right to relief. However, the able-bodied had only a conditional right for which 'a test is to be applied to their alleged destitution, and that test is a task of work'.[106]

To appreciate how the poor-law reformers could consider the act of 1834 as a piece of humane and charitable legislation, it is necessary to understand their attitude towards the poor. In the first place, they distinguished sharply between the indigent classes and the poor. Secondly, they believed the needs of those groups could be best met by two separate social policies. The indigent, those unable to labour or unable to obtain the means of subsistence by their labour, deserved relief in time of misery and distress. The poor on the other hand, the 'large section of the human race whose lot it is to earn their subsistence by their labour', should not be encouraged in idleness and indolence by 'eleemosynary' provisions and lax poor-law policies.[107] Legislation for the working classes, Sir James Graham observed, should be shaped so that it was 'conducive to the interests of the moral, the industrious, and the provident labourer, as contradistinguished from the idle and the improvident'.[108] In all of this one can detect a sense of confidence in the ability to separate the industrious from the improvident and to transform the idle into industrious labourers by the administration of certain elementary and uniform rules.

The poor-law commissioners, in their effort to reduce the allowance system, followed what they considered to be a middle ground between the total abolition and the liberal extension of outdoor relief. As they put it in a letter to Sir James Graham on 11 December 1846:

> In a matter beset with difficulties, arising both from the social condition of the poorer classes, and the divided state of public opinion, the Commissioners have endeavoured to follow a safe

and prudent, and at the same time consistent course; they have to the utmost of their power given effect by their regulations to the views of the Legislature, and sought to enforce the principles of sound administration, so far as circumstances appeared to permit.

Guided by experience in accord with local circumstances the commissioners established procedures which, in their view, would provide humane relief when required and at the same time remove the stimulants to idleness and improvidence which existed in the allowance system. By 1846 therefore, as they pointed out to Sir James Graham, the administration of the new poor law was directed only to an elimination of outdoor relief for the able-bodied in rural areas. The indigent could still receive outdoor relief in rural areas and even the able-bodied could obtain outdoor relief in urban areas.[109] The response of the advocates of poor-law reform to allegations of administrative cruelty, therefore, was much like their response to allegations of administrative despotism. Viewing the new poor law as a measure based on cautious experience, the poor-law reformers believed it adequate both for establishing the proper relationships between local and central government and providing a humane system of poor relief.

V

In 1847, after thirteen years of controversy climaxed by the bone-crushing scandal at Andover, the central poor-law authority was reconstituted with a president sitting in parliament. While the supervisory powers of the central board were not reduced, all the duties and responsibilities of that agency were transferred to the new Poor Law Board.[110] More than anything else, the legislation of 1847 was a gesture to gain public confidence by making the central poor-law authority more directly responsible to parliament. Existing evidence suggests that the poor-law commissioners themselves approved of the changes made in 1847. In a letter to George Grote in 1847, George Cornwall Lewis stated that he had no objection whatever to the Government measure. The next year, in a letter to Sir Edmund Head, Lewis wrote: 'In England the Poor Law is no longer heard of. The experiment of direct responsibility to Parliament has been successful.'[111]

E

The major criticism of the new poor law, and this is one of the more important implications of the evidence presented here, fits into the historical model of political behaviour described in the introduction to this book. The critics of the new poor law raised humanitarian objections to the legislation of the 1830s and 1840s which, as the poor-law commissioners recognised,[112] gave them an enormous rhetorical advantage. These humanitarian considerations, however, were linked to a political position which idealised parochial institutions sanctioned by custom and the ancient constitution as the chief repositories of social and political value. John Walter's resolutions against the Victorian poor law in 1843, for example, specified that a remedy to the cruel suffering imposed by the administration of poor relief could be provided by making the new poor law 'conformable to Christianity, sound policy, and the ancient constitution of the realm'.[113] There is much about these attitudes which is reminiscent of what Professor Richard Hofstadter has called the paranoid style of politics. Like the radical-right in America described by Daniel Bell, the critics of the new poor law responded in a heated and often exaggerated fashion to government growth and state intervention as a conspiracy against political and social values whose wisdom was countenanced by centuries of English history.[114] Faced by a world growing increasingly complex and complicated, and seeing what they believed to be the subversion of parochial government, the opponents of the Victorian poor law reacted by calling for a return to the institutions and values of pre-industrial England.

It is not surprising that Conservatives should oppose the new poor law by stressing the values of parochial government with legal and constitutional arguments; however, it is striking that Liberals explained their opposition in the same manner. That John Walter, Thomas Wakley, and G. F. Muntz should use notions like England's 'ancient constitution' in their criticisms of the new poor law indicates they were less prophets of the future than captives of the past.[115] Two conclusions follow from a consideration of the radical opposition to the Victorian poor law. First, a recognition of its role in the criticism of the new poor law tends to undercut the Tory-paternalistic interpretation of Victorian social reform. Radicals, perhaps even more than Conservatives, raised humanitarian and political objections to the legislation of 1834. Second, the use of the myth of the 'ancient constitution' suggests that Victorian radicalism was not dominated solely by a Benthamite ideology, for such a notion was completely alien to Bentham's anti-Whiggish temperament.

The attitudes of the poor-law reformers, in contrast, conform to an incremental model of political behaviour. Proceeding according to modest goals and pragmatic methods, they sought neither to restore an idealised past nor create a future society according to an utopian blueprint. Rather, they engaged in cautious modifications which, at least in their view, would reduce existing corruptions and preserve existing values and benefits. Consequently the work of the poor-law reformers cannot be described either as an application of Malthusian principles or as a collectivised nationalisation of poor relief.

The new poor law cannot be considered Malthusian because the Royal Commission, in theory as well as practice, opposed the complete abolition of poor relief.[116] Similarly, the poor-law commissioners, while their efforts were directed to the elimination of the allowance system and the reform of local poor-law administration, were aware that outdoor relief could be eliminated only in certain cases and after a careful examination of local circumstances. On the other hand, the new poor law should not be considered collectivistic legislation since its proponents conceived of it as a measure which was limited in both function and form. They intended it as neither a mechanism for the elimination of poverty nor for the promotion of social mobility. The most it was intended to accomplish was the transformation of the idle and improvident into industrious members of the working classes. Furthermore, poor relief was neither to be administered by a national agency nor financed out of national taxes. Local authorities retained responsibility for the administration of poor-relief financed out of local rates.

To be sure, the new poor law constituted an extension of state action. Sir James Graham, to take but one important example, was under no illusions about the critical state of the social order in the hungry forties. Government intervention, in his view, was becoming more rather than less necessary because the numbers of the poor were constantly increasing.[117] In addition, it must be recognised that the new poor law served as an important precedent for government growth in the future. Yet, after all this has been said, it would be inappropriate to describe, as Professor H. L. Beales has done, the new poor law as a measure of 'social fascism'.[118] Conceived as an instrument to supervise the local administration of poor relief the new poor law helped to stimulate the reform of local authorities by the establishment of uniform policies for the reorganisation of local institutions dispensing poor relief. By retaining the distinction between central supervision and local administration, the Victorian poor law was calculated to bring together the best features of both.

Notes to Chapter 2 will be found on pages 192–9.

Chapter 3 CENTRAL AND LOCAL GOVERNMENT II
Politics and Public Health in the 1840s

All England is afraid of being put under a central board in London.
. . . The parochial soul is on fire—provincial patriotism is big with
indignation at the project of a central despotism. But the cry is too
hasty; the alarm and indignation are premature. The administration
will still be local.

The Times (15 June 1847)

I

THE MOVEMENT for sanitary reform began in the late 1830s as part
of the work of the Poor Law Commission, which found that the
'nuisances by which contagion is generated and persons are reduced to destitution' constituted one of the most important
pressures on the poor-rate.[1] The medical accounts which Dr Neil
Arnott, Dr James Kay-Shuttleworth, and Dr Southwood Smith
attached to the poor-law reports indicated, for the first time, the
relationships between sanitary conditions and pauperism. However, the public-health issue was distinguished from the poor-law
controversy in two ways: first, pauperism was an habitual matter
and health was an intermittent consideration; second, pauperism
was a class matter, but the question of health touched all levels
of society.

The concern for the health of towns varied from time to time
and place to place. It was particularly evident on the occasion of
demographic crisis, such as the impact of the Irish emigration to
Liverpool and Glasgow, or the unhappy visitation of the Asian
cholera to the British Isles. The nineteenth century witnessed the

decline of traditional diseases such as the bubonic plague and smallpox, but suffered an increase in the incidence of others.[2] Typhus chiefly afflicted working-class districts because it was nurtured in conditions of squalor, overcrowding, and insanitation. Chadwick's famous sanitary report of 1842 was directed to an investigation of the typhus epidemics which besieged the country in 1826–7, 1831–2, 1837, and again in 1846. Cholera, a waterborne disease, broke out twice in the first half of the nineteenth century. In 1831–2 and again in 1848–9 it ravaged England after spreading from India to Russia and the Baltic Sea.[3] Even typhus and cholera, however, were outstripped as mass killers by tuberculosis, which, as an urban disease, thrived on unventilated living and working conditions, undernourishment, and physical debilitation.

The public-health issue was perceived as part of the Condition of England Question which affected all social classes. Lord Ashley (Conservative: Dorsetshire) believed the health issue was 'essentially a working man's question'.

> . . . it affected the whole of the working man's life: it began at home; it affected his capacity to eat and sleep in comfort, to go abroad, and to gain a livelihood by which he might be enabled to rear his family in comfort and respectability. He knew this question was well comprehended by the working classes, and was one of the questions they really had at heart.

Ashley, however, recognised the matter of disease as an issue which extended beyond working-class considerations. 'This intolerable evil', as he referred to it, might break out in working-class districts and quickly 'desolate some contiguous and wealthier region' taking its toll in increased 'bills of mortality', increased rates, and 'increased demands on private charity'.[4] As Sir John Simon, the medical officer for the City of London from 1848 to 1854 and the medical officer for the Central Board of Health after 1854, acknowledged, 'no station can call itself exempt' from the evils of sanitary mismanagement.[5]

The crusade for the 'sanitary idea' was conducted, throughout much of the history of the public-health movement, by an enlightened minority.[6] Doctors, bureaucrats, and members of parliament provided the leadership for the movement which finally produced sanitation legislation. According to Professor M. W. Flinn, the doctors of the nineteenth century, such as Arnott,

Southwood Smith, and Simon, more than any other group 'were responsible for stirring the social conscience'.[7] Chadwick, Kay-Shuttleworth, the fledgling professional bureaucrats, and the Office of the Registrar-General conducted the investigations and detailed local surveys providing statistical demonstrations of the threat which insanitary conditions posed to health, morality, and even civilisation itself.

By the mid-1840s the highest political circles were aware of the importance of public-health reform. In 1845, the Queen, appearing before the Commons and Lords assembled, announced that legislation should be prepared to promote improved sanitary conditions in working-class districts.[8] In the view of Viscount Mahon, William Alexander Mackinnon (Conservative: Lymington), and Lord Portman, parliamentary legislation and government action were required to cope with the problems of sanitation and disease.[9] During the 1840s a small group of members of parliament pressed for public-health legislation. These included Robert Aglionby Slaney, the advocate of rural and economic reform, who was also, as the last chapter reveals, a strong proponent of the Victorian poor law. Slaney, an active health investigator between 1843 and 1846, reported on the sanitary condition of Birmingham as well as fourteen other towns.[10] During Peel's administration Lord Lincoln, the First Commissioner of the Woods and Forests, brought in two health of towns bills which served as models, paving the way for the legislation of Lord John Russell's government. George William Frederick Howard, Viscount Morpeth (Liberal: Yorkshire), who served Liberal governments as Chief Secretary for Ireland and First Commissioner of Woods and Forests, was responsible for the formulation of the legislation of 1847–8, which passed into law as the Public Health Act (1848).

The public-health movement had no organisation for mobilising public opinion until 1844. The medical journal *The Lancet* realised that only the active co-operation of the government and the medical profession could limit the physical deterioration of the cities.[11] For the most part, however, *The Lancet* was little concerned with public opinion and addressed itself almost exclusively to the medical profession. In 1844, the Health of Towns Association was formed for the purpose of diffusing among the people the information by recent inquiries, as to the physical and moral evils that result from the present defective sewerage, drainage, supply of water, air and light, and construction of dwelling-houses; and also for the purpose of assisting the legislature to carry into practical operation any effectual and general measures of relief, by preparing the public mind for the change.[12]

With the coalescence of the efforts of the Health of Towns Association, the doctors, the bureaucrats and members of parliament, the movement for public-health reform was strengthened, quickened, and came into its own.[13] The beginning of Queen Victoria's reign, as Sir John Simon observed, marked the beginning of a new era in the concern for the health of the nation. In 1847 G. F. Muntz (Radical Reformer: Birmingham) remarked in his quaint way: 'There was a mania now for sanitary measures. In fact, there was an insanity in sanity'.[14]

Most interpretations of early Victorian public-health reform have stressed its centralising qualities. According to this view, the Public Health Act (1848) was modelled on the new poor law and incorporated within it, in the form of the General Board of Health, the 'unwelcome and novel interference by a Central Department'.[15] However, the health measures of the 1840s, considerable evidence suggests, were not completely centralist in their emphasis because the recommendations for sanitary reform, from the report of Slaney's Select Committee in 1840 to the Public Health Act itself, contained a careful concern for local administration. The opposition to public-health reform was rooted in the same reverence for local institutions and administration which characterised the opposition to the new poor law. Sanitary-reform measures, these critics charged, were measures of 'centralisation' which would be both politically corrupting as well as politically expensive. To support their position the critics of public-health measures used historical and constitutional arguments drawn from the traditions of English Common Law and English limited government. The advocates of the health of towns bills denied the charge of administrative centralisation by stressing the localist character of their measures. In addition, they emphasised the relationship between the physical environment and social problems, asserting that, since the community could not afford the consequences of insanitary conditions, health measures were justified on economic grounds.

II

A new concern for environmental conditions, as Professor Flinn has suggested, was co-extensive with the decline of public-health conditions in the 1830s and 1840s. Local boards of health were established to deal with epidemic conditions on a temporary basis and local improvement acts were directed to the problems of lighting, sewerage, and paving towns. The Municipal Corporations Act (1835) was an attempt to reorganise borough governments along more rational lines. Boroughs adopting these measures had less urgent need of sanitary legislation. However, these reforms were just beginning in the 1840s and could not meet the immediate sanitary requirements of that decade. For the country, taken as a whole, administrative reform to meet sanitary problems was required on all levels.[16] The attempt to provide administrative solutions for these problems began in 1840 with the work of the Select Committee of the House of Commons chaired by R. A. Slaney. The most famous investigations into the sanitary state of the nation were conducted by Edwin Chadwick, who had long been associated with the Poor Law Commission. Chadwick was the author of the report on the sanitary condition of the working classes (1842) and the report on intermural interment (1843). These reports were supplemented by the report of the commission chaired by the Duke of Buccleuch (1844–5).

Following these investigations the Earl of Lincoln, in 1845, brought in a public-health measure. Since it was introduced late in the session that bill was withdrawn and reintroduced in 1846. However, Lincoln's bill was not acted on in 1846 because of the corn law crisis.[17] In 1847, Lord Morpeth, a member of Lord John Russell's government, introduced a health of towns measure which was, in certain important respects, based on Lord Lincoln's bill. Morpeth's bill failed to pass in 1847, in part, as Greville noted, because it was 'wrong to bring in such measures so late in the session, and the measures were not framed in a manner to get through with short discussion'.[18] In 1848, Morpeth brought in his measure again, and in that year it passed. The general thrust of these investigations and sanitary measures reflects the growing role of the state in social concerns. This is especially evident in the recommendations of the Buccleuch Commission and Morpeth's bills, which called for the creation of a central agency, sitting in London, to concern itself with the health of the nation. However, it would not be correct to assume that the growth of the state meant the elimination of local control and local administration. All the recommendations and measures for sanitary reform, including Chadwick's sanitary report and the Public Health Act, retained the concept of local authority and direction.

The report of the select committee of 1840[19] reflects the tendency of early Victorian social reformers to retain administration and direction of sanitary affairs in the hands of the local authorities. The committee, in fact, recommended that additional powers be granted to such local officers as the sewer commissioners. Its report called for the creation of local boards of health to examine those conditions in their jurisdictions which might be 'prejudicial to the general health of the inhabitants'. These local boards were not to be created by the central government or by parliamentary statute, but by the local board of poor-law guardians, the town councils in corporate towns, or directly by the ratepayers.[20] The precise relationship between the local board of health and the central government was left vague. The report merely stated that local boards should report annually to the central board of health, 'if such a Board be constituted', or to the Home Secretary. The purpose of such reports was not to provide central control over local authorities, but to provide information on sanitary matters 'by which means publicity would be insured to their proceedings, and much useful information collected and diffused'.[21] This select committee also called for the appointment of local inspectors of health, either directly by the ratepayers or by the poor-law guardians, who would be authorised to proceed by indictment for the abatement of threats to the public health. The officers of health would also be responsible for making periodic reports to the local board.[22] It is clear that the authority of this official was to be local in character and was to have no relationship to the central authority.

There is, however, another side to the report of 1840. As it indicated, the central government did have a role in establishing sanitary reforms. That role, however, was clearly legislative rather than administrative:

> It appears to Your Committee, that where such evils are found to follow from the neglect or inability in these respects of local authorities that it is the duty of the Legislature to take efficient steps to protect so numerous and valuable a portion of the community.

Legislative intervention was to take the form of general parliamentary acts to establish uniform regulations for the construction of working-class housing and for the care of the sewage of densely populated districts.[23] Intervention of this kind, as the select committee recognised, constituted a violation of private property. But, such a violation was justified 'on the plea of the general good' and was intended to be no more extensive than the interference provided for in various acts of parliament concerned with the construction of roads, railways, and canals. In addition, the report stated, it was the policy of the select committee to interfere 'as little as possible with private property' and to go no further 'than the strict necessity of the case justified'.[24]

The most famous investigation into the sanitary condition of England was conducted by Edwin Chadwick, who used information gathered from poor-law assistant commissioners, medical officers, clerks, guardians, doctors, and factory inspectors.[25] George Cornwall Lewis, one of Chadwick's principal antagonists on the Poor Law Commission, saw considerable merit in the sanitary report, but apparently believed Somerset House was having sufficient difficulties in the administration of the new poor law without being saddled with more of Chadwick's work. On 13 March 1842 Lewis wrote to George Grote:

> Chadwick has been writing a long report on the means of preventing disease by drainage, cleansing, etc. It contains a great deal of good matter, and, on the whole, I prefer it to anything else he has written. We shall present it shortly as *his* report, without making ourselves responsible for it.[26]

Chadwick has been often considered a 'fanatic for administrative uniformity and centralization',[27] and a doctrinaire executor of Bentham's blueprint for a centralised administrative state. A close reading of the sanitary report, however, necessitates some qualification of this view.

Chadwick's career, taken as a whole, reflects his thoroughgoing contempt for parliament, public opinion, and unreformed local government.[28] However, the sanitary report of 1842 indicates no desire on Chadwick's part to eliminate local administration and vest absolute control of public health in a central authority. To be sure, it provides ample evidence of Chadwick's distrust of and dissatisfaction with the existing local authorities. While emphasising the importance of inspection as a means to reform local administration, the report makes no reference to a central board and goes only so far as to recognise that public health was 'the acknowledged province of the legislature'.[29] In Chadwick's view, the law for the protection of public health and the constitutional institutions for its restoration, such as the courts leet, had fallen into disuse. The consequence was a 'multiplication of badly appointed officers in addition to the evils of excessive cost and bad quality of the service to the rate payers'.[30] Chadwick's primary solution for these problems, as found in the sanitary report, was to remove the local public-health administration from 'the influence of petty and sinister interests' and the appointment of well qualified and responsible local officers. To this end, local boards of health must possess both executive authority and responsibility, inspectors must be appointed to detect debilitating conditions, and local public works must be conceived and carried out by responsible and skilled civil engineers. Chadwick's general rule for the improvement of local sanitary conditions was: 'In proportion as science is securely allied to local administration is its respectability enhanced and the attainment of its objects ensured'.[31] The keynote in all of this was effective and responsible local administration.

In addition to its emphasis on the reform of local government, the sanitary report possesses a strong empirical quality. Late in life Chadwick claimed that he had never followed anyone in his work, not even Bentham, and that his conclusions had been derived 'solely from close and important collections of evidence'.[32] Curiously, the sanitary report does bear a reference to Blackstone, Bentham's great antagonist in the campaign for legal reform, but contains no reference to Bentham himself.[33] Rather than basing his argument for sanitary reform on a theoretical blueprint, Chadwick drew upon the social investigations of A. J. P. Parent-Duchâtelet (1790–1826) and Louis René Villermé (1782–1863) in France; M. Ducpetiaux, the Inspector-General of prisons in Belgium; and nearly 2,000 investigators in England.[34] He adopted a similar method the next year in his report on interment in which he cited evidence collected in Boston, Frankfort, Berlin, Paris, Munich, Wurtemberg, and Russia:

> The remedial measures hereafter submitted for consideration have been deduced directly from the actual necessities experienced within the field of inquiry, and such only are submitted as clearly suggested themselves without reference to external experience. The following preliminary view of the experience of other nations is presented for consideration on account of the confirmatory evidence which it contains, as well as the instances to be avoided.[35]

Just as Chadwick's report was based on the facts discovered by social investigators, it also contained an examination of the existing laws relating to the protection of the public health and included a consideration of both the statute law and Common Law traditions.[36] The sanitary report, as Professor Finer has indicated, was not the final statement on sanitary administration. Its conclusions were general rather than precise and were set forth as hypotheses requiring further test rather than doctrines for immediate implementation.[37]

In 1843 a Royal Commission, chaired by the Duke of Buccleuch, who was lord president of the Privy Council at the end of Peel's administration, was appointed for inquiring into the condition of the large towns and most populous districts.[38] Chadwick played an important role in the continuing work of this commission and in the end drew up the major part of its report. While confirming Chadwick's analysis of existing evils and supporting his programme for correction, the Buccleuch Commission went beyond the report of 1842 and conducted a more systematic investigation, pointing with greater precision to the more subtle particulars of legislation.[39] The commission's report, as Professor Finer has argued, was to the public-health movement what the poor-law report (1834) was to public assistance, since it served as the basis for all the sanitary legislation of the early Victorian period.[40]

Unlike Chadwick's sanitary report, the report of the Buccleuch Commission called for a greater role to be played by central government. Yet, like Chadwick's report, it also specified a continuing role for the institutions of local government in the protection of public health.

Both parliament and the Crown, the Buccleuch Commission recognised, had important functions in the task of preserving the health of towns. While many evils could be removed under existing legislative provisions, it was necessary for parliament to make further enactments before sanitary reform could be 'fully accomplished'. In addition, the existing confusion and overlapping of local acts for sanitary purposes required clarification and rationalisation by the passage of general acts for general purposes.[41] The commission also recommended that the Crown should play a greater part in public-health arrangements by being empowered to 'inspect and supervise the execution of all general measures' for sanitary purposes. This power of inspection, the commission maintained, would enable the Crown to determine the extent to which local authorities were effectively administering the law. If those authorities were found wanting, the inspector was to be authorised 'to enforce upon the local administrative body the due execution of the law'. In addition, the report specified, the Crown should have the power to approve the regulations of the local magistrates concerning the operation of lodging houses and the appointment of local medical officers, as well as the power to protect the independence of the auditors of local accounts. The Buccleuch Commission recognised 'the necessity of a superior authority for supervising' the execution of local acts which detailed projects for drainage, paving, and cleansing.[42] Therefore, it is clear that the commission envisaged a larger role than previous committees and reports had for the central government in the care of the public health. The Buccleuch Commission, it is important to emphasise, did not call for a superior authority to administer or control the machinery for the protection of the health of towns. The sole duty of a central authority was one of supervision.

The report of the Buccleuch Commission also discussed the responsibilities and obligations of the local authorities in the government of sanitary affairs. In the first place, the commission stressed the need for the reorganisation and rationalisation of the local health institutions. The arrangements for drainage, paving, cleansing, and water supply should be placed under a single authority and men qualified by education and training should be appointed to administrative positions for local improvement.[43] In the second place, the commission recommended that local authorities should be vested with the power to provide the kind of services sometimes associated with 'gas and water socialism'— characteristic of English local government later in the nineteenth century. Local administrative bodies, it suggested, should be authorised to construct sewers, branch sewers, and house drains. In addition, those authorities, the commission indicated, should be obliged to provide a sufficient supply of water to all the inhabitants. To that end, the local authorities should be enabled to purchase the interests of established water companies when the latter chose to sell, and new conditions should be established for the creation of new independent water companies so that the local authorities could purchase their works after the lapse of a specified period of time.[44] Furthermore, the commission maintained, local sanitary authorities should be empowered to raise money for the purchase of property necessary for the widening of streets, alleys, and courts. Finally, the Buccleuch Commission urged that certain powers of compulsion should be placed in the hands of the local authorities. Local administrative bodies, in those districts where the inhabitants were exposed to the 'noxious exhalations of any factory', should be authorised to investigate the cause of nuisance and to take legal proceedings to end it. If, on the complaint of the medical officer, any house were found to be in 'such a filthy or unwholesome state' as to constitute a threat to the public health, the local authorities were to 'require the landlord to cleanse it properly without delay'.[45] Thus, the Buccleuch Commission placed considerable emphasis on responsible and effective sanitary administration by local public-health authorities.

The legislation suggested by these investigations was put forward by Peel's government in 1845–6 and Lord John Russell's government in 1847–8. In each case, these health measures were brought before the House by the First Commissioners of the Woods and Forests—the Earl of Lincoln and, his successor, Viscount Morpeth. Morpeth's bills differed from Lincoln's in several respects. Both called for a central authority, but Lincoln vested it in the office of the Home Secretary and Morpeth in a board connected to the Privy Council. Both placed emphasis on local administration, but Lincoln proposed to establish new electoral authorities for the administration of sanitary affairs, whereas Morpeth proposed to invest the town councils with this power. Lord Lincoln excluded London from the scope of his bill, but Morpeth, in his early bills, included it.[46] Lord Morpeth's measure, which was finally enacted in 1848 as the Public Health Act, contained a double emphasis similar to that found in the new poor law. It was not completely centralist since it did not call for the assumption of the administration of the machinery for the protection of the public health by a central agency. Yet, it did call for the central government to fill an important function in ensuring the protection of the health of towns. The Public Health Act, like the Poor Law Amendment Act, combined elements of central supervision with elements of local administration.

The House of Commons passed the Public Health Act only after considerable debate and compromise. Some historians have regarded these compromises as so damaging as to render the act ineffective.[47] This view was also held by some contemporary observers. On 28 September 1848 George Cornwall Lewis wrote to Sir Edmund Head:

> The Health of Towns Act passed after a multitude of changes, and Chadwick has at length been installed as the paid Commissioner, where I hope he may remain quiet. The Act does not apply to the metropolis or to the large towns, and will, I presume have no important operation. It was so emasculated by Henley in Committee that its powers will not amount to anything in practice.[48]

An examination of Morpeth's bills of 1847 shows the extent to which they were subject to the process of legislative compromise; they clearly provided for a more explicit exercise of central power than is found in the act of 1848.[49] However, and this is the significant issue, in spite of a greater and more explicit degree of centralism, Morpeth's early proposals contain the same distinction between central supervision and local administration found in the act of 1848. The function of the central authority and central inspection, as these bills specify, was to aid local officials in the execution of health measures. The order in council implementing the legislation, Morpeth stated, would confer 'the necessary powers *on a local administration* for the purpose of carrying all the sanitary arrangements which may be required into effect'.[50]

The fundamental distinction contained in the act of 1848 was between central supervision and local administration. The Public Health Act called for the creation of a General Board of Health to consist of the First Commissioner of Her Majesty's Woods and Forests and two other persons. The board, as the act specified, was established 'for superintending the Execution of this Act'. To that end, it was authorised to appoint a secretary, clerks, servants and superintending inspectors. However, the general board could not initiate a local inquiry into sanitary conditions without a petition signed by one-tenth of the locally rated inhabitants, or unless the average annual mortality rate exceeded 23 per 1,000. After inquiry by the general board and the superintending inspectors, 'the Queen with the advice of Her Privy Council' could order the act into effect. In emergency conditions the act could be put into effect by a provisional order in council without the petition of the rated inhabitants. The general board was authorised to sanction the appointment and dismissal of the local health officers, the dismissal of the surveyors, and the debts incurred by local boards. It was, in addition, given jurisdiction over burial grounds and interments. No vaults or graves were to be constructed beneath a place of worship and no new burial ground was to be opened after the passage of the act without the permission of this board.[51] The general board was, therefore, created for purposes of the supervision but not for the administration of public-health provisions. It was empowered to initiate the investigation that would lead to the application of the act and was given some powers of sanction over the local boards. However, it was the local boards which were to carry the burden of sanitary administration.

The act of 1848 placed the powers of sanitary administration completely in the hands of the local authorities. In corporate boroughs (boroughs reformed according to the Municipal Corporations Act) the town councils were to act as the local boards of health. Local boards of health for districts composed of corporate boroughs and non-corporate districts were to consist of members selected by the town councils of the corporate borough and members elected by the property holders of the non-corporate

F

districts.[52] The act of 1848 called for the consolidation of the local authorities for water supply, sewage, drainage, and the paving of streets 'under a single local management and control'. The local boards of health were also enabled, by this act, to purchase 'the Rights, Priviledges, Powers, and Authorities vested in any Person for making Sewers', and land for the improvement of streets.[53] Charged with the responsibility of providing adequate supplies of water to the inhabitants of their districts, they were authorised to erect waterworks where necessary. In order to effect these purposes local boards could borrow funds and levy both special and general district rates.[54] The audit of these accounts was not to be conducted by an officer of the general board. In keeping with the concept of local administration, the audit of the accounts of the local boards of health was to be conducted by the 'auditors of the Corporate Borough whereof the whole or part is within such District'.[55] Under this act the local authorities were given certain compulsory powers. They could compel property owners to install drains and to provide water if it was available at a rate of less than twopence per week.[56]

All of this suggests that the Public Health Act was not a centralising measure in the sense that its critics used that expression. That is, it was not a usurpation of local administrative authority and responsibility. The act called for the creation of a new central agency, which obviously constituted an important increase in the role of the central government. However, the function of that agency was to supervise local administration, not conduct the administration of public health itself. In this it did not deviate from the general tendency of the proposals for sanitary reform which had been suggested since 1840. Moreover, the act of 1848 vested new powers in reformed agencies of local government, for it placed authority for sanitary administration either in borough governments reformed according to the Municipal Corporations Act or in the hands of officials responsive to the votes of property holders and ratepayers.

The public-health measures of 1847–8, as the division lists show, received overwhelming support in the House of Commons. The division of 18 June 1847, on the motion for going into committee and rejecting Sibthorp's motion for postponement, is typical. It passed by a vote of 191 to 50. An analysis of that division makes a number of things evident.[57] First, support for the measure came from all quarters with a majority of Conservatives and Liberals favouring it. However, and here voting on public health diverges from voting on the new poor law, Liberals supported the measure more extensively than Conservatives—97·6 per cent of the Liberals as opposed to 57 per cent of the Conservatives. Second, opposition to the public-health measure came largely from the Conservative side of the House—43 per cent of the Conservatives as compared to only 2·4 per cent of the Liberals. To be even more precise, opposition to the bill came largely from the Protectionist wing of the Conservative party—88 per cent of the Peelites voted for the public-health measure and 56 per cent of the Protectionists voted against it. This Protectionist rump which opposed the bill was joined by a handful of members, such as Thomas Slingsby Duncombe, G. F. Muntz, and Henry Galgacas Redhead Yorke (Reformer: York), who sat on the Liberal side of the House.

A statistical analysis of this division list reveals, with greater precision, the relationship, or rather the lack of it, between public health and other interventionist issues in the 1840s. The social investigations conducted under the aegis of the Poor Law Commission, it is widely known, initiated the discussion of public-health issues. As this book shows the controversy over the public-health bill raised issues similar to those raised in the discussion of the new poor law. It would be easy to surmise, therefore, that those who voted for the new poor law also favoured sanitary legislation. A comparative analysis of voting on the new poor law, factory legislation, and public health reveals quite a different and contrary picture. As such an analysis using scalogram techniques indicates, voting on the public-health issue can be placed on a statistical scale representing the traditional radical programme (free trade, political reform, attacks on the Church of England). Votes on the poor-law and ten-hour issues, however, form another scale representing an entirely different ideological dimension. To put the matter another way, voting on the poor-law issue was unrelated to voting on the public-health measure. Members of the House of Commons did not perceive these issues in the same terms and considered them unrelated questions.[58]

What is known about wider opinion outside the House of

Commons confirms the evidence of the division lists: opposition or support for one variety of government growth did not necessarily require consistent support or opposition to others. Evangelical humanitarian proponents of ten-hours legislation and slave-trade abolition had little interest in the campaign for sanitary reform. Perhaps they did not see the health question as a part of their main objective: the reform of England by the propagation of the evangelical way of life.[59] On the other hand, *The Times*, which had been so bitter in its opposition to the new poor law, supported the sanitary measures of 1847–8. While continuing to hold the general view that central superintendence should be vested in 'cautious and considerate hands' and that local responsibility was an important part of the English political tradition, *The Times* viewed the problems of poverty and public health as different kinds of political issues requiring different kinds of political solutions. Poverty was a social and moral issue which did not demand state intervention because pauper relief was a matter for charitable and philanthropic agencies and could be determined best by local authorities. Sanitation, on the other hand, was a physical and material issue which required the intervention of government agencies.[60] *Fraser's Magazine*, similarly, published articles supporting sanitary reform in contrast to its previous opposition to the new poor law. It continued to emphasise the importance of parochial administration, but recognised that the system of local self-government had failed in matters of sanitary administration.[61]

III

The public-health measures of the late 1840s evoked opposition from a number of different quarters: corrupt oligarchies fearing the loss of political power, property owners opposing an increase of local rates, engineers and other professional men who objected to inspection agents of the general board, commercial water and gas companies resisting the intrusion of public authorities into the area of private profit, and business men confronted with no direct threat to their interests but who had little confidence in the administrative skills of the central government. The City of London, in particular, served as a locus of the opposition to the

Public Health Act.[62] The measure of 1847-8 was opposed, Sir John Simon observed, 'because in its mere novelty it was an offence to those prejudices and vague timidities which at first resist all new legislation'.[63] In the House of Commons the largest body of opposition consisted of Conservative Protectionists who were joined by a small group of members from the Liberal side of the House. The hostility of these Liberals, it has been suggested, was derived in large part from their pride in their growing cities in the North of England and their confidence in laissez-faire.[64] The parliamentary debates, however, reveal that these men opposed public-health measures for some of the reasons given by the Protectionists. Both venerated local administrative autonomy. The same combination of attitudes, as this book has shown, can be seen in the opposition of certain Radicals and Liberals to the new poor law.

Critics of public health employed a variety of arguments in opposition to the measures of 1847-8. Some denied any correlation between disease and crime, and others refused to attribute the increasing mortality rate to cholera. Still others despaired of any legislative attempt to rid towns of disease.[65] The primary themes, however, in the arguments against public-health measures resembled, in tone and substance, the criticisms of the new poor law. These attacks emphasised the importance and value of the institutions of local self-government. Critics saw the General Board of Health as an instrument for usurping the administrative powers which ought to be retained by the local authorities. As in the case of the attack on the new poor law, this point of view was justified by a kind of historical arcadianism, which used legal, constitutional, and historical arguments to establish the legitimacy of institutions of local government by relating them to the ancient Anglo-Saxon constitution and the Common Law tradition. To depart from these time-honoured institutions, in the view of the critics of public-health measures, meant the decline of politics into corruption, social disorder, and increasing expenditure.

At the heart of these criticisms stood the fear that the Public Health Act would provide an irresponsible, despotic, arbitrary, and unconstitutional administrative system which would undermine the wholesome institutions of local government. David

Urquhart (Conservative: Stafford) regarded the public health bill as

> ... un-English and unconstitutional—corrupt in its tendency—it was an avowal of a determination to destroy local self-government, and, if carried, its effects would be to pass a roller over England, destroying every vestige of local preeminence, and reducing all to one dull and level monotony.[66]

Joseph Warner Henley (Conservative: Oxfordshire) believed the public-health measure would give the Privy Council the novel, unconstitutional, and dangerous power to nullify all local acts.[67] Colonel Sibthorp denounced the investigatory powers of the superintending inspectors of the general board.

> He condemned the inquisitional power of the inspectors, which would almost authorize them to go to the house of the Lord Mayor of York and see what he had for dinner, and whether he went sober to bed, which he was sure the right hon. Gentleman always did.[68]

Toulmin Smith compared the general board to the Court of the Star Chamber, declaring it was an instrument of despotism and arbitrary rule foreshadowing 'the destruction of that Responsibility of all entrusted with authority which it is the end of all our national institutions to secure'.[69] For Charles Pearson (Radical Reformer: Lambeth), this bill would deprive the local authorities of their powers of independent action 'which was the glory of our Saxon institutions'. Both David Urquhart and Toulmin Smith viewed the bill as contrary to English Common Law. Urquhart complained that the framers of the bill were ignorant of the Common Law and suggested that if they would but consult *Blackstone's Commentaries* they would find sufficient legal means for combating health hazards.[70]

In addition to their almost paranoid fear of government growth, these critics possessed an uncommon confidence in the power of unreformed local authorities to solve the sanitary problems of the 1840s. Toulmin Smith believed the English constitution provided the fullest opportunity for the introduction of improvements designed to promote the social, political, and moral welfare of the nation. For him, only institutions of local self-government could properly protect the interests of each local district because they had worked social and political miracles even when imperfectly developed. The sewers of London were, for Smith, 'the greatest wonder of the world'.[71] This same confidence in local government was shared by others. Muntz and Sibthorp, having ample confidence in the cleverness and resourcefulness of local officials, did not believe that London experts were required to explain the duties and obligations of corporate governments.[72] Charles Pearson maintained that centralised forms of sanitary administration were inferior to local forms and cited mortality statistics for Paris and London to make his point.[73]

The opposition to government growth, therefore, was linked to a reverence and respect for the institutions of local government 'by which England had risen to her present position in the scale of nations'. The critics of the public-health measures feared that the ancient political institutions of England, which had been sanctioned by the ancient Anglo-Saxon constitution and Common Law, would be eliminated by the growth of the central government and state power.[74] This emphasis gives the controversy, like that over the new poor law, a sentimental, arcadian, and romantic character. The respect for the ancient and hoary institutions of England long past shows the extent to which political controversy in the nineteenth century used the political ideas and concepts of the seventeenth century and the constitutional notions implied by the Whig interpretation of history. The antiquarian flavour of these arguments, however, stands in sharp contrast to the new demands made on local institutions by urbanisation and epidemic disease.

The critics of the Public Health Act predicted certain dire results as a consequence of its implementation. For them government growth would lead to political corruption, extensive government expenditures, social disorder, and threats to private property. Most frequently the fear of political corruption was stated in terms of opposition to political patronage and jobbery. Toulmin Smith regarded the measure of 1848 as an act 'to legalize universal jobbing, to create universal patronage'.[75] In part, objection to patronage and jobbery was a partisan criticism. Henley, for example, was concerned lest the superintending inspectors of the general board be put in the service of the Liberal Government for electioneering purposes. Some members of parliament were even more direct in the use of this allegation to attack the Liberal party. John Stuart (Conservative: Newark) felt certain the Government would be charged with corruption in the country because the Whigs had a reputation for creating positions at substantial salaries for their political supporters.[76] A pamphlet entitled *A Letter to Lord Morpeth* related the political success of the Liberals to their ability to manipulate the patronage generated by government growth:

> The Whigs have invariably exhibited the wisdom of the unjust steward; they owe their tenure of office, and the difficulty of ejecting them or keeping them out of it when ejected—their strength as an opposition, and their viability as a political party— to their dexterity and tact in seizing, and the want of tact with which they are allowed to seize, every opportunity for the creation of Boards and Commissions, not only with extravagant salaries, but with patronage, and powers, and sources of influence, ramifying in a thousand channels through every electoral district. Let them carry this bill, and nothing short of violent revolution and a Chartist Government will ever turn them out.[77]

Lord George Bentinck (Conservative: Lynn Regis) used this argument for a personal attack on Lord Morpeth. Morpeth, he argued, was not troubled by the centralising features of the bill because he would have all the despotic powers and patronage conferred upon him.[78] Colonel Sibthorp, however, did not see the issue as a partisan one. He objected to the increased power of patronage the measure would give the Government, but he did not condemn the measure as a 'Whig' measure. Indeed, he had more confidence in a Liberal than a Tory government because there was less 'deceit and hypocrisy' in the former than the latter. Political corruption, Urquhart maintained, should stand as a warning to centralisers of all parties, for it was disease of this kind which had produced revolution in France.[79]

The notion that government growth would bring an increase in the cost of government was closely related to the charge of political corruption. Indeed, Asa Briggs has suggested that the criticism of sanitary reform stressed the question of economy as much as the issue of centralisation.[80] For Toulmin Smith money was being squandered on 'absurd crotchets' which would only tend to satisfy 'individual vanity at public expense'. Richard Spooner (Conservative: Birmingham) asserted that, given the current state of the economy, the retail merchants and small tradesmen would be unable to pay the increased rates this measure would require. England, Charles Pearson predicted, would follow the same course taken by France and other countries with a centralised administration. He claimed that in France, out of an income of £54,000,000 a year, £18,000,000 was spent paying 500,000 placeholders in the civil administration. These views had common currency in the parliamentary debate on the public-health measures and were emphasised repeatedly by such men as Sibthorp and Urquhart.[81]

Finally, the public-health measure of 1847–8 was criticised as an invasion of private property. This was a minor theme in the controversy over public health, but one which recurred with some frequency during the 1840s and 1850s. As early as 1841, Lord Melville condemned public-health measures as a threat to the rights of private property. In 1844 Henry Tufnell (Liberal: Devonport) objected to the metropolitan buildings bill because it constituted an 'unwarrantable interference with the rights of property'. The Public Health Act, Lord Seymour (Liberal: Totnes) charged in 1854, had permitted the government to interfere with every trade and occupation in the most arbitrary and despotic manner.[82] *The Economist*, however, held the most strident opinions on this point. In 1848 it attacked the Public Health Act because the general board was permitted to interfere with the business and house of any individual. In addition, *The Economist* detected attitudes in the public-health movement which opposed industrialisation and urbanisation. It alleged that the formulators of public-health legislation intended it as a means of limiting the extensions of businesses which they regarded as offensive. Further, *The Economist* believed the proponents of the legislation of 1847–8 'object to towns, and they are to check their growth'.[83] Thus, the health of towns measure was condemned on all sides. Corrupting and costly, it was regarded as a threat to the political and economic structure of the country.

Detailed examples of most of the themes discussed here can be found in the writings of Joshua Toulmin Smith.[84] During the controversy over public health and the attempt of the City of London to exclude itself from a general sanitary measure, Smith was the chairman of a sanitary committee in a metropolitan district as well as the chief spokesman for the anti-government forces. Smith's Anti-Centralisation Union provided the organisational focus for the attack on the General Board of Health in 1854. After the reconstitution of the general board, the Anti-Centralisation Union served as the organ for a general campaign against bureaucracy and government, publicising cases of governmental impotency which occurred during the Crimean War as evidence of the necessity for returning to the system of local self-government.[85]

Smith, in addition to being the most vocal and outspoken critic of the Public Health Act, was the most thoroughgoing and consistent theoretical opponent of government growth. Drawing on intellectual and literary themes which had wide emotional appeal in the 1840s, Smith categorically rejected all forms of 'government by commissions'. This led him to denounce the General Board of Health, the Factory Commission, the Poor Law Commission, the railway department of the Board of Trade, and the Committee of the Privy Council on Education. In spite of Smith's use of popular historical and political themes, his extreme position was an anomaly in political circles because his categorical rejection of all forms of state intervention was not generally shared by members of parliament.[86] Perhaps Smith recognised that his position was not widely held in parliament when he wrote:

> Were there but two or three Members of the House of Commons who had thoroughly mastered the true spirit and principles of Local Self-Government, and its practical development in the Common Law of England,—and who had the earnestness and the moral courage to fulfil their duties in their places in Parliament,— it would be sufficient to stem the tide of this whole system; and to make felt the importance and necessity of holding fast to those only foundations of freedom and lasting welfare which are to be found in the practical activity of true Institutions of Local Self-Government.[87]

None the less, Smith's writings provided a vast storehouse of argument and evidence from which critics of government growth could draw, no matter what their particular grievance or political goals.

There may have been a personal as well as a theoretical aspect to Smith's opposition to government growth. Smith was subjected to an investigation by a central department of the government when, in 1846, agents of the Board of Excise searched his house in Birmingham for an illegal still. Smith protested violently against this intrusion upon his rights and property. His protest was carried to the floor of the House of Commons by Richard Spooner, who moved for an inquiry into the activities of the Board of Excise. The chief business of the House on 14 May 1846, as Peel noted in his official correspondence to the Queen, was devoted to a discussion of Toulmin Smith's case against the excise commission.[88]

Toulmin Smith rejected government growth and state intervention completely and absolutely. For him every kind of government took one of two forms. It was characterised either by local self-government or centralisation. In Smith's view the designation of governments as monarchial, aristocratic, or democratic was unrealistic because these were only superficial distinctions which did not portray, in any meaningful sense, the true nature of national political life. For him the nature of the political system determined the extent to which a nation would be free, happy, progressive, prosperous, and safe.[89] Thus, Smith considered centralisation and local self-government as administrative and political opposites. In the former a small number of people, having no knowledge of or personal concern in a particular situation, controlled and managed the political system. In the latter the largest number of people, having the greatest knowledge of and personal concern in an administrative matter, controlled and managed it.[90] Centralisation, for Smith, was all that was bad in government practice, consisting of 'irresponsible control, meddling interference, and arbitrary taxation'. He went so far as to consider it a form of communism because 'Its object is to take away the free action of every man over his own property; to stay the free use of every or any man of his own resources and his own ingenuity'. In Smith's view, the whole system of centralisation tended to discourage individual thought and action by conditioning men to accept any '*vade mecum*' offered to them by boards and commissions.[91]

The attack on government growth made by Toulmin Smith extended further than the criticism of the central agencies in which centralisation was manifested. Smith was moved to a complete condemnation of the authorities and instrumentalities through which those authorities had been created. This led him to attack the Crown, parliament, and statute law. Thus, Smith denounced, as a violation of Common Law, Crown-appointed commissions of inquiry. Under the fundamental laws of the country, he maintained, the king and his ministers were prohibited from adopting any proceeding or appointing any officers without the previous consent of the nation. The function of the Crown was 'to *set in motion*' the institutions of local self-government whenever it was necessary to implement the law.[92]

Similarly, Smith's criticism of centralisation led him to attack the supremacy of parliament. For Smith, parliament had departed from its most important function: the preservation of the 'supremacy of certain Fundamental Laws and Institutions'. By this deviation parliament had helped centralisation triumph over free institutions. Indeed, Smith dated the growth of centralisation from 1688, the date of the beginning of parliamentary supremacy.[93] In Smith's view, the authority of parliament was limited to matters concerning the entire nation and the conduct of foreign relations.

> Parliament has, and can have, no original authority of its own. It is a result, and not a source. Its authority is not, like that of the folk and people, self-derived and inherent. No doctrine can be more self-evidently absurd than that of such original authority; while the implication of it is the true ground-work of centralization. There are institutions in this country far more fundamental than Parliament itself. The latter exists only as derived from the folk and the people of the realm, and as the result of the working of the institutions of Local Self-Government. On the full and perfect working of the latter must always depend the lawful character of the former, and the constitutional character of all and any of its acts.[94]

Smith's anti-parliamentary posture led him to object to statute law. Statute law, he argued, was 'theoretical' and had a tendency to infringe on free institutions and responsible action, whereas Common Law was 'practical' and was associated with the spirit of freedom.[95] Smith even objected to local acts of parliament because they violated the fundamental laws of the country by conferring arbitrary powers curtailing the liberty of the subject. Local acts constituted the creation of an *imperium in imperio* within

England, which threatened the unity and cohesion of the country. They were alien elements which did not derive from nor contribute to the organic unity of the country.[96] Toulmin Smith associated all individual, political, and social values with local self-government. For him, this system produced and nurtured the elements necessary for personal happiness and prosperity as well as civic peace and harmony. Local self-government and English Common Law stimulated individual and local responsibility, and, as a consequence, energy, activity, and self-reliance. He also believed political values and benefits stemmed from local self-government. For him, free institutions could only be sustained by the active participation of citizens. The life and vitality of free institutions require a conscious recognition of their reality, which could be stimulated only by the personal experience of civic activity.[97] Therefore, even local representative bodies for legislative purposes did not constitute the essential feature of English local government. Local government, historically, was characterised by and found the sources for revitalisation in the processes of direct democracy:

> It is quite clear from the ancient records, that, until a comparatively late period, the size of all towns and cities being much smaller than at present, and the population of Counties much less, no authoritative Local Representative Bodies existed for legislative purposes. The inhabitants themselves were summoned, in primary folk-motes [sic], to decide every question. This would not have been possible to work well but for the perfection in which the Institutions of Local Self-Government existed in England. Each shire being divided into hundreds, and each borough and city of any size into wards, the members of each of which divisions met regularly and frequently, and the inhabitants were well prepared to express an opinion when assembled in the general folk-motes [sic].[98]

This system of local participatory democracy had, from Smith's point of view, provided the means for the development of patriotism and the political education of the people, and constituted 'the rock of our safety as a free state'.[99] Local self-government was, in addition, the best bulwark against social tension and dislocation. The revolutions on the continent in 1848, Smith implied, had been produced by centralisation and government by commissions. He suggested that similar occurrences could only be prevented in England by a return to the institutions of local self-government. As Smith conceived of the issue, one of the great values of local government was that it, instead of stimulating conflicts between classes or interests, had the 'humanising effect' of uniting society in a common recognition of common interests.[100]

Toulmin Smith's position was much like Richard Oastler's in that both held arcadian social and political views characterised by a reverence for the ancient institutions of England's past. However, there are certain important differences between the views of these men. Toulmin Smith had little of the Tory-aristocratic tone which is found so frequently in Oastler. Smith was concerned primarily with urban life whereas Oastler associated himself almost entirely with rural life and rural values. More importantly, Smith's position, as extreme and as consistently unrealistic as it was, was supported by a wealth of learning which Oastler lacked completely. As a consequence, Toulmin Smith's views reflect a hardness and toughness which is missing in Oastler's sentimental yearnings. The intellectual materials Smith brought to bear on his subject were largely antiquarian and legal, but he also utilised a knowledge of Teutonic languages, literature, and folklore. His arguments were strewn with references to Magna Carta, Coke, the Petition of Right, and English Common Law.[101] In addition, Smith also made exegeses from the Saxon to give credence to his views on local government and centralisation.[102] Much of the tone and force of Smith's argument and rhetoric—in this case through the use of the *axis mundi* image—is shown in his use of Teutonic folklore to characterise the struggle between the forces of local self-government and centralisation:

> Centralization is the foul Dragon that is ever gnawing at the root of Yggdrasil, the great World Tree of Freedom:—Local Self-Government is the true Urda's spring, whose pure waters can alone keep freshened, for ever, the strength and growth of Yggdrasil.[103]

In sum, the critics of public-health legislation opposed this measure as a violation of Common Law, the English constitution, and English historical practice. Political deviations of this kind must, in their view, produce political corruption, increased expense, and political dislocation. In spite of the provisions of the act of 1848 permitting local boards of health to limit the freedom of action of private householders, gas companies, water companies, and to engage in enterprises producing public services, there were few attempts to condemn the measure with analogies drawn from free-trade arguments. *The Economist* alone argued from a laissez-faire posture. While denying that its position was based 'on any mere popular prejudice against centralisation', it believed the best political results were obtained by leaving man to the working of 'uniform material laws'. It was a general rule of moral philosophy, *The Economist* held, not to attempt coercion where natural motives already existed.[104] Toulmin Smith, it is true, valued private enterprise and individual initiative. However, for him these capitalistic values could only be produced and nurtured by the ancient institutions of local government. Toulmin Smith, therefore, did not place these values within the context of laissez-faire propositions. His values, like those of other critics of public-health legislation, were formulated in a framework emphasising the ancient Saxon constitution and the Common Law.

IV

The public-health measures of 1847–8 were supported by men of all political affiliations, with the most extensive support coming from the ranks of the Liberals and Peelites. Like the advocates of the new poor law, the proponents of public-health legislation struck a political posture which differed strikingly from that of their opponents. Instead of drawing on the deep tradition of Common Law and the ancient Saxon constitution, the public-health reformers turned to the investigations of the health of towns for justification of their policies. Recognising epidemic disease as a social and a moral hazard, they believed preventive measures were the most effective and economical means for coping with sanitary threats. The public-health reformers realised, consequently, that parliamentary legislation, central supervision, and central inspection were required for adequate preventive measures.[105] This meant the extension of government into one more aspect of national life. Nevertheless, and this indicates their essential traditionalism, the advocates of public-health measures attempted to show how their provisions for government growth fitted into the context of local institutions and local authority.

The public-health reformers attempted to meet the challenge of their most severe critics by denying that their policies consisted of absolute 'centralisation'. Lord Morpeth's legislation, as he emphasised in 1847, left the control of sanitary measures in the hands of local authorities. Indeed, Morpeth believed the bill accorded too few compulsory powers to the central agency since it could only interfere with the local authorities by bringing public opinion to bear on the issue of sanitation. Yet, as he stated in the debate on the public-health measure in 1848, Morpeth regarded the local authorities as the proper agencies to be charged with sanitary concerns. In his view, the function of the central authority should be limited to providing advice for the creation of local sanitary districts, the arbitration of disputed questions, the formulation of some uniform procedures, and the auditing of accounts.[106] William Mackinnon rejected the charge of 'centralisation' because local health officials were to be selected by the ratepayers and not by the Crown or the General Board of Health. The general board, as Lord John Russell maintained, could not be considered irresponsible, arbitrary, or despotic since the Chief Commissioner of the general board was also the First Commissioner of the Woods and Forests, who was responsible to parliament for anything done in his department.[107] Further, *The Times* pointed out on 2 July 1847, the function of the general board was not to usurp the powers held by local authorities, but merely to inquire, to report, and to assist those authorities. Continuing to value the parochial traditions of England, the public-health reformers insisted that the legislation of 1847–8 did not contain provisions which would introduce a system of centralisation constituting a threat to English liberties.[108] Even Edwin Chadwick, who is frequently portrayed as a centraliser of the first water, was vexed by the continuing accusations that the general board had violated the rights of local government and had disregarded local opinion and local considerations.[109]

The public-health measure of 1847–8, as its proponents conceived of it, was legislation which provided the opportunity for central and local authority to function side by side in a co-operative effort to eliminate threats to public health. Past experience had shown them, as Shafto Adair's resolution to the Health of Towns Association indicates, the necessity of combining in sanitary legislation effective local administration responsible to the rate-payers with supervision by a central authority responsible to parliament.[110] As Lord Normanby noted in 1844, a central authority should be established having the same relationship to the local health authorities as the poor-law commission had to the boards of guardians.[111] For Chadwick, sanitary reform was not to be thrust upon localities without their sufferance, nor were local bodies to be completely independent of central supervision. As Professor Finer has shown, 'Chadwick tried to steer a course between a compulsory public health measure and unfettered local autonomy'.[112] Similarly, Lord Morpeth wanted to leave the administration and execution of sanitary reform in the hands of local authorities. In turn, those local authorities should be aided by the knowledge and special skills which a central agency could offer:

> The part of central control is to provide indispensible prelimi-naries, to suggest useful methods, to check manifold abuses, but to leave the execution and detail of the requisite proceedings to local agency and effort.[113]

All improvements, Joseph Hume argued, should be implemented by local authorities on a local basis. The function of the general board was to suggest courses of action when the local agencies neglected their duty.[114] *The Times* acknowledged a concern for central and local co-operation on 9 May 1848 when it stated that the state should neither extend its power and take over the govern-ment of towns and cities, nor should each city consider itself an independent body politic. 'The State, the city, the people, the property, must all be taken into account with only one object in view. *Salus populi suprema lex esto.*'

Since they were frequently alleged to be enemies of local administration, the public-health reformers felt compelled to deny this charge explicitly. *The Times*, on 15 April 1847, expressed 'the utmost concern' to find itself in opposition to those who criticised the public-health measure as a violation of local government:

> All honour to corporations and local commissioners, and to the many worthy citizens who have not only thought with Themi-

G

stocles that disagreeable functions were sweetened and ennobled by a faithful discharge, but have also been content with a less splendid sphere for their sanitary labours than the cincture of the Acropolis, the port of Piraeus, and the celebrated walls that linked Athens with her Mediterranean empire.[115]

Lord Morpeth claimed he could not have supported the legislation of 1847–8 if its effect was to usurp local authority or limit local efforts. Morpeth had intense respect for those principles of local administration which 'so much distinguished English political life'.[116]

Yet, the advocates of sanitary reform did not have confidence in the local authorities in so far as they were oligarchical, corrupt, and unreformed. As a subscriber to *The Lancet* indicated, public corporations were subject to the same defects of human nature as private individuals and if left to their discretion would fail to function properly.[117] Lord Morpeth recognised some general supervision must be maintained over the local authorities or all sanitary reform efforts would be a mockery. The measure of 1847–8 was a means, therefore, of instituting reformed and effective local administration for sanitary matters. In R. A. Slaney's view, therefore, the bill would extend the powers of local bodies and improve them.[118] The measure, Lord Morpeth suggested, would place the united authority for cleansing, sewerage, draining, and paving in the hands of the governments of 158 corporate towns which had never enjoyed such authority before. Consequently, Morpeth believed his bill would improve local administration rather than undercut it. As he put it:

It is very well to talk of the rights of Englishmen. He wished them to be respected and vindicated. But some attention was due also to the lives of Englishmen; and so far, while he believed this Bill would be found most justly to deserve the name of 'a Bill for promoting health', it might with almost equal accuracy and truth be termed a Bill for consolidating, strengthening, and making more effectual the functions of local bodies in the various municipal towns of England and Wales.[119]

Central action, the advocates of the public-health measure believed, was a means for fortifying local government when it failed to meet its obligations. It was 'an ally of real loyal self-government against spurious local self-government'.[120]

Those promoting the public-health measure believed several benefits would accrue from fruitful co-operation by the central and local authorities. Collaboration between central and local agencies, in the first place, would facilitate the application of professional expertise to the technical problems of sanitary improvement. In Chadwick's view, major preventive measures could only be implemented by utilising the skills possessed by civil engineers. The Buccleuch Commission recommended that all local improvements should be planned and put into effect by persons trained in the principles of engineering and that sanitary officials should be properly qualified for their jobs by 'possessing the necessary scientific attainments'. As the Metropolitan Sanitary Commission recommended, the object of sanitary reform should be the application of qualified, paid professionals to the tasks involved in sanitary administration. These commissioners expected the quality of the training of these officers to be even higher than the normal standards of professional preparation.[121] The quantity and quality of expertise required for sanitary reform would very likely be greater than local experience and administration could supply. Local effort, *The Times* suggested on 15 April 1847, could be supplemented by the central authority, which could bring to bear its greater stock of experience derived from a greater number of sanitary investigations.

A second advantage which the public-health reformers expected from the measure of 1847–8 was a greater application of general knowledge to local problems. Realising that health was a national issue, not a local one, they attempted to find a mechanism for dealing with the national implications of dirt and disease. Central inspection was part of such a mechanism. As Lord Lincoln indicated in 1848, one of the chief values of central inspection was its service as a channel of information between the central and local health authorities. The General Board of Health, Lord John Russell observed in 1854, was an important instrument of public policy because it could furnish information and advice to local boards of health which they might use for a more effective administration of local sanitary affairs. Chadwick himself viewed the central agency as an instrument for the collection and diffusion of information to the local authorities. The central authority was intended, as Tom Taylor put it, to act for the entire nation to turn 'local facts to general use, whether by way of warning or example'.[122]

Finally, many believed a public-health measure would replace the confused and varied local efforts by general and uniform solutions to sanitary problems. As *The Lancet* pointed out, sanitary reform could not be attained by piecemeal legislation but instead required a general and comprehensive plan.[123] Lord Normanby agreed with the importance of local administration, but emphasised the critical character of general principles established nationally. In 1847, J. A. Roebuck expressed gratitude to Lord Morpeth for attempting 'to unite all the scattered and disorganised elements, and consolidate them into one measure for the general benefit'.[124]

The advocates of the public-health measure recognised a factor ignored by their critics, for they perceived a direct relationship between the physical environment and the condition of the working classes. As Lord Ebrington argued in a speech to the Health of Towns Association, sanitary conditions affected the condition of the working population in two ways: disease attacked their health and tranquillity, and also influenced their Christianity and morality.[125] These two themes were widely emphasised in the controversy over public health. The report of the select committee of 1840 pointed out the incongruity of an opulent thriving community existing side by side with a working-class population which could not be expected to maintain similar standards of health and cleanliness since it was subject to all manner of physical contamination.[126] An article in *Fraser's Magazine* attempted to demonstrate the close relationship between working-class health and working-class wealth. In its view, subsistence, the support of wife and family, comfort, independence, hope of improvement, all depended upon the health of the worker.[127] The health of the working classes, R. A. Slaney believed, should be guarded as a matter of justice, not as a matter of compassion. Since laws existed to protect the property of the rich, laws should exist to protect the property of the poor, which consisted in 'his health, his strength, his sinews, his power to labour'. Joseph Hume, as early as 1845, maintained that the physical condition of the working classes was a matter of national importance. To allow the working classes to be deprived of their strength and vitality would, from Hume's point of view, mean the collapse of the strength and stability of the country.[128]

These reformers also recognised that insanitary conditions constituted a threat to the moral and religious condition of the working class. The select committee of 1840 reported that some of the most important effects of disease were crime and social discontent, and that life in an unhealthy environment went far to offset the moral and religious inclinations inculcated by the churches. In the opinion of this committee, diseased environments produced a decline of the 'moral character' and an 'indifference to the common decencies of life'. This kind of environment, the committee maintained, removed incentive and acted as a check on the normal impulses to industry and self-improvement.[129] Chadwick was in substantial agreement with these views concerning the relationship between health and morality. He stated in his sanitary report:

> . . . the population so exposed is less susceptible of moral influences, and the effects of education are more transient than with a healthy population.[130]

Chadwick went further and was more explicit in his description of the effects of interment practices on morality. Burial practices which corrupted the physical environment also demoralised and degraded human sensibilities and engendered a disrespect for human suffering and an indifference to death.[131] Similarly, the Buccleuch Commission realised that unhealthy physical conditions encouraged crime, which stemmed from 'intemperance and the indulgence of vicious propensities'.[132] The moral condition of the poor, R. A. Slaney observed in 1848, corresponded in every respect to their physical condition. Physical dirt and degradation resulted in discontent, drunkenness, and crime.[133]

The public-health reformers were extremely sensitive to the allegation that government growth to facilitate programmes for the health of towns would lead to uneconomical and vastly increased expenditures. They realised the popularity of such a charge and knew it would have to be met in a forthright manner.[134] Even Chadwick, not always the most solicitous about public opinion, acknowledged the necessity of demonstrating the cheap and economical character of sanitary reform.[135] Thus, Sir John

Simon maintained 'sanitary neglect is mistaken parsimony', Lord Ashley believed disease was expensive and health cheap, and Lord Palmerston regarded health as a local, a commercial, as well as a pecuniary matter. In the view of the apologists for the legislation of 1847–8, a reformed system would be cheaper to administer and, in the long run, more economical than existing arrangements. Such economy, Chadwick suggested in his sanitary report, would result from the application of inspection and a reorganisation of the existing fragmented and unsystematised sanitary and health services.[136]

In particular, many believed the chief economic benefits resulting from a public-health measure would be a relaxation of the pressure on the poor-rates and charity funds. Disease, they realised, brought an additional burden on the poor-rates and charities since illness made it impossible for workers to fulfil their obligations to their families. An increase in the mortality rate, as a consequence of disease, meant an increase in the numbers of widows and orphans seeking relief under the poor law. Public-health measures, therefore, as the testimony of Dr Neil Arnott, Dr Southwood Smith, and the conclusion of the select committee of 1840 indicated, would reduce both disease and expenditures as well as contributing to the economic independence of those who now looked to the community for support.[137] In the debate on the health of towns bill in 1847 Lord Morpeth noted, 'besides its other advantages', the measure would provide both real and tangible economic benefits.[138] R. A. Slaney also viewed the matter as an economic issue, estimating the country would regain more than ten times its initial investment in the reduction of the poor-rates. Slaney observed in 1848:

> Hon. Gentlemen complained that the Bill would entail a great expense on the country. Instead of causing additional expense, it would effect a considerable saving—it would be a measure of economy. It would not merely be a benefit to the poor, but it would also be a saving to the rich. It would diminish the poor-rates, and it would also diminish crime, inasmuch as it would remove many of the causes of crime. The country would repay itself doubly and trebly by the adoption of this measure.[139]

The investment required for a public-health measure, Viscount Ebrington argued, was a 'reasonable sacrifice' for a Christian nation, a 'politic expenditure' for a wise nation, and a 'lucrative investment' for a trading nation.[140]

The advocates of the public-health measure, while eschewing narrow legal and constitutional considerations, viewed the matter of economy in a much broader sense than their critics did. While retaining a belief in the importance of local administration, they realised the wealth of the nation was bound up in the health of the nation. The economic health of England, Francis Head argued, depended upon the physical health of the working classes and, therefore, it was in the interest of national prosperity to purify the environment in which the working classes lived and worked.[141] In the opinion of William Guy, the public-health bill was a measure for making as well as saving money, for it would produce men out of children, create productive out of unproductive citizens, and would provide the nation with 'its best riches and its cheapest defence—the arm strong to labour, and, if the sad necessity arises, to fight'.[142] Viewed from this broader perspective, the question of expense and economy was related to the issue of English national strength and prestige. A public-health measure, as Lord Normanby put it in 1845:

. . . would be a blessing to future generations; that through its means might be born, with all the freshness, strength, and vigour of life, a race of men, gifted with that physical superiority that once distinguished, and might again belong to Englishmen, and which, connected with their higher moral energies, constitute the surest foundation for our national greatness.[143]

Understanding the question of economy in this broader perspective the public-health reformers believed sanitary legislation would contribute to the improvement of the condition of the working classes producing a reduction of local taxes, and a strengthened national economy producing an increased national wealth.

In 1848 the sanitary affairs of England, with the exception of the Metropolis, were placed under the government of procedures contained in the Public Health Act. The failure to include London in the general act of 1848 was the subject of vigorous debate in

the House of Commons. Critics of the legislation of 1848, such as
Sibthorp and Hudson (Conservative: Sunderland), as well as its
advocates, such as J. A. Roebuck, objected to the exclusion of an
urban centre having obvious need of sanitary reform.[144] Lord
Morpeth acknowledged the necessity of sanitary improvements in
Metropolitan districts, but believed such requirements could be
adequately supplied in a separate bill. He reminded the House, in
the spirit of compromise and practicality, that everything could
not be accomplished simultaneously. If parliament attempted to
take up all things at once it might very well end its labours with
nothing to show for its efforts.[145] The Metropolitan districts, as
a consequence, were placed under a consolidated commission for
sanitary matters which was independent of the General Board of
Health.

The Public Health Act of 1848 was a significant interventionist
measure since it marked the extension of state activity into areas
traditionally reserved for private and local action. There was clear
demand, both in parliament and from the public at large, for the
state to play an increased role with regard to the question of
national health even if the rights of private property were violated.
As Lord Ellenborough declared in 1841, the rights of property did
not extend so far as to allow individuals to endanger the health of
the community. If 'avarice had its rights', so too did humanity.
The government, Joseph Hume observed in 1847, should be ready
to restrict 'self-interested associations' and 'consult alone the
interests of the many'.[146] As *The Times* noted on 9 May 1848, the
propertied classes could not be depended upon for providing
health measures necessary for the community since they went only
so far as to satisfy their legal obligations, leaving the remainder to
Providence. Consequently, some central authority was needed to
combat the selfishness of the propertied classes, compelling them
to do their duty. The state must step in with the coercive power
of the law, William Guy insisted, 'whenever the rights of property
became the wrongs of the poor'.[147]

This strong sentiment for state intervention should not be
construed as the basis for a characterisation of the Public Health
Act as a collectivist measure nationalising the health services of
England in a tightly organised and centralised system. As this book
shows, the social investigations of the 1840s suggested some kind

of central authority, but they also stressed the necessity of local administration for sanitary improvements. Moreover, the Public Health Act, which created a General Board of Health, specified that local authorities would have the responsibility for administration of the measure under the general supervision and superintendence of the central authority. Indeed, Royston Lambert confirms this in his analysis of the function of the state in sanitary matters after 1848. As he puts it, the role of the central government after 1848 had a 'part-time, almost philanthropic, extra-governmental flavour'.[148]

The controversy over public-health reform, it should be emphasised, did not consist of a conflict between individualist principles with analogies to free trade as opposed to state collectivism.[149] Rather, the conflict, like that over the new poor law, was between two different conceptions of politics. The critics of sanitary reform, with their organic view of society and politics, drew their arguments from English history and Common Law and attacked the act of 1848 as unconstitutional in its formulation, arbitrary and despotic in operation, and as a stimulant to political corruption and government expenditure. The advocates of public-health reform, on the other hand, had both a broader and more complex view of the issues involved in the sanitary question. Realising the importance of the social investigations of the 1840s, they adopted a political stance which allowed them to reaffirm the importance of local administration and at the same time support measures which would provide effective solutions to growing environmental problems. In their view the extension of state authority in the Public Health Act of 1848 was accomplished gradually in the context of local government and local authority. While dealing meaningfully with disease and filth, they could retain the confidence that their actions were not inconsistent with the historical structures of English government and administration.

Between 1848 and 1854 the Public Health Act was under constant attack by Toulmin Smith, the Anti-Centralisation Union, and other localist elements. Lord Morpeth was subjected to personal criticism even before the act of 1848 was passed, and Lord Ashley accepted a position on the General Board of Health in full realisation of the unpopularity which would follow.[150] In 1854 the legislated lifetime of the general board expired and Lord Palmerston, the Home Secretary in Aberdeen's cabinet, took steps to renew it by reorganising the general board under the aegis of the Home Office. The weakness of Aberdeen's government, and its indifference to sanitary matters, left the general board to the untender mercies of its enemies.[151] Legislation in 1854 reconstituted the General Board of Health to consist of a group of *ex officio* ministers presided over by a permanent salaried president charged with the formulation of policy and responsible to parliament for the actions of his department.

Even after 1854, however, the concern for public health did not lapse into absolute localism. Under Sir Benjamin Hall (Reformer: Marylebone), the first president of the reconstituted board and one of the most energetic critics of the general board, the role of the state in matters of public health assumed the character of a permanent department of the government with its permanent inspectorate and ministerial responsibility.[152] In 1858 the Local Government Act allowed localities to adopt voluntarily the provisions of the legislation of 1848. In spite of its title, the Local Government Act was not completely localist, for eighteen of its clauses placed discretionary powers in the hands of the central authority. In the 1850s, as in the 1840s, the state's powers were extended in matters of public health.[153]

Notes to Chapter 3 will be found on pages 199–208.

Chapter 4 PRIVATE OPPORTUNITIES AND PUBLIC RESPONSIBILITIES
Early Victorian Railway Legislation, 1840-1847

These undertakings originate, as is well known, entirely in the motives of public advantage: it is the pride and boast of our country that such vast works can be executed by the enterprise of private individuals, without assistance from the public purse; and far be it from Parliament to check this valuable and characteristic spirit. But it is this very circumstance which calls for redoubled vigilance on the part of the Legislature.

Let care be taken that public good is not sacrificed to private advantage!

What Will Parliament Do With the Railways? (London: 1836)

I

RAILWAY LEGISLATION, at first glance, with its necessary concern for economic and technical considerations, seems to have little relationship to the issues raised in the controversies over the poor law and public health. Closer scrutiny of the railway question, however, reveals that railway legislation, as it was formulated in the 1840s, conformed to the general pattern of early Victorian state intervention. On the one hand, the railway issue was appreciated as something other than a mere technical matter. As an anonymous author put it in a pamphlet addressed to Sir Robert Peel: 'It is not a question of engineering only—there are moral, social, and political considerations of importance which must enter into the argument.'[1] Moreover, railway development was seen, as the quote at the head of this chapter suggests, as a public matter having advantages to the community at large, and not as a narrow question concerning only the profit margins of capitalists. As another anonymous writer declared:

> ... we may henceforth hope that railways will be considered, not as 'legalised nuisances' to be abated, not as eager and grasping monopolies, invading private property, and wringing enormous profits from an injured community to satisfy the avarice of a few bloated capitalists, but as truly national enterprises, deserving of every support and encouragement which an enlightened government can give. . . .[2]

Moreover, just as the poor-law and public-health reformers considered their measures as means for the co-operation of central and local agencies, so, too, as this statement reveals, did the proponents of railway legislation attempt to find ways in which the government and railway companies could co-operate in the public interest rather than engage in conflict. The relationship between the government and the railways, Professor Parris concludes, was characterised less by hostility than by signs of partnership.[3]

In the second quarter of the nineteenth century there were three periods of boom in the development of English railways. The first occurred immediately following the opening of the Stockton and Darlington railway in 1825, and the second resulted, at least in part, from the extension of the great trunk lines from London to the North, South, and West of England after 1836. The third surge of railway speculations and projections, the so-called 'great railway mania' of the early Victorian period, took place in the mid-1840s. A simple table reveals the rapid extension of the British railway system in the first half of the nineteenth century.

	Acts	Miles opened
1801–1840	299	3,000 (about)
1841	19	15
1842	22	67
1843	24	91
1844	48	797
1845	120	2,883
1846	272	4,790
1847	184	1,663
	988	13,306

Arthur W. Hart, a contemporary, noted a continuing increment in railway income. Between 1845 and 1848 the value of the annual traffic increased from £6,670,000 to £10,000,000.[4] The impact of this railway development is beyond dispute. Railways stimulated a demand for coal and iron products, and also created an enormous demand for labour in its own right. The railways accomplished a transportation revolution by reducing transport costs and by broadening local markets. Even as it produced these economic changes, the railway stimulated social change, resulting in the interpenetration of town and country, and the blurring of social distinctions. In short, the railway was an important instrument in ending what Marx called 'rural idiocy' and in fostering the *embourgeoisement* of the country. Samuel Smiles echoed similar sentiments when he observed:

> Railways virtually bring towns and cities into close approxima-
> tion; they open up for agriculturalists new markets for the sale of
> their produce; they circulate freely the great necessities of life,
> coal, provisions, and clothing; they offer to the denizens of the
> cities the ready enjoyment of rural beauty, and to the rural
> population they give the advantages of towns and cities; and
> thus, by their means has Great Britain become as one great city,
> the streets of which are the iron roads which now stretch across
> it in all directions.[5]

The function of the railways, the *Westminster Review* stated with a gust of national pride, was to 'perfect the civilisation' begun by the road and the printing press.[6]

The railway companies, deriving their authority from private acts of parliament, stood outside the existing legal structure. With no place under English law for a public prosecutor, and with the concept of administrative enforcement outside the existing legal machinery still in its infancy, there was no means for government either to check the abuses of railway companies or to aid in effective railway development. The established interpretations of early Victorian railway legislation, therefore, emphasise its restrictive and limiting character.[7] Yet, as the evidence presented here indicates, the relationship between the state and the railways was as symbiotic as it was antagonistic. The influence of the government increased in railway development at least in part because the officers of the railway department of the Board of

Trade were 'models of ability, industry, and integrity'.[8] Consequently, Professor Parris suggests, the railway department was a microcosm of the more general pattern of government growth by which the English state was adapted to the imperatives of an industrialised society.[9] Cleveland-Stevens regards early Victorian railway legislation as a reasonable and viable alternative to government ownership of the railways. By state supervision, state purchase became unnecessary, since the monopolistic tendencies inherent in railway development were rendered harmless.[10]

In spite of government growth in the field of railway development in the 1840s, state control over the railways was far from complete—far less complete than its control over the emigrant passenger traffic, so admirably documented by Professor Mac-Donagh.[11] The most frequent explanation of the limited character of railway legislation is to point to the power of the railway interest in the House of Commons.[12] While the railway lobby was undoubtedly a powerful political force in the 1840s, the extent of its influence in shaping the details of legislation is less clear. The political power of vested interest is not always sufficient to hold off threats to its privileges, as the case of the corn laws makes abundantly clear.[13] Therefore, in attempting to identify the character of early Victorian railway legislation and the attitudes men held towards it, this book turns away from the rough and tumble of political arm-twisting and seeks to find those elements in the parliamentary debates, the sessional papers, and the pamphlet literature. Railway legislation in the 1840s, the evidence suggests, should not be considered collectivistic, since it did not nationalise the railways under a public authority. Moreover, the public controversy over public railway bills indicates a dual and ambivalent attitude on the part of the British political community. Apparently wide segments of those men alert to public affairs saw both advantages and dangers in public legislation. They appreciated the value of government growth to curb abuses and to encourage railway development. Yet, they realised the possibility that extensive regulation could stifle railway development. Just as the Poor Law Amendment Act and the Public Health Act attempted to establish an effective equilibrium between central and local government, so too the railway acts in the 1840s sought to set the spheres of the public and private interest in political equilibrium with each other.

II

Railway development in the 1840s, with its tendency towards amalgamation, and therefore monopoly, suggested to many, both in and out of public life, the necessity for some kind of government intervention. England, however, had no model after which she might pattern a system for public regulation. The French railway department was almost solely concerned with the problems of encouragement rather than restraint, and the Belgian model for state regulation came too late to influence English considerations. As Professor Parris has suggested, the English problem was novel, as was its solution.[14] English railway legislation in the 1840s, taking advantage of nearly a decade of administrative experience with regard to the poor law and the factory system, established the means for central supervision and inspection, through the Board of Trade, while leaving the details of management and administration to the railway companies.

In 1839 a Select Committee of the House of Commons[15] reported its recommendations concerning the state of English railways. One of its principal recommendations, to use the language of the report, was

. . . a supervising authority should be exercised over all arrangements in which the Public are interested. It would seem that this control should be placed in the hands of the Executive Government, and it might be expedient to vest it in a Board to be annexed to the Board of Trade, of which the President and the Vice-President should be members, together with one or two engineer officers of rank and experience.[16]

This recommendation contains two themes which run through the entire nineteenth-century revolution in government: supervision by a central authority, and the application of professional expertise. In particular, these themes characterise the railway legislation of the 1840s, beginning with the bill proposed by Lord Seymour and James Loch (Liberal: Wick), a director of the Liverpool and Manchester railway, in 1840, and extending through the acts of 1842, 1844, 1845, and 1846. Since the content of this body of legislation has already been examined in considerable detail,[17] it would not be fruitful to duplicate such efforts here. However, it is appropriate to elucidate the character of the early Victorian railway legislation in terms of the two themes suggested above.

The legislation of 1840, sponsored by Lord Seymour and James Loch, charged 'the Lords of the Committee of Her Majesty's Privy Council appointed for Trade and Foreign Plantations' with the responsibility for supervising railway development.[18] The Board of Trade initially set out to run its railway department on a limited experimental basis. Since a good deal of its work was related to the statistical branch of the Board, the railway department was annexed to it and only later acquired an independent position. The main business of the railway department was handled by a law clerk, a junior clerk, and an inspector general. Samuel Laing, Henry Labouchere's private secretary, was named the first law clerk. Lieutenant Colonel Sir Frederick Smith became the first inspector general and was succeeded in 1841 by C. E. Pasley.[19] The Board of Trade was authorised by the legislation of 1840 to insure compliance with all provisions of acts regulating or chartering railways. Any lack of compliance was to be certified to the Queen's Attorney General for England or Ireland, or to the Lord Advocate for Scotland, who were to recover all penalties and forfeitures and enforce the performance of all such provisions.[20]

The inspection of railway lines, the most effective means of applying national standards of expertise to railway development, was the most important function of the railway department. The Board of Trade was authorised by the act of 1840 to appoint officials for inspecting railways and their attendant stations, works, buildings, engines, and carriages. No man could be appointed to such a position if, in the year preceding, he had been a railway director or had held a position of trust and responsibility in any company.[21] The legislation of 1840 was limited in one important respect: it could not prevent the opening of a line even if inspection showed it to be unsafe. The act of 1842, however, remedied this limitation by providing the Board of Trade with the power to postpone the opening of a line, continuing on a month to month basis, if inspection revealed the existence of danger to the travelling public.[22]

Inspection by the railway department enabled it to act as an arbitrator as well as serve in an appellate capacity. The legislation of 1840 removed railway regulation from the jurisdiction of the local judicial system by repealing the clauses of acts requiring the approval of justices of the peace on regulations of railway companies. Further, all provisions empowering justices to decide disputes between landowners and railway companies concerning certain construction problems were repealed and the authority to act as an arbiter was vested in the hands of the Board of Trade.[23] The legislation of 1842 further extended the power of the Board of Trade by charging it with the responsibility of arbitrating disputes between railway lines. The Clauses Consolidation Act of 1845 also expanded the authority of the railway department by authorising it to act in an appellate capacity when landowners were injuriously affected by deviations from the established plans of railway projections.[24]

The collection and validation of railway statistics, a necessary aspect of inspection and the application of expertise, was a major task of the railway department of the Board of Trade. The legislation of 1840 required railway companies to provide a month's notice to the Board of Trade before opening any portion of a new line. In addition it called for companies to submit information about the operation of the line, such as the records of passenger and freight traffic with a table of tolls and fares charged, and a statement of accidents involving personal injuries.[25] The railway act of 1842 required companies to inform the railway department of any accidents resulting in injuries within forty-eight hours and obliged them to submit statistics on all accidents whether injuries occurred or not.[26] In addition, as the act of 1840 specified, the bylaws and regulations made by companies for the government of their lines were not to be effective until two months after being submitted to the Board of Trade, which was authorised to evaluate and approve them.[27]

One important aspect of early Victorian railway legislation was the attempt to remove the power of arbitration and appeal from institutions of local government, placing them in the hands of the railway department of the Board of Trade. This is not to suggest, however, that central authorities arrogated all privileges and responsibilities of local government. Parish authorities retained

H

certain specific powers with regard to prosecution and rating. The Clauses Consolidation Act (1845), for example, specified and defined the responsibilities of local government. Construction on a line could not begin until a plan or section of all alterations from the original plan had been placed in the hands of the clerks of the peace in the counties through which the line was to pass. If a landowner objected to the acquiring of land for railway purposes because it was essential 'to the beneficial Enjoyment of other neighbouring Lands belonging to him', a justice of the peace could summon the company before two other justices, who could order the return of the contested lands. Any question of damage done by a railway company to other roads was to be referred to the determination of two justices of the peace. Railway companies were to make annual accountings of their receipts and expenditures and report them to the clerks of the peace and the overseers of the poor in the various parishes through which the line passed.[28]

The legislation of 1844, sponsored by W. E. Gladstone as President of the Board of Trade, deserves a separate discussion as a special and important case because it has been frequently taken as a collectivistic measure. John Morley, for example, believed the act gave government 'the full right of intervention in the concerns of the railway companies', and E. Cleveland-Stevens regarded it as a direct attempt to give the state a hand in the operation of railways.[29] The legislation of 1844, following the recommendations laid down in the third report of Gladstone's Select Committee in 1844, gave government the option of revising rates charged by companies or purchasing the shares of companies projected after 1844 after twenty-one years had elapsed. In addition, it obligated railway companies to provide travelling accommodations at moderate rates for the lower classes. The administration of this act, like other railway legislation before 1846, was to be supervised by the railway department of the Board of Trade through its system of inspectors.[30]

The revision and purchase clauses of the act of 1844 are, of course, the elements which admit of a collectivistic interpretation most directly. Yet, a consideration of the report of Gladstone's select committee, the debate on the bill, and the act itself, indicate that such an interpretation is excessive and unwarranted. Intervention in the management of railways, the select committee of 1844 realised, was an improper intrusion into the business affairs of companies. Legislation which was excessively rigorous or rigid, it believed, might well cripple the legitimate operations of a company. The function of the railway department, as the select committee conceived it, was not to restrict the operations of the company but to serve as a mediator between the government and the railway lines in an effort to accommodate legislative requirements to existing circumstances.[31] Further, the inspection clause of the act of 1844 specified that no inspector could 'exercise any powers of interference *in the affairs* of the company'.[32] Gladstone himself stated an unequivocal objection to a general interference by the state in the 'management of these companies', and described the legislation of 1844 as both mild and restrained:

> I contend that this measure, so far from being a measure of violence, of an extreme or doubtful character, is a measure of utmost importance, and that the option of revision and purchase is characterized by the utmost temperance and moderation.[33]

Both Gladstone and Henry Labouchere (Liberal: Taunton) insisted the purpose of the bill was not to call for the immediate revision of tolls or the purchase of railways, but rather to give the government authority to reconsider the status of the railway system at some time in the future. As Gladstone put it:

> We are content . . . with making a mere provision for the limitation in the future; the whole effect of which provision is, that instead of Parliament having its hands tied and fettered as they are now, they shall be free to deal with these matters for the public good. . . .[34]

As this discussion indicates, the function of the legislation of 1844 was not to provide for the public ownership or control of the railways. Moreover, the proponents of the legislation carefully eschewed government meddling with the day-to-day management of railway affairs.

In 1846 a Select Committee chaired by James Morrison[35] proposed to reorganise the railway department of the Board of Trade as an independent railway commission 'so constituted as to obtain public confidence'. The railway commission, as described by Morrison's select committee, would have authority to process all proposals for the construction or amalgamation of lines, to inspect existing as well as projected railways, to hear and inquire into complaints made against railways by local bodies, and to make suggestions concerning proper fares and tolls. For these purposes the select committee recommended that it possess all the powers formerly exercised by the railway department of the Board of Trade.[36] Lord John Russell's government turned these recommendations into law, creating the Railway Commission in place of and holding all of the powers of the railway department.[37] In effect, the new agency was a central board connected to the executive, since it was appointed by the Queen's ministers rather than the legislature, but with a salaried president and officers who might sit in the House of Commons.[38]

Early Victorian railway legislation, it is possible to conclude, simultaneously extended and limited the role of the central government in railway matters. Central authority was extended by legislation making it the appropriate business of government to concern itself with the details of construction plans, junctions, amalgamations, and the leasing of rights to other lines. Central authority was limited in the sense that it possessed no regulatory powers. It could not inspect established lines, demand special—even if safer—equipment, or in any way determine the appropriate use of equipment or schedules.[39] The preponderance of the evidence, therefore, suggests it is misleading to regard railway legislation in the 1840s as collectivistic, since it neither asserted a public control over railway management nor obliterated the legal distinction between the public responsibilities and the private opportunities of railway companies. Therefore, it would appear most fruitful to emphasise the complementary and co-operative relationships which existed between government and the railway companies between 1840 and 1846.

Railway legislation in the 1840s, as the division on Gladstone's bill in 1844 indicates,[40] was not an issue over which parties contended. Rather than being a party issue, the railway question was one on which parties were divided internally. It is clear, however, that the Liberals were more deeply split than the Conservatives. In the division on 11 July 1844, 82·5 per cent of the Conservatives and 39 per cent of the Liberals supported the bill, while 17·5 per cent of the Conservatives and 61 per cent of the Liberals opposed it. It would be tempting to interpret the heavy Conservative support as a manifestation of the landowners' opposition to the invasion of their rural privacy by mechanised intruders and the opposition of Liberals as a consequence of their faith in abstract laissez-faire dogmas. The House of Commons, a reading of the parliamentary debates reveals, was more concerned with practical political issues than it was with a hatred of modernity or a blind confidence in political economy.

III

Opposition to railway legislation was not always unqualified and many who objected to state intervention generally understood some cases might require government action which restricted the independence of railway companies. For example, William Ewart criticised 'undue interference' with railway companies, but, believing parliament was obligated both to allow the public the benefit of free competition and to protect it from dangerous overspeculation, supported measures which would allow the government to collect information in order to avoid excessive speculation.[41] Thomas Gisborne (Reformer: Nottingham) opposed limiting stockholders' dividends but maintained that parliament might properly revise the schedule of tolls at twenty-year intervals. John Bright objected to a revision of tolls by the government but admitted that railways must submit to some forms of regulation. And Richard Lalor Sheil (Repealer: Dungarvon), objecting to the 'inquisitorial powers' which the act of 1844 placed in the hands of the government concerning the financial operations of companies, approved of the powers of supervision and inspection given by the same act.[42]

Even George Hudson, the magnate known in his own time as the railway king, did not expect an absolute application of a principle of non-interference, especially when such interference worked in his own interest. Testifying before a Select Committee in 1844, he suggested it might be well for the Board of Trade to exercise more authority in requiring companies to give accommodations to adjoining lines. The rash of railway investment in the mid-1840s encouraged Hudson to favour government intervention for the solidification of railway development by limiting excessive speculation. As a consequence, Hudson believed the railway measure of 1846 would have the 'effect of placing the parties interested in railways on a solid basis'. Hudson himself presented a clause to be inserted in all railway acts which would provide intervention by the government in the form of protection for railway projectors. Hudson, as his biographer observes, was well aware of the threat which excessive speculation might provide to his empire.[43]

In general, the position of *The Times* was similar, since, while maintaining there was little need for public legislation on railway matters, it held that government was obligated to interfere 'on proper occasions in all public undertakings'. Close examination of *The Times*'s position reveals the expression 'proper occasions' allowed considerable latitude for government intervention, including the investigation of railway plans before construction began, the authority to determine maximum fares, the power to require guarantees from companies lest they fail to maintain the fares originally specified, the determination of the number of carriages for each type of accommodation, and the authority to require sufficient railway employees to protect the public safety.[44] The position of *The Times*, it might be observed, while denying the *necessity* of government intervention on railway matters, went considerably beyond the legislation of the 1840s, when it came down to recommending specific actions by the state.

The critics of railway legislation raised two kinds of objections to government intervention. The first, in minor mode, was based upon political considerations. The second, in major mode, was based upon economic considerations. In some ways the political criticisms of railway legislation were framed in the same rhetoric as the criticisms of the new poor law and the Public Health Act. That is to say, these political objections were not based on laissez-faire arguments drawn from the campaign for free trade. Rather, they focused on the dangers of 'centralisation' and the concentration of political power, which were based on the assumption that government growth was unconstitutional, despotic, and contrary to the political customs of the nation. Consequently, as a letter to the editor of *The Times* on 1 July 1844 indicates, railway legislation was identified, at least in part, with other manifestations of state intervention:

Sir,—Most people thought that when we got rid of the Whigs we also got rid of their pet system of centralization and commissions, but it seems the system is 'too good' to be abandoned, and accordingly beside our present Poor Law nuisance, we are to have an embryo board for railways.

Early Victorian railway legislation, since it was regarded by its critics as a deviation from the natural political order, was considered despotic, corrupting, and unconstitutional. Matthew Talbot Baines (Liberal: Hull) maintained it was improper for the central government to establish an 'inquisitional or vexatious' system for inquiring into the operation of railways. Benjamin Hawes detailed the ways in which he believed railway legislation provided despotic infringements upon the liberties of Englishmen. The legislation of 1840, he believed, gave government access 'at all hours' to information concerning the operation of railway companies. Hawes feared this power would be applied against other forms of enterprise such as canal companies or joint-stock banks.[45] For Captain Henry George Boldero (Conservative: Chippenham) the inspecting authority of the railway department would allow it to invade the offices of companies and peruse its 'most private concerns'. John Campbell Colquhoun expressed his concern that government growth was politically corrupting when he characterised the legislation of 1844 as

. . . so unfair, so ruinous, to railways, so unjust to the public in the long run, so unfair to all classes, so full of patronage, corruption, jobbing and mischief.[46]

John Bright raised the constitutional implications of government intervention in railway matters. In his view the constitutional issues implicit in the legislation of 1844 were sufficient for him to oppose it even if the bill were perfect in other respects. Like Colquhoun, Bright objected to the amount of patronage railway legislation placed in the hands of the government because increased patronage would foster the concentration rather than the diffusion of political power. As Bright observed:

He wished to see a powerful Government—powerful in the opinions of the people, but not in the amount of patronage at its disposal. . . .[47]

An additional set of criticisms, related to these political objections, stressed that railway legislation was contrary to the traditions, customs, and indeed, the very personality of Englishmen. As Charles Buller (Radical Reformer: Liskeard) maintained, the legislation of 1844 had no precedent in existing law and was 'contrary to all our habits and institutions' as well as the accepted patterns of political behaviour. In England, in contrast to the continental countries, private corporations independent of the government constructed roads and were responsible for the lighting of towns. His chief reason for opposing government growth in the form of railway legislation was the inconsonance of such measures with the best features of the English national character:

> The English were a self-relying, a self-acting people. They were not accustomed to look to the Government for their bread. The system of centralization tended to make men machines instead of making them powers; it made them slaves instead of free men.[48]

Lord Hatherton, in general agreement with Buller's position, declared it was the particular genius of the English people, a genius stimulating private enterprise and leading to the creation of the empire, which made them keep such matters in their own hands.[49] These arguments, utilising a perspective drawn from an appreciation of custom and tradition, represent the use of historical insights in the controversy over railway legislation and are analogous to similar lines of argument in the poor-law and public-health controversies. Significantly, this position was not argued by Conservatives alone. Rather, it was stated and defended by Baines, Buller, Bright, and Hatherton—all Liberal or Radical in their political views. This evidence reconfirms conclusions reached in the discussion of the new poor law and the public-health movement: that reactionary intellectual themes, finding their substance and inspiration in an understanding of England's past, informed the political left as well as the political right in early Victorian England.

Aside from these political considerations, marking a sharp divergence from the cases of the Victorian poor law and the Public Health Act, the main criticisms of railway legislation stressed economic arguments. The major assumption lying behind these economic considerations was the notion that the free employment of capital, the basis of past as well as future progress, produced public benefits and private profits. This assumption, it is significant to note, was as close as the discussion of early Victorian railway legislation came to using the concepts of classical political economy. Generally, however, the value of the free employment of capital was stated as a practical consideration rather than as an abstract dogma applicable to all situations. The free employment of capital was understood as an appropriate guide to national policy, not because of its theoretical significance, but because of its practical benefits for the country at large as well as the railway companies. For example, Charles Poulett Thomson (Liberal: Manchester), the President of the Board of Trade in Liberal governments during the 1830s, regarded the fact that government had not interfered with capital as the reason for England's economic superiority. G. F. Muntz and Richard Lalor Sheil accepted the same notion when they opposed the legislation of 1844 because it threatened to 'check the spirit of enterprise', preventing the expansion of the railway system.[50]

Opponents of railway legislation raised the spectre of the exportation of English capital if government began to interfere with railway development. In George Hudson's view, foreign capital was invested in England because of the assurance of secure and profitable investment. In the event parliamentary enactments limited the security of investment possibilities, Hudson believed capital would find its way to France, where the government was prepared to guarantee any amount of investment. Government interference 'would end in a way disastrous to the Government, injurious to the public, and destructive to the interests of the shareholders'. Lord George Bentinck used a similar argument when he warned that English capital would be employed in Greek or Spanish economic development unless speculation in the improvement of communications in general, and the construction of railways in particular, was left to follow its own course.[51] The major consideration in this position was not whether or not the free application of capital conformed to the appropriate rules of political economy; rather, government intervention was seen as a factor leading to a crisis of confidence in the business community producing the export of English capital. Samuel Shaen, therefore, recognising the economic importance of railways as well as the precarious character of railway capital, warned against 'crude and empiric, or uncertain and hasty legislation'.[52]

The critics of railway legislation frequently emphasised the public character of the railways as a complement to their private role. In the view of these men, the railway companies, in spite of the fact that they were private corporations, conferred great advantages upon the public at large. John Bright stressed this claim in an effort to show how the railway system was not monopolistic. Since monopoly, according to Bright's definition, never benefited anyone but the entrepreneurs involved, it was clear the railways could not be considered monopolies because they provided cheap and safe transportation for the entire country.[53] Two conclusions were drawn from the assertion of the public character of English railways. First, it was believed that public accommodations could not be effectively regulated by government. In George Hudson's view, parliament could not prevent lines which competed for the same traffic from reaching private agreements amongst themselves concerning tolls and charges. Thomas Gisborne believed it was impossible for government to control railway speculation, for capital was subject to the direct influence of other factors: the labour and money markets.[54]

A second conclusion, however, was drawn from an understanding of the public qualities of railway enterprise. If public benefits were to be maximised, the responsibility for the management of railway lines should be left in the hands of company directors and not arrogated to a central government agency. Sir John Easthope (Liberal: Leicester) believed there was little need to regulate railway affairs because

> . . . there was . . . the strongest grounds for affirming that the individuals to whose direction the railways throughout the country were confided, fully felt and understood that their own true interests, and the interests of the proprietors of these public undertakings, were identical with the interests of the public; that their interests were best promoted by looking to a minimum rather than a maximum of charge; and he thought it would be impossible for his noble Friend to show any clear and intelligible evidence to the contrary.

Birkham Escott (Conservative: Winchester) supported only those railway measures which would leave 'the most unlimited discretionary power' in the hands of the directors of the railway companies because 'they had the strongest interest to give way to public opinion, and to promote the public security and accommodation'. William Ewart believed non-interference should be the cardinal principle of railway legislation because to interfere with the personal responsibility of railway directors would increase, not reduce, the danger to the public. Greater benefit would accrue to the public, George Hudson argued, if responsibility was left in the hands of railway directors than if it were assumed by parliament or the Railway Commission.[55]

Naturally, critics of the railway acts were not solely concerned with the public benefits of railway enterprise. As one would expect, they believed railway companies, as private corporations, should receive the profits and benefits of investment and risky speculation. Far from feeling that profits should be restricted, those who objected to railway legislation maintained that profits of companies were insufficient. Consequently, Samuel Shaen, declaring the railways had been subject to both unfair risks and unfair regulations, believed there was no basis for the charge that railway profits were unusually large, and Charles Hindley (Whig: Ashton-under-Lyne) regarded the remuneration received by railway companies as unobjectionable because railway projections were great patriotic undertakings. G. F. Muntz maintained that railway investors took great risks and, therefore, should receive great profits. As he pointed out, if these investors had suffered losses on their speculations there would have been no great public demand for indemnification.[56]

The criticism of railway legislation in the 1840s was based only in part on political arguments using a perspective adduced from an historical and organic vision of economics and society. For the most part, the opposition to railway legislation rested upon a concern for the public role railway development played in the national economy. Just as the critics of the new poor law and the Public Health Act wished to solve the problems of poverty and disease within the framework of parish and county government, the critics of the railway acts wished to deal with the problems of railway development in the context of authority controlled by the directors of railway companies. For all the talk of profits and the value of railway enterprise as an aspect of individual initiative and the English character, only rarely did this take a form which might be interpreted in the context of the campaign for free trade. Far from denying the public character of the railways, the opponents of the railway acts recognised it and viewed government intervention as a threat, not only to railway profits, but to the national economic advances which had occurred as a consequence of railway development. A plea for the national interest, rather than a concern for the abstract dogmas of political economy, stood at the heart of the criticism of early Victorian railway legislation.

IV

The attitudes of proponents of railway legislation can, most appropriately, be described as incrementalist. Concerned neither with dogma nor a legislative blueprint, they proposed qualified and pragmatic legislation which would on one hand extend the authority of the state, and on the other hand avoid a violation of institutions which were considered crucial for the economic development of Britain. To straddle such a political fence was difficult indeed, but the advocates of state intervention believed these goals could be reached if they followed the guidelines established by administrative and political experience. Again and again in these discussions, experience was invoked as a means for coping with delicate and difficult issues. Experience, the officers of the railway department observed in a report to the President of the Board of Trade in 1841, determines the necessary precautions and regulations which government should enforce to secure the public safety. When Gladstone introduced a bill in 1842 to extend the power of the Board of Trade he was careful to point out both the restricted nature of the measure and his intention to expand the powers of the central authority 'only on specific points *where experience* showed they were called for'. Edward Strutt (Reformer: Derby), Chief Commissioner of Railways from 1846 to 1848, placed the same emphasis on experience in his speech on the railway bill of 1846. As he indicated, the legislation of 1846 was not a 'complete measure' and further experience would call for additional alterations and improvements.[57]

The incrementalist insistence on experience as a guide to the gradual extension of state authority led the proponents of railway legislation to a restrained and modest position on these matters. Seeing the limits of state intervention, they had no desire to provide government management for the railways. Yet, recognising the public character of the railways and appreciating their monopolistic tendencies, the threat of excessive speculation, the possibility of capital waste, and the lack of uniformity in railway development, many public persons pressed for increased state action. Significantly, government intervention in railway affairs was conceived, therefore, not merely as a restrictive device, but as a positive instrument for the improvement of the railway system in the private as well as the public interest.

The proponents of railway legislation, it must be emphasised, had no intention of allowing the state to usurp the management of the railways. To put the matter positively, there was considerable sentiment among those advocating state intervention—and here they were in substantial agreement with their critics—that while government might inspect and supervise, the conduct of railway affairs must continue to rest in the hands of railway companies receiving their authority by parliamentary enactment. The officers of the railway department of the Board of Trade, as much as they wished greater uniformity in the operation of railways, did not believe such an objective should be obtained by the unilateral exercise of parliamentary power. They stated, 'we think it better to attain this object gradually and by the co-operation of the railway companies themselves' than by the use of authorities contained in the legislation of 1840. Similarly, the select committee of 1844 began its investigation with a 'strong prepossession against any general interference' by the central authority in the operation of railways, and found no reason to change its opinion on the subject.[58] When Gladstone addressed the House of Commons on his motion to consider new provisions for future railway acts he had no doubt about the prerogative of parliament to interfere in railway matters but believed the House was disposed 'to restrain the exercise of this right within proper and moderate bounds'.[59] Moreover, the advocates of state intervention believed the public safety and advantage were best protected when railway companies retained responsibility for the management of their lines. As Lord Seymour indicated, the purpose of the inspection clause in the legislation of 1840 was 'not to take away from the railway directors that responsibility to which they were already subjected'.[60] Sir Robert Peel believed that to carry intervention 'beyond its proper limits' would not provide increased security for the public but would produce diminished returns:

> The railway companies would . . . feel relieved from the responsibility. They would then shield themselves from public indignation, on account of the Government having the superintendence of the regulations. Then their vigilance would be relaxed; and they would have the power of asserting, that as the Government had relieved them from the responsibility, the Government ought to assume it.[61]

Even the officers of the railway department had no desire to regulate matters of detail with regard to railway management because they believed the railway directors bore the legal responsibility for such concerns.[62]

Far from being dogmatic proponents of nationalisation the advocates of state intervention acknowledged the political and economic limitations which they perceived to railway legislation. Politically, they recognised that the intervention of a central department required public confidence in the constitution and composition of such an agency, a point which the select committee preparatory to the legislation of 1840 readily admitted. Regrettably, the railway department never gained such a degree of political confidence because it seemed to operate behind a veil of secrecy, its reports were sometimes regarded as unreliable, and some critics believed that decisions were made by clerks rather than responsible officials.[63] When the Railway Commission was established in 1846 one of the important considerations was its political viability. Again, public confidence was conceived as the most important criterion for its continuing effectiveness. As Henry Goulburn (Conservative: Cambridge University), who served as Peel's Chancellor of the Exchequer, put it:

> The object of the Government in introducing this bill was to appoint men in place of the former Commissioners, who would command the confidence of the public, which from some reason or other, the late Commissioners did not, not withstanding their great talents and fitness for office.[64]

Political credibility, consequently, was an important consideration in an age when government growth and the use of central agencies was coming into its own as a means for organising and ordering an industrial society.

Economic considerations, as the proponents of railway legislation conceived them, provided other limits to state intervention.
Advocates of state intervention, no less than their critics, wished
to avoid any kind of state action which could potentially limit
railway development. A method of control and supervision should
be applied to the railway system, the second report of the select
committee on railway acts enactments maintained, but this should
be accomplished without discouraging 'legitimate enterprise'.[65]
Even James Morrison, an inveterate critic of the railways, believed
state intervention to protect the public interest should be balanced
by provisions for the encouragement of railway investment. In
1846, after a speech in which he suggested the eventual acquisition
of the railways by the state, Morrison moved for a select committee
to inquire into those conditions necessary for promoting the public
interest but 'without discouraging legitimate enterprise'.[66] The
legislation proposed in 1844, Gladstone indicated, was not to be
applied to existing railway lines lest investment in railway projections be restricted. Moreover, Gladstone was prepared to
modify his bill in order to avoid the diversion of capital, normally
invested in railway development, into areas which were 'not beneficial to British skill and industry'.[67] Government, Earl Grey
stated in 1846, could legitimately interfere to ascertain the extent
to which a company was capitalised, to determine whether the
capital was sufficient to carry out the projection, to decide whether
a project was in the public interest, or to determine whether a
project unnecessarily violated private property. However, he could
not subscribe to the 'irrational' and 'unconstitutional' principle
that government had the right to interfere in the enterprises of
private citizens or that it could limit the amount of capital to be
invested in railway projects.[68] Consequently, the advocates of
state intervention in railway matters believed 'proper' legislation
was compatible with 'legitimate' railway speculation. Their conception of the important role railways played in the economic
development of the country served as an effective limitation on
both the quantity and quality of government intervention. The
interventionist measures proposed by the advocates of railway
legislation were neither complete nor absolute and capital investment was to be uninhibited so long as it complemented the public
interest.

In spite of these reservations, the public interest and the public character of railways were used as the basis for justifying state intervention into railway matters. Proponents of railway legislation conceived of the railways as public associations having public responsibilities. The second report of the select committee on railway acts enactments described railway companies as analogous to other associations with a public character: turnpike trusts, canal companies, and associations for local improvements. These corporate bodies, the select committee maintained, were not constituted permanently and, as a consequence, parliament could subject them to regulation or, if necessary, withdraw their authority completely. Of these public associations, the railways were appreciated as the most significant. As the select committee put it in 1846:

> But of all the means of communication between different parts of a country, that by railways is by far the most important. If it be necessary for the public welfare that a country should never divest itself in perpetuity of its right of property in its ordinary highways, it is still more important that it should not part with the right to control its railways.[69]

These assumptions were used to justify state intervention in the areas of speculation, rates and charges, and public safety. Advocates of railway legislation were prepared to sanction state intervention on at least four grounds: they conceived of the railway system as a dangerous monopoly; steps should be taken, they recognised, to check excessive speculation which had accompanied the rapid railway growth of the 1840s; national resources should be properly allocated to prevent capital waste; and, greater uniformity should replace the chaos of railway development.

One of the most significant dangers perceived by the advocates of intervention was the monopolistic tendencies of railways. As James Morrison argued as early as 1836, the parliamentary acts chartering railway companies gave them the equivalent of a monopoly. Parliamentary dispensations permitting amalgamation of railway lines further reduced the possibilities of competition which might check monopolistic tendencies.[70] Monopoly, therefore, was taken as a direct threat to the public interest. The select committee in 1839 recognised that the economic interest of the railway companies, a good return on their investments, did not square with the national interest: safety, speed, and economy. The select committee on railway acts enactments acknowledged that monopolies constituted an 'intolerable abuse' because they were 'subject to no responsibility and under no effective checks or control'.[71] Railway monopoly, Henry Labouchere realised, was an innovation in English economic life and stood outside the ordinary competitive mechanisms which might possibly restrain it.[72] Gladstone, as one of his most famous statements on this question reveals, shared Labouchere's scepticism concerning the ability of competition to regulate monopoly. Gladstone observed:

> It was said, let matters . . . be allowed to go on as at present, and let the country trust to the effects of competition. Now, for his part, he would rather give his confidence to a Gracchus, when speaking on the subject of sedition, than give his confidence to a Railway Director, when speaking to the public of the effects of competition.

Competition, for Gladstone, was insufficient because railway investment required large amounts of capital and the parties providing it were few in number. Consequently, even rival companies found it easy to engage in price-fixing with regard to tolls and charges.[73] Joseph Hume, for one, did not consider his support for railway legislation and his opposition to the corn laws as an ideological contradiction when C. N. Newdegate, the Protectionist whip, charged him with inconsistency in 1847. Newdegate, the Radical Reformer responded, did not know what 'free trade' was. Hume favoured the free employment of capital in any fair and legitimate enterprise, but, as a free trader, he objected to privilege and abuse. For Hume, railway monopolies, no less than the corn laws, constituted such privilege and abuse.[74]

Proponents of railway legislation also justified their policies by alluding to what they conceived to be the dangers of excessive speculation. The successful employment of capital, Edward Cardwell (Conservative: Clitheroe) declared, must be balanced by measures preventing reckless speculation. The act of 1844, in his view, would stabilise the money market precisely because it would discourage financial adventurism. Even F. T. Baring (Liberal: Portsmouth), who had opposed legislative interference with the utilisation of capital, supported anti-speculation resolutions in 1846. Baring stated his concern as follows:

I

It was . . . only an appeal from Philip drunk to Philip sober; an inquiry whether a voyage projected with fair breezes and smooth water, was to be persevered in when clouds were gathering, and the waves so rough as at present.

In 1847 Joseph Hume made a motion before the House of Commons which would compel railway companies to call up all of their first credit before trying to raise additional capital, because he was certain widespread speculation threatened all the institutions of the country.[75] Critics of the railway system believed unrestrained speculation would produce both financial and moral consequences. The mania of railway investment in the 1840s, Lord Dalhousie asserted, could impair other parts of the country's economic structure and Labouchere saw it as the force which produced a confusion 'prejudicial to individuals and not creditable to the commercial character of the nation'.[76] In addition, some members of parliament regarded unrestrained speculation as a threat to morality. While having no objection to '*bona fide*' investments, Lord Monteagle objected to the 'little-go' system of speculation, which permitted men of modest means to invest in joint-stock operations. Since he believed the lower classes were incapable of judging their interests in these affairs, Monteagle hoped government would restrain the 'reckless and irrational practice of low gambling in railway speculations'. Similarly, Lord Brougham deplored the practice of 'trusting to chance, instead of exertion and labour, and honest industry', and James Morrison believed speculation had produced a 'disasterous influence' on English morality.[77]

In addition, without some measure of state intervention to avoid unnecessary duplication in rival lines, proponents of legislation feared the investment capital of the British public would be wasted. As Poulett Thomson was careful to explain, he was not hostile to railway enterprise, but government should take steps to ensure that the capital of the country 'was not improvidently or unwisely applied'. In the view of the select committee on railway acts enactments, the best railway system was one constructed at the least expense, with the least sacrifice of soil, and which afforded the greatest facilities and encouragement to the total economy. 'Economy in the outlay of capital, and in the application of the surface of the country to its railways, ought always to be aimed at.'[78]

Along with the dangers of monopoly, excessive speculation and wasted capital, the critics of the railway system objected to the apparent chaos of railway development. Therefore, they justified state action as an instrument for ordering and rationalising development. In Samuel Smiles's view, the disorder of railway projections could have been avoided by a 'well digested scheme of railways, superintended by scientific men appointed by the government', and the Marquess of Londonderry predicted in 1836, 'the greatest mischief and confusion must follow' unless the government laid down general principles for railway companies.[79] The report of a select committee in 1844 also called for a more uniform pattern of railway development. Since railways took a national rather than a local character, it suggested, future lines should be considered as something more than mere projects for local improvement: they should be planned as parts of a national system of communication serving the entire country.[80] As both Colonel Sibthorp and Joseph Hume protested, railway development had been excessively concerned with local and private interests and had been insufficiently concerned with the national interest.[81] These notions received the support of anonymous contemporary pamphleteers. As one put it, the development of English railways marked the beginning of an important awakening of her economic energies: 'Let Parliament see that the step is sure, and that the ground beneath her feet is solid and lasting'.[82]

As the concern for favourable allocations of resources and greater uniformity in railway development indicates, the proponents of railway legislation were not solely motivated by an antipathy to railway companies. As much as they wished to limit abuses, they wanted legislation which would facilitate and improve railway development. A select committee on railways in 1844 affirmed the importance of positive legislation which would contribute to the encouragement of railway enterprise. Gladstone hoped measures could be contrived for both 'the advantage of the public and the improvement of the railway system'. Lord John Russell's position was essentially the same when he indicated, in 1847, that the object of railway legislation was 'to improve our railway system without any unnecessary interference with railway property'.[83] These sentiments were also echoed in the public at large. A pamphlet addressed to Sir Robert Peel in 1837 suggested that an investigation of the railways, 'judiciously applied', would not necessarily be restrictive but, on the contrary, would contribute to railway improvement by guaranteeing 'the adoption of sound principles'.[84] *A Letter to the Right Hon. W. E. Gladstone, M. P. President of the Board of Trade, On Railway Legislation* (1844) admired the effects of government action on railways since 1840 and, while insisting on the importance of private ownership, recommended increased state intervention. Since, as the author of this pamphlet believed, the benefits of railways had not been fully realised, government and railway companies should seek out a common ground for private as well as public advances.[85] This anonymous writer proposed, as terms of the alliance between government and the railways, that the former should be entitled to revise the fares of railway lines each five years with the maximum dividend remaining at 7 per cent. Government, in this author's view, should also retain the right of returning the ownership of lines to the public at some time in the future. On their side, railway companies would benefit by government intervention to reduce the expense of railway projections and by the extension of government credit to railway companies.[86] These benefits would have the effect of providing cheaper transportation, expanding 'to the utmost the power and the spirit of the capitalist', and creating additional railways by cheapening construction costs.[87] Railway legislation, as these examples show, was calculated as a stimulant to private enterprise in an effort to maximise the co-operative potential between public and private spheres rather than stressing restrictive antagonisms.

For the most part, the major themes stressed by advocates of railway legislation rested on pragmatic assumptions and modest limited goals. There was little doctrinairism, save for a small group of men whose support for interventionist legislation, paradoxically, was based upon either a concern for private property or a strict anti-modernist opposition to industrialisation. For example, William Clay (Reformer: Tower Hamlets) was chiefly concerned about urban private property. When sixteen railway schemes were projected for one of the parishes in his constituency, resulting in the razing of 1,284 'houses and tenements', Clay demanded immediate intervention by the legislature 'to see that the public interests should not be injuriously or capriciously affected by such

speculation'.[88] Men such as Clay might oppose what Toulmin
Smith called 'government by commissions', but in their zeal to
protect private property they supported measures which increased
the sphere of action of the central government. An anonymous
pamphlet, *Railways and the Board of Trade*, criticised the railway
department for 'irresponsibility' and rashness, and excoriated
Gladstone as 'rash, busy, and of abundant vanity' in using unconstitutional remedies to deal with the problems of railway development. Yet, the same pamphlet called for strong parliamentary supervision of railway projections to ascertain their usefulness to the public, their profitableness to investors, and the
extent to which they interfered with private property.[89]

Colonel Sibthorp was one of the more fascinating, if eccentric,
critics of the railways. Apparently, considering his opposition to
the reform bill, the attempts to reduce electoral corruption, and
the Crystal Palace, Sibthorp's opposition to railways rested on a
thoroughgoing hatred of modern devices and life-styles. The
Colonel's speeches in the House of Commons make it clear that
he was totally opposed to railways and saw no advantage in them.
In 1842, noting an increase in railway accidents, Sibthorp hoped
a bill would be introduced 'for the annihilation of railways'.[90] In
1844 he remarked:

> The railway companies might, no doubt, say that they were at
> all times anxious to consult the public interest; but it was his
> belief that they were more anxious to put 10 or 15 per cent in
> their own pockets. He never travelled by railroad, he hated the
> very name of the railroad—he hated it as he hated the devil.

For Sibthorp, the railways were 'dangerous', 'delusive', 'unknown
to the constitution' and a threat both to the rights of the poor and
private property. Like all things modern, the railways posed a
threat to the archaic values which Sibthorp admired and respected.
As a consequence, ironically considering his opposition to the Poor
Law Commission and the General Board of Health, he supported
measures which increased the power and jurisdiction of the
central government.[91]

V

Railway legislation in the 1840s, like the new poor law and the

Public Health Act, attempted to establish an equilibrium between local authorities—in this case the railway companies—and central political authority. While increasing the sphere within which government could act, the railway acts did not call for government to concern itself with the details of railway management. The railway acts, consequently, were not collectivistic: they preserved a fundamental dualism in the way Victorians viewed railway enterprise. As the prescript at the head of this chapter indicates, railways were conceived of as public as well as private bodies. Chartered by parliament and conferring benefits upon the country at large, they were initiated, financed, and managed by private corporations. Early Victorian railway legislation, therefore, preserved this dual character, institutionalised it in the structure of government, and attempted to maintain an equilibrium between the public and private interests by means of legal discipline.

Proponents and critics of railway legislation shared a wide area of agreement on the question of state intervention. They were agreed that, generally speaking, capital should be invested without hindrance, that the responsibility for railway management should rest with the directors of railway companies, and both were in agreement concerning the public-private character of railways. The antagonism in the controversy concerning the railway acts centred on the distinction between the proper spheres for private opportunities and public responsibilities on the part of the railway companies. To put the matter another way, the area of disagreement focused on the degree of intervention, the implications and results of such intervention, and the degree to which the problems of railway development could be solved within the context of government supervision.

The critics of railway legislation relied largely on economic arguments without falling back on narrow dogmatisms. Without resting their case on abstract formulations in a laissez-faire context, opponents of state intervention and government growth feared railway legislation would restrict railway development, English capital would be invested in the economic development of other countries, and England would lose the advantages which she had gained as a consequence of the railways. The proponents of railway legislation, concerned to protect the public interest by reducing the abuses of monopoly, excessive speculation, capital waste, and disorderly railway construction, believed their work should be guided by pragmatic experience. As one knowledgeable person wrote in an open letter to Sir Robert Peel:

> The experience of the last few years, and, particularly, searching examinations which have taken place in the last session of Parliament, have brought forward many new facts, and questions, which were before only matters of opinion, have now been put to the test of experience. We are, therefore, in a position to reason with more safety on the subject than we have hitherto been.[92]

Seeing no necessary contradiction between state intervention and a prospering railway system, the advocates of railway legislation hoped to encourage and guide railway development by effective state action. Remarkably, compared to the poor-law and public-health controversies, the discussion of railway legislation included few allusions to historical anachronisms. To be sure, all sides understood railways to be historical and legal analogies to canals and turnpike-roads, but the use of archaic values played only a slight role in the evaluation of the railway acts in the 1840s. When such archaic references were used, they appeared on both sides of the discussion: Benjamin Hawes opposed railway legislation as a restriction on the ancient liberties of Englishmen, and Sibthorp favoured railway legislation because railways were alien to the English constitution.

The mildness of railway legislation in the 1840s is often attributed either to the strength of the railway lobby in the House of Commons or to the doctrinal power of classical political economy. The peculiar way in which Victorians conceived of the railways may suggest another reason for their hesitancy in utilising government to regulate and control this valuable means of transport. On all sides of the discussion of railway legislation, as this chapter has indicated, Victorian politicians viewed the railways as having both a private as well as a public character. Since railways conferred benefits on the country as a whole in the form of lowering transportation costs, in opening new markets, in generating capital and new industry, government intervention could be sanctioned only in so far as it did not curtail the public benefits flowing from railway development. As W. L. Burn has pointed out, everyone had an interest in the railways from the landowners, railway magnates, and coalowners to the average man who was able to recognise the sharpest evidence for progress in their extension.[93] Government intervention into an enterprise of such magnitude might be necessary, but it also had to be limited and cautious.

Notes to Chapter 4 will be found on pages 208-12.

Chapter 5 THE RESTRICTION OF LABOUR AND ECONOMIC GROWTH

Early Victorian Factory Legislation, 1833-1847

One of the prominent mistakes of modern Statesmen has been to devote their attention to things rather than to human beings,—hence the popular belief that cheapness must be nationally advantageous. . . . The supporters of factory regulation had the honourable merit of beginning with the consideration of human beings; there was, therefore, between them and their opponents an impassable gulf. True, the avowed end of both was the same, namely the improvement of all, but the means leading to the end were opposed: the free school of economists said—'All interference is wrong, get cheapness, and whatever else is needful will follow in its train.' The supporters of factory regulation said—'Check excessive and unnatural labour, care for health and morals, and whatever else is needful will follow in their train.'

'Alfred', *The History of the Factory Movement* (1857)

I

THE FACTORY question, which politicians perceived in both economic and moral terms, was perhaps the most famous and most controverted state interventionist issue in early Victorian Britain. Colonel Robert Torrens saw factory legislation as the most 'delicate and important' matter to be brought before the reformed parliament and Lord John Russell conceived of it as matter which involved the most important and far-reaching consequences. Karl Marx recognised the ten-hours act as the first victory of working-class political economy and John Morley regarded the act of 1844 as 'an exertion of the power of the state in its strongest form, definitely limiting in the interest of the labourer the administration of capital'.[1] This attempt to see the factory acts as an aspect of modern collectivism has found its place in more recent discussions of these issues. G. M. Young, for example, described the ten-hours bill as one of the signs of a 'new State philosophy' marking the turning point of the age, and Professor Roberts identified the factory act of 1833 as the beginning of a 'centrally directed collectivism'.[2]

While there is a good deal to commend these views, it is probably too extreme to characterise the factory acts as 'socialistic' or 'collectivistic'. The essential tension over the factory question, considerable contemporary evidence suggests, was not between ideological stances such as socialism and capitalism or collectivism and individualism. As the prescript at the head of this chapter indicates, the proponents and the critics of ten-hours legislation were agreed upon general social goals. They were divided, however, by different ways of viewing the industrial system and different concepts of political action, with the former seeking the improvement of the working classes through legislation to limit the hours of labour and the latter seeking the same objective through an expanding economy.[3]

The nineteenth-century movement for factory reform began in 1802 under the leadership of Sir Robert Peel, the father of the prime minister. Fourteen years after his successful efforts to pass the Health and Morals of Apprentices Act (1802), the elder Peel led the movement for a more general regulation of child labour in the factories, culminating in the act of 1819. In the 1820s, Sir John Cam Hobhouse, the radical politician and friend of Lord Byron, proposed legislation designed to make Peel's acts effective, which was passed into law in 1825. In the early 1830s the ten-hours movement began and was led at the outset by Thomas Michael Sadler (Conservative: Aldborough). Sadler chaired a select committee to investigate the conditions of factory labour and sponsored a ten-hours bill in the House of Commons of 1832. When Sadler was not returned to the reformed parliament, Lord Ashley, whose interest in the factory question had been aroused by the report of Sadler's committee, took his place as the principal promoter of the ten-hours bill.[4] The government rejected the bill in

1833 and established a royal commission to investigate factory conditions and, if possible, to discredit Sadler's report. Lord Althorp brought in a bill in 1833 which, while it did not reduce the labour of children to ten hours, established an administrative system for the inspection of factories. In the 1830s and 1840s Lord Ashley, John Fielden and Joseph Brotherton (Liberal: Salford) provided the chief parliamentary leadership for a ten-hours bill, and Richard Oastler, Joseph Rayner Stephens, and G. S. Bull led extra-parliamentary agitation for such legislation. During the legislative sessions of 1843 and 1844 Sir James Graham brought factory measures before the House of Commons. Since these bills did not include a ten-hours provision Ashley used them as vehicles for ten-hours amendments. In 1846 Ashley brought in another ten-hours bill, which failed because of the more pressing business of the corn laws. When Ashley relinquished his seat because of his position on the corn-law issue, John Fielden took his place as parliamentary leader of the ten-hours movement. In 1847 Fielden brought in a ten-hours bill which was passed into law.

Efforts to establish the legislative requirements for factory reform in the 1830s and 1840s may be said to have had two aspects: the movement for ten-hours legislation chronicled by Samuel Kydd and later by John Trevor Ward, and legislation, such as the acts of 1833 and 1844, which created an administrative system for the supervision of work in the factories. It must be emphasised, as this chapter seeks to show, that opposition to ten-hours legislation did not necessarily mean a total rejection of government intervention in factory affairs, nor was it predicated upon a narrow anti-humanitarianism. Critics of the ten-hours bills sought to find in alternative economic strategies, such as the repeal of the corn laws and a concern for the expansion of the national economy, alternative solutions to working-class distress in the factory system. In addition, factory legislation, even the attempt to pass ten-hours legislation, was not the special work of Tory paternalists, but had broad support from both sides of the House of Commons. Lord Ashley and other Conservatives were joined by Liberals and Radicals such as Fielden, Brotherton, Sir George Grey, Russell, Buller and Howick. Consequently, the ten-hours movement was a common meeting ground where the liberal views of men like Buller and Howick were offset by the reactionary views of Oastler and Joseph Rayner Stephens, who, with their evangelical fervour, adopted positions which were often sentimentalised idealisations of the past. Ironically, in some important instances, the support for ten hours was linked to an opposition to the kind of government growth and administrative intervention found in the new poor law, the Public Health Act, and even the factory acts of 1833 and 1844.

II

The legislation for the reform of the factory system, as *The Times* noted on 21 September 1833, was of two very different kinds. On the one hand, an attempt was made to restrict the hours of labour of women and young persons, and, on the other hand, early Victorian factory legislation attempted to provide administrative machinery for the inspection of factories and for the supervision of child labour and education. The acts of 1833 and 1844 focused on the questions of governmental administration and supervision while the bills and amendments of Sadler, Ashley, and Fielden and the act of 1847 emphasised the restriction of the hours of labour to ten hours per day.

The act sponsored by Grey's government in 1833, as well as that of Sir Robert Peel's government in 1844, was characterised chiefly by its concern for the regulation and supervision of factory labour and the education of factory children. This legislation directed itself only secondarily to the restriction of the hours of labour. Indeed, the Royal Commission[5] which conducted the investigation preparatory to the act of 1833 rejected the ten-hours proposal.

The report of the Royal Commission recommended legislative restrictions on the labour of children because they were not free agents and therefore incapable of protecting themselves. Yet, it rejected ten-hours legislation because 'we have been careful not to lose sight of the practical limits within which alone any general rule admits of application'.[6] The commission regarded the ten-hours proposal as both insufficient and excessive. The proposal was insufficient in so far as it made no provision for the well-being of children either before or after their hours of labour: it contained no provision for elementary or moral education. The ten-hours proposal was excessive, from the Royal Commission's point of view, in so far as it would restrict the labour of adults, contributing to both the reduction of wages for the working classes and the reduction of profits for the factory masters.[7]

Children under the age of nine, the Royal Commission suggested, should not be allowed to work in mills or factories and the labour of children under the age of fourteen should be limited to eight hours. Above the age of fourteen, however, young people were to be considered adults. The rationale for these limitations on the hours of child labour was that, since children were not free agents, their wages were frequently appropriated by their parents or guardians. In addition, the labour they performed was not regulated by their capacities but by the length of adult labour, a detectable and permanent deterioration of the physical constitution was evident among working children, and factory children had been excluded from the means of elementary and moral education. To balance the economic effects of the reduction of child labour, and to prevent the shut-down of industrial units because of reductions, the Commission recommended the employment of double shifts of young persons to keep the factories in operation.[8]

The recommendations of the Royal Commission, exclusive of the hours question, went far beyond the ten-hours bill. It recommended that a paid staff of professional inspectors be appointed for the enforcement of factory legislation. It called for the appointment of three inspectors, who were to travel through the factory districts with the authority to enter all factories where children were employed, to order the fencing-off of machinery, to direct sanitary arrangements, and to investigate the conditions of education of working children. In addition, the inspectors should be empowered to hear cases of infractions of this law and to fine offenders. These inspectors, the commission recommended, should meet as a board and report to the government for purposes of further legislation.[9]

As the Royal Commission recognised, an important means for the improvement of working children was to secure the advantages of education for them. Three or four hours of education per day, it indicated, would accomplish at least two important objectives. It would prevent the same child from working in two factories on the same day and would also qualify the children to adapt themselves to alternative modes of employment should the 'vicissitudes of trade or other causes' make it necessary that they find other work.[10] Finally, the Royal Commission recommended that 'pecuniary responsibility' for accidents occurring to children under fourteen years of age should rest upon the employer. The employers should be required to pay for medical attendance, all the expenses incurred, and half salary until the person could return to work. Such a responsibility, the Royal Commission asserted, would make the owners more eager to institute protective measures because by this means 'we combine interest with duty, and add to the efficiency of both'.[11]

The factory act of 1833, based upon the evidence and recommendations of the Royal Commission, was framed by Edwin Chadwick.[12] It did not include a ten-hours clause but it, nevertheless, regulated the hours of child labour. Persons under the age of eighteen were prohibited from working at night and were restricted to twelve hours labour per day.[13] Children under thirteen years of age were restricted to nine hours of labour per day and the employment of children under the age of nine was prohibited. All working children were required to present surgeon's certificates testifying to their strength and fitness.[14]

The act of 1833 empowered the government to appoint four persons as factory inspectors. The inspectors were charged with the duty of entering all mills and factories where children were employed, and all schools attached to them, to investigate the conditions of employment and education.[15] The inspectors were authorised to formulate all rules and orders necessary for the execution of the act, to enforce school attendance on the part of working children, and to require a register in each factory showing the names of the children employed there with their hours of work. Such registers and records kept in compliance with the act were to be open to the inspectors for examination. Inspectors were, under this act, to possess the same powers, authority and jurisdiction over constables and peace officers as those possessed by the justices of the peace. Further, the inspectors and the justices of the peace were to preside over any proceedings for the enforcement of the act. The inspectors were required to submit reports of their proceedings to the Home Secretary twice each year.[16] The factory inspectorate, therefore, was to serve as a professional corps of examiners whose authority was supplemented by magisterial and judicial powers in order to provide for an efficient execution of the act. The legislation of 1833 also provided an educational requirement for children employed in the factories. Children under thirteen years of age were required to attend a school selected by their parent or guardian. In the case of orphans, the employer, under the supervision of the inspector, was to make a deduction from the weekly wages of the child to pay for his schooling. Before being allowed to work, each child was required to present a voucher from a schoolmaster, showing he had indeed attended classes. This part of the act of 1833 takes on increased significance when it is appreciated that one of its chief purposes was to encourage the 'Health and Means of Education' of the children employed in mills and factories.[17]

The Commission for Inquiring into the Employment and Condition of Children in Mines and Manufactories (1843), like the royal commission ten years earlier, did not attribute the evils of the factory system to factory work itself or to the hours of labour. It placed responsibility for the evils in the factory system on the circumstances surrounding factory labour. This inquiry was conducted by four of the most experienced social investigators of the early Victorian period: Thomas Tooke, Thomas Southwood Smith, Leonard Horner, and John Saunders. They stated in their report:

> With few exceptions there is nothing in the nature of the employments included under the present inquiry directly injurious to the health, but they are often pursued under circumstances which manifestly interrupt the nutritive functions, and check the growth of the body. . . .[18]

As the commission acknowledged, children frequently began work at a very early age and often worked long hours. However, the report noted, it was in the trades and manufactures where the master was considered exonerated from responsibility for child labour because the workmen hired the children themselves where the hours were the longest and the labour most oppressive. The work in which children were employed, the commission maintained, was 'seldom in itself oppressive, or even laborious', but the factory children, in their long hours of labour, were not sustained by a sufficient standard of nutrition or dress.[19] The report of the commission in 1843 focused less on the question of hours than on the educational and moral condition of children employed in factories. It deplored the apparent fact that there was no agency capable of dealing with the deteriorating moral condition of children in the factory districts. The commission attributed this low moral condition to a 'general ignorance of moral duties and sanctions', produced by the absence of 'moral and religious restraint'. The lack of restraint among the working classes was in turn imputed to an absence of moral and religious training.[20] Because of this emphasis on moral and religious instruction the commission's report in 1843 is, in some ways, a more important document in the history of the movement for national education than it is for the history of factory legislation.

The act introduced by Sir James Graham to amend the laws relating to labour in factories (1844) did not deal in great detail with the hours of labour. It was more largely concerned with the supervision and inspection of the factory system. The act did, however, limit factory labour to persons above the age of eight and restricted female labour to twelve hours per day.[21] The act of 1844 went a long way to a further definition of the factory inspectorate and its functions. Although the authority of inspectors to act as magistrates or to make rules, regulations, and orders for the government of factories as provided by the act of 1833 was removed, their authorisation to enter and inspect all factories and schools was continued.[22] The inspectors, under the direction of the Home Secretary, were to make use of a central office, to appoint the surgeons who were to issue certificates specifying the age of children, and to fix the fees to be paid by the factory owners to the certifying surgeons. They were further empowered to annul any surgeon's certificate if the child was 'of deficient health or strength, or by Disease or bodily infirmity incapacitated for labour'. The act, in addition, authorised the Home Secretary to direct the inspectors to prosecute in order to compensate any person receiving bodily injury in a factory.[23]

The legislation of 1844 also redefined the education requirement for working children. All parents or persons deriving direct benefit from the labour of children were to require the attendance of such children at school three hours for each day of employment. The factory owners had to obtain certificates of attendance of children working in their factories and to pay the school fees deducted from the wages of the children. The inspectors were authorised to supervise the education of children employed in factories and to annul the certificates issued by incompetent schoolmasters.[24]

In contrast to the legislation of 1833 and 1844, the bills of Sadler and Ashley and the Act of 1847 were of an entirely different character and were narrowly concerned with the restriction of the hours of labour. This is not to suggest that the proponents of the ten-hours measure did not favour education and other ameliorative measures. However, they believed the restriction of labour was a prior condition to the development of such programmes. As the preamble to Ashley's ten-hours bill (1832) shows, the most important condition to be improved was the unreasonable and unnatural length of time that children were forced to work.[25] No persons under the age of eighteen, the bill specified, should be employed for more than ten hours in any one day nor more than eight hours on Saturday. Persons under the age of nine were prohibited from finding employment in mills or factories.[26] Ashley's bill made no explicit provision for the education of children, nor did it provide for a professional inspectorate for the purposes of supervision and enforcement. Similarly, the ten-hours act of 1847 limited the labour of young persons under the age of eighteen and the labour of women to ten hours per day. But, in contrast to the lengthy and complex legislation of 1833 and 1844, the act of 1847 was both simple and limited. It contained no provision for the education of children employed in factories nor did it establish or define the administrative machinery necessary for enforcement.

Both in the form of administrative intervention, as in the case of the factory acts of 1833 and 1844, and in the form of legislative intervention, as in the case of the ten-hours act, the role of the state in industrial affairs was expanded in the 1830s and 1840s. However, it should be emphasised, intervention in either form was sharply limited. In no case was government authorised to do more than supervise the conditions of labour in the factories. In no case was government au horised to interfere with the management of

K

factory operations unless, of course, those operations had been involved in illegal practices. In the instance of poor-law and public-health legislation, distinctions were retained between central supervision and local administration. The factory acts, like railway legislation, retained the distinction between governmental supervision and corporate management.

One of the most popular and recurring explanations of the political support for ten-hours legislation is that it was the special work of the Protectionist wing of the Conservative party. A significant role in the factory movement, a recent historian of these issues argues, was played by Tory paternalism, evangelical piety, and 'early manifestations of Tractarian social sympathies'. Conversely, the same historian asserts, the opposition to factory legislation was led by dogmatic free-traders—by implication at least political liberals and radicals—with an unrealistic faith in an individualistic social ethic.[27] While there is some appeal in a clear and simple explanation of this kind, the picture is actually far more complex, as recent scholarship, the division lists, the cabinet minutes and the parliamentary debates reveal.

There was, in reality, a considerable confusion of political attitudes on the factory question. As Charles Cavendish Fulke Greville, the courtier and political diarist, observed in 1844:

> I never remember so much excitement as has been caused by Ashley's Ten Hours Bill, nor a more curious political state of things, such intermingling of parties, such a confusion of opposition; a question so much more open than any question ever was before, and yet not made so with the Government; so much zeal, asperity, and animosity, so many reproaches hurled backwards and forewards.[28]

Recent research has taken cognizance of this situation. Examinations of parliamentary division lists, for example, indicate the complex relationships between the factory question and other political issues. Analysis of this sort suggests that voting on the ten-hours question bore no statistical relationship to voting on the liberal-radical programme (the chartist petition, free trade etc). To put the matter another way, political attitudes towards the ten-hours issue bore no relation to political attitudes on other issues in early Victorian politics. Voting on the liberal-radical programme, as a consequence, cannot be used to predict voting on the ten-hours question. Between 1844 and 1847, however, supporters of the liberal-radical programme increasingly came to oppose the ten-hours bill and *vice versa*.[29]

To turn to the specific issue of party support, before 1847 the Liberals were the strongest supporters of the ten-hours bill while, in 1844 at least, the Conservatives opposed it by a small majority. Since Conservative support for ten hours became overwhelming only in 1847, it is fair to conclude that their concern for this issue was the result of a 'sudden conversion' rather than of long-term interest.[30] Even in 1847, however, Liberal support was not lost and more than half of their number joined with Conservatives in the passage of Fielden's bill. A simple comparison of the parliamentary division lists produces figures supporting these conclusions.[31] In 1844 a minority of the Conservatives voting (46 per cent) favoured the reduction of hours, but their support had increased to 78 per cent by 1847. To take the Protectionists alone, in 1844, 57 per cent supported the shorter working day. This figure increased to 94 per cent in 1847. On the Liberal side of the House of Commons, both in 1844 and 1847, a small but clear majority (57 per cent and 58 per cent respectively) favoured the ten-hours bill. Moreover, in both years a majority of every Liberal group, with the exception of the Reformers in 1844, favoured the reduction of hours.

If parties were divided internally on the factory issue, Peel's ministry was no less so. During the discussion of the factory bills in 1844, as Gladstone's memoranda of 23 and 25 March indicate, the Duke of Buccleuch and Gladstone argued for a compromise on an eleven-hour measure. Peel, Graham, and Stanley, joined by Lord Ripon and Lord Haddington, resisted this effort and remained firm in their opposition to a revision of working hours. In 1846, G. F. Muntz recalled the ministerial confusion of two years earlier when a minister had said to him:

> I assure you, Sir, we are so pestered by contradictory representations and intelligence from all sides upon this matter of the Factory Bill, that we don't know what to believe or what to do.[32]

Sir James Graham's anxieties were so great on this occasion that he believed the legal proceedings against Daniel O'Connell had not proceeded rapidly enough and feared the Liberator would return to England to throw his weight against the Government on Ashley's ten-hour amendment.[33]

The simpler bipolar explanations of the factory acts, with their attempt to place Conservatives and Liberals in opposition to each other on the factory question, also suggest that the ten-hours measure of 1847 was an act of political revenge against Peel and the Liberals for the repeal of the corn laws. This allegation, some evidence in the parliamentary debates indicate, was contrived by Liberal opponents of the ten-hours bill. Thomas Milner Gibson (Liberal: Manchester) implied Lord George Bentinck's support for ten hours was an attempt to interfere with the vested interests of manufacturers because manufacturers had violated the vested interests of agriculture. As J. A. Roebuck put it:

> The landlords were attempting, if possible, by this measure, to make the manufacturers share in the mischief which they said would be entailed upon them by the repeal of the corn laws.[34]

The Protectionists rejected this charge themselves. C. N. Newdegate regarded it as an 'unfair accusation' since he had supported ten-hours legislation, as had others, some time before the repeal of the corn laws. Similarly, Lord John Manners declared his position on the factory question was determined by a regard for justice rather than a special concern for agricultural prices.[35]

To see the conflict over the factory question in terms of simple bipolarities, such as business versus land, or ideological dichotomies, such as liberalism versus conservatism or even laissez-faire versus collectivism, seems incomplete and unsatisfactory. The discussion over these matters, as the parliamentary debates reveal, was far too rich to fit into these neat categories. Consequently, it seems most appropriate to turn to the contemporary controversy over the factory issue to assess the extent to which insights derived from other cases of state intervention can be used in an explanatory sense here. It will be recalled that the controversies over the new poor law, the public-health movement, and the railway acts utilised two very different ways of viewing politics. On the one hand, constitutional, legal, and customary arguments, often encased in an historical vision, were brought to bear against legislation which fostered government growth. On the other hand, a practical concern to modify the structure of governmental relationships, often accompanied by evidence and polemical ammunition derived from parliamentary investigations, was used to make the case for increased state action. Both of these elements, in one form or another, are to be found in the debate over the factory question. However, these themes were used in surprisingly different ways and often with different effect.

III

The most common interpretation of the opposition to ten-hours legislation in the 1830s and 1840s stresses the concern for a crude individualistic economic and social philosophy, with a corresponding emphasis on unrestricted labour as the basis for such opposition.[36] To be sure there was some discussion of the value of free labour, but this should be appreciated in the context of the larger concern for the strength and vitality of the national economy which pervaded this controversy. Critics of the ten-hour measures, most of whom did not oppose all factory legislation categorically, objected to the principles of 'false humanity' which they believed motivated their opponents. Indeed, there was little opposition to 'centralisation' amongst the critics of ten hours, nor were there many dogmatic objections to the limitation of hours as a general matter. Consequently, the major themes in the criticisms of the ten-hours measures included a defence of the factory system and a series of broad economic arguments which stressed that a ten-hours bill would work to both the disadvantage of the working classes and the nation, since such a measure would reduce wages as well as curtail industry and trade. The condition of the working classes, the opponents of ten hours reiterated, could best be improved by governmental and fiscal policies which, while protecting the working classes from the abuses of industrialism, would improve economic and social conditions by stimulating rather than depressing the economy.

The focus of the attack on early Victorian factory legislation was the question of hours and the limitation of labour, not the structure of administrative machinery required to enforce such legislation. Unlike the controversy over the new poor law and the Public Health Act, the cry of 'centralisation' was not raised against the factory acts. There was no great outpouring of pamphlet literature against the centralising features of the acts of 1833 and 1844 such as that which greeted the new poor law.[37] In the House of Commons, similarly, debate was marked by an absence of discussion on administrative centralisation. In 1833 the discussion of the factory inspectorate did not include objections on legal or constitutional grounds and what little discussion there was related solely to the practical issue of the efficiency and effectiveness of the inspectorate.[38] Other objections were raised in the 1840s when Mark Philips (Reformer: Manchester) opposed the appointment of men of inferior character and station as assistant inspectors. In 1844 he objected to the nomination of assistant inspectors and the establishment of the central factory office, maintaining that the inspectors should be gentlemen 'selected from persons of the highest class' with their offices located in the districts for which they were responsible.[39] Captain Henry John Rous (Conservative: Westminster), who in his lifetime was 'universally regarded as the dictator of the turf', played a Sibthorpian role and predicted the factory acts would create a great army of government functionaries 'which would entail a great expense upon the country'.[40] In 1848 *The Economist* saw the work of the factory inspectorate as a demonstration of the 'unmistakable characteristics of a most vexatious law'.[41] These objections to government growth, however, did not bulk very large in the context of the factory question. The central controverted point was with regard to the restriction of the hours of labour.

Even the question of the restriction of the hours of labour did not bring forth absolute or dogmatic objections in large numbers. The doctrinaire statements of such men as Lord Brougham, the Earl of Radnor and Mark Philips were the exception rather than the rule. As Peel observed in 1846, all but perhaps ten members of the House believed parliament should intervene in questions having social consequences and that the principles of free trade had no necessary bearing on such legislation.[42] The concept of parental authority was often used to oppose legislation for the protection of children in the early years of the controversy over the factory question. Parents, the Earl of Rosslyn argued in 1819, were the natural guardians of their children.[43] Even William Cobbett regarded factory legislation as a slur on the honour of English parents. In his view, the factory bill

... was going to say to the world: 'English parents are such cruel beings, that we are obliged to pass a law to prevent them from sacrificing their hapless offspring.' ... How came it that English parents should be branded with such cruelty? How did it happen, that a people the most humane and the most feeling in Europe, should have such a charge made against them?[44]

While the protests of Lord Brougham and the Earl of Radnor against the Government bill in 1844 contained pleas on behalf of parental authority,[45] objections to the limitation of the hours of children had in the 1840s largely disappeared and most members of parliament, even the most inveterate critics of the ten-hours bill, supported such legislation. The most generally accepted formulation was that children, because they were not free, should be protected, while free adult labour should remain unregulated. Daniel O'Connell considered it generally inexpedient to interfere in the relations between the employers and the employed, but such an interference was justifiable in order to protect the interests of children. The restriction of hours or the regulation of wages, Joseph Hume believed, was 'mischievous', but he also believed 'the case of children was an exception to that rule'. J. A. Roebuck, his biographer notes, opposed interference with adult labour as a general principle but yet 'earnestly advocated placing restrictions on the employment of children of tender years'. Roebuck made his position clear on the floor of the House of Commons.

... he had always opposed legislation for adult labour upon every occasion. It was only in those cases in which those who were not *sui juris* able to offer opposition, and to defend their own interests, that the law should step in; and on such occasions he had repeatedly contributed his assistance for the purpose of allowing the law to step in.

The most defensible aspect of factory legislation, Sir James Graham remarked in 1844, was the extension of protection to children since they were defenceless and compelled to work because of the poverty of their parents.[46]

The critics of the factory legislation were faced with the difficult task of defending the new industrial system in the light of obvious abuses existing in the factory districts. They attempted to counter the attacks on the factory system by suggesting the criticisms of the system were frequently based upon the allegations of irresponsible people who wished to destroy it, asserting that the factory system had much to recommend it over and against the other sectors of the economy, and by arguing that working-class conditions could be attributed to sources other than the factory system itself.

In the early days of the factory agitation the complaints against the factory system were sometimes seen as part of an active conspiracy by irresponsible elements in society. As Sir James Graham suggested in 1818, the petitions in favour of legislative interference originated with 'a set of idle, discontented, and good for nothing workmen' who believed that they did too much work for the wages they received. Much of the agitation in favour of the ten-hours bill, Sir George Phillips warned, was the work of 'paid and hired agitators, who lived in idleness, upon the contributions of others'.[47] Others claimed that criticisms of child labour originated with enemies of the factory system. Mark Philips, in an argument to be repeated by John Bright in 1846, charged the workers in the handloom industries with stimulating hostility against cotton manufacturers in order to reduce the production in factories so the prices and export of their own goods would be increased. William Henry Hyett (Whig: Stroud) proposed that the enemies of the factory system were exaggerating the condition of the children in the factories in order to limit the productive capacity of the country.[48]

Opponents of the ten-hours bill also defended the factory system by claiming the conditions of labour in the factory districts were not as bad as they had been often portrayed. As Thomas Gisborne suggested in 1833, the factory system had been improved and injurious abuses 'had been all but entirely remedied by the introduction of improved machinery'. Sir William Clay argued that, except for the male spinners in the cotton factories, factory labour was very light and consisted merely in observing the machinery and tying the threads that break.[49] Others took the more realistic position that conditions of labour in the manufacturing sector were superior to those in other economic sectors and that life in the factory districts was more wholesome than life in the agricultural districts. Those working in factories, J. A. Roebuck maintained, were warm and protected from the weather and had good food and good pay. The agricultural labourers, on the other hand, were 'exposed to the cold, wet, and frost, and with bad pay, bad clothing, and bad lodging'. Henry George Ward (Liberal: Sheffield) said in support of this view:

It was well known that those labourers who had come into the manufacturing towns from the agricultural districts had declared that they would rather be transported than go back to the agricultural districts again.

Many of the criticisms of the factory system could be just as easily applied to other branches of manufacturing as to the textile industries. The antiquated handloom industries were most open to unfavourable comparison. As William Bolling (Conservative: Bolton), a manufacturer, pointed out, the condition of the handloom weavers called 'much more imperiously for attention than that of [the] classes employed in factories'. Henry Warburton (Radical Reformer: Kendal), citing the report of the commission on the handloom weavers, argued that their condition could not be taken as a model of domestic happiness because 'no where were prudence and economy less habitually exercised than in the cottages of these weavers'.[50]

Finally, the critics of ten hours met the attacks on the factory system by claiming the condition of the working classes could not be attributed solely to the length of hours worked and therefore a ten-hours bill could not alleviate social problems. The comparative mortality rate, Bright declared, was greater in commercial centres such as Bristol and Liverpool than it was in industrial centres, and as T. M. Gibson indicated, the infant mortality rate in Bethnal Green, London, though it had no factories, still approached 60 per cent. Several, therefore, considered the health of working-class districts a more relevant variable than the hours of factory labour as an explanation of working-class conditions. From Lord Morpeth's point of view, the condition of the working classes was chiefly marked by its unhealthiness. Health, Morpeth maintained, was not a function of hours so much as it was a function of cleanliness, ventilation, and space. Sir Charles Wood (Liberal: Halifax), ready to support sanitary improvements in the manufacturing towns because they could not be effected by individual means, supported government intervention in the form of a public-health measure but opposed it in the form of a ten-hours bill. Sir Robert Peel also favoured sanitary improvements rather than the restriction of labour in order to improve the condition of the people.[51] Several other alternatives, in addition to sanitary improvement, were suggested in place of the ten-hours measure. Francis Place believed population control rather than ten-hours legislation would improve the condition of the labouring classes.[52] Joseph Hume favoured the reduction of impediments to labour and the removal of combinations among masters.[53] Wood, Brougham, Hume and Roebuck all favoured national education as a crucial ameliorative measure.[54]

One of the most favoured alternatives to ten-hours legislation raised the most sensational and emotional issue in early Victorian politics: the question of the price of bread. In the 1830s and 1840s the repeal of the corn laws was frequently suggested as the best way to improve the condition of the people. As Colonel Robert Torrens maintained in 1832, the causes of working-class distress were deeper than the ten-hours advocates thought. Torrens stated:

> The poor were distressed, because the tax-gatherer took from them a large portion of their produce, and because they existed in a country where, on account of the Corn Laws, a great quantity of labour was necessary to get a small quantity of food.

Richard Fryer (Radical Reformer: Wolverhampton) believed necessity compelled children to undergo severe and lengthy labour. Necessity could only be removed by a policy of free trade in corn, which would take the monopoly of food out of the hands of the great landed proprietors. For Joseph Hume the corn laws had produced most of the evils which were ascribed to the factory system and adverse economic conditions forced factory owners and occupiers to exact extensive labour from their workers. If the corn laws were repealed the distress of the manufacturers would be mitigated and the hard treatment of factory workers could be relieved.[55] Views similar to these were held by Charles Villiers, Edward Baines, John Bright, and Richard Cobden, all important participants in the effort to have the corn laws repealed.[56]

As the parliamentary debates reveal, before 1846 there was little attempt to relate opposition to the ten-hours bill to a general free-trade philosophy.[57] However, in 1846 several members began to identify their opposition to the shorter day with their position on the corn laws, stressing the importance of commercial freedom and sound legislation for the welfare of the working classes. H. G. Ward regarded the ten-hours bill as a retrogressive step because its principles were inconsonant with his views as a free trader. For Sir James Graham it was inconsistent to pass a factory bill which would 'impose fetters hardly less galling than those which we have struck off'. John Bright advanced the notion that the agitation for short time was based on a concept of political economy which the House of Commons had, in 1846, 'most emphatically declared to be unsound and rotten'. The corn laws and the ten-hours bill were both 'protective' because the former increased rents at the expense of the consumer and the latter raised wages at the expense of capital. He supported corn-law repeal and opposed ten-hours legislation because in both cases Bright hoped to promote the welfare of the working classes.[58]

Criticism of the ten-hours measure was based largely upon economic considerations. The question of the shorter day, many agreed, raised difficult and complex economic problems.[59] Sir James Graham put it this way:

> . . . the subject is delicate, it is like a house built of cards, from which one can not be removed without danger to the whole fabric, and evils may be created which I tremble to contemplate, but certainly, foreseeing those evils, I am bound with the whole power and influence of the Government to guard against them.[60]

The complexity and importance of the factory question was sometimes evaluated in quite precise terms. According to Sir George Phillips's estimate, two-thirds to three-fourths of Britain's exports would be affected by ten-hours legislation. Ashley's amendment, Peel remarked in a letter to the Queen on 19 March 1844, would affect the cotton, woollen, silk and textile manufactures, constituting '35 millions out of 44 millions of our export trade'.[61] Consequently, while the critics of the ten-hours bill did not ignore its moral or humanitarian implications, their perspective focused on the commercial aspects of the ten-hours issue. Again, to use the words of Sir James Graham:

> I have said, on the one hand, that the physical and moral condition of a large class of the community is now brought under

discussion, on the other hand justice compels me to say, the question of commercial prosperity and manufacturing industry of this country is tonight materially involved in the question upon which we are deliberating.

Indeed, Henry Warburton alleged that Ashley had abrogated his responsibilities as a statesman by failing to consider the ten-hours question in the light of its commercial consequences.[62] Viewed from this economic perspective, the ten-hours question had significance for the prestige and power of England as well as for its culture and civilisation. Restrictive legislation, W. H. Hyett declared, would reduce the country, whose civilisation had advanced because of commerce and manufactures, into a 'state of immediate misery and confusion, such as no heart could conceive, and no tongue describe'. In Henry Warburton's view, the restriction of manufacturing power would make it impossible to maintain the colonies and dependencies of England. J. A. Roebuck attributed England's military success over Napoleon to the 'surplus produce' of the manufacturing districts. To cripple England's productive powers, therefore, would make her unable to defeat her new enemies, the chief of which was the famine which had devastated Ireland and which, in Roebuck's view, was about to invade England. To restrict industry, Roebuck also believed, would serve to impede England's financial powers.

. . . when they came to a vote of supply, the Chancellor of the Exchequer would feel all his energy crippled, he would find that his finances were cut short, by the right hand of England being withered.

The Economist warned against restrictive legislation by identifying the factory system as the central feature of life distinguishing modern from ancient times. In Cobdenite fashion, the factory system was conceived not only as the element which made progress inevitable, it was also the element which, in conjunction with commerce, would guarantee world peace.[63]

The chief objection to the ten-hours bill was that it would place English industry in an unfavourable competitive position. Lord Althorp expected a reduction of hours to drive English manufactures out of the market. William Bolling believed a difference of two farthings would tip the scale against British manufactures and, therefore, the ten-hours bill was an instrument of economic suicide. The legislation of 1802 and 1819, H. G. Ward suggested, had not harmed English industry because then England was in possession of the markets and politicians could deal with the question in a 'liberal and kindly spirit'. Now, England enjoyed no such commercial superiority and could not afford such luxuries. John Dennistoun, the Glasgow banker and Radical reformer, indicated another difference between the legislation of 1846–7 and the earlier factory acts. Previous legislation merely limited the labour of women and children where the bills of 1846 and 1847 would, he feared, limit the power and capacity of the steam engine itself.[64] The economic results of the ten-hours bill were understood, therefore, to constitute a threat to the strength, prestige, and industrial superiority of the nation.

In spite of a concern for the economic condition of British manufactures, this commercial perspective did not ignore the condition of the working classes. The condition of the workers, some argued, was directly related to the condition of the industrial system: the former could not prosper without the latter. An article in the *Westminster Review* stated:

A system which promotes the advance of civilization, and diffuses it over the whole world—which promises to maintain the peace of nations, by establishing a permanent international law, founded on the benefits of commercial association, cannot be inconsistent with the happiness of the *great mass of the people*.[65]

For Sir James Graham, the 'peace, happiness, and future prosperity of the country' were inseparably linked with commercial prosperity. H. G. Ward, citing Adam Smith to show how the long-run interests of capitalist and labourer were identical, expected no permanent improvement in the condition of the working man without an increase in the capital of the country.[66] As critics of the ten-hours bill concluded, restrictive legislation would not serve the best interests of the working class. Lord Althorp, in 1833, expected the ten-hours bill to be 'one of the greatest acts of cruelty that could be inflicted' and, in Lord Stanley's view, Ashley's legislation would 'frustrate his own benevolent objects'.[67] Thus, critics of the ten-hours bill maintained that parliament should avoid sentimentality and 'false humanity' and should act to protect and guarantee the 'permanent interests' of the people. It was 'false humanity' to enact legislation which would increase unemployment and reduce wages. Conversely, the permanent interests of the workers could best be ensured by a governmental policy which would widen the scope of industry and employment at a high wage level.

One major threat to the well-being of the working classes, the opponents of the ten-hours bill insisted, was the reduction of employment by restrictive legislation. As early as 1832, Peel warned that the zeal of legislators to reduce the hours of factory labour might cause workers 'to be thrown out of employment altogether'. In 1844, John Bright predicted restrictive legislation, crippling English trade, would prevent the constantly increasing population of the country from obtaining constant employment. To restrict the implementation of capital, Joseph Hume warned in 1847, would 'risk the removal of a certain portion of those employed by capital'.[68] In 1846 and 1847 the critics of the ten-hours measure compared the condition of workers in England favourably with that of Irish workers. In Joseph Hume's view, the Irish population suffered because of the absence of employment and would gladly take the place of those on behalf of whom Lord Ashley was acting. T. M. Gibson regarded it as an anomaly that in England they were trying to solve the problems of the people by the limitation of labour and in Ireland they were trying to improve the condition of the people by extending employment.[69]

The threat of reduced employment was sometimes presented in theoretical terms. Using arguments having their probable origin in Locke, Smith, and Ricardo, many believed the ten-hours bill would deprive the worker of his labour: the only property he possessed. Graham stated it this way:

> Talk of confiscation!—this Clause, if passed, will be a confiscation of the most extensive and of the very worst kind; it would be a confiscation without compensation—it would lead to the depriva-tion of a large portion of the only property the great mass possess —a confiscation of one sixth part of their work which is their capital.[70]

This point was also made by Peel, T. M. Gibson and Lord Brougham.[71] To restrict the labour of the working classes would make them powerless. It would rob them of the only commodity with which they could trade and would leave them adrift in that hard world which accommodates only those with the powers and skills requisite for life in industrial society. To deprive men of their only power in the name of humanity was delusion rather than amelioration. This point was also made in more practical terms. The result of the restriction of the hours of labour would not only confiscate the working man's capital and property, it would also reduce working-class wages. In his letter to the Queen of 19 March 1844 Peel gave this as one of his chief arguments for opposing Ashley's amendment. The ten-hours amendment, he said, 'must lead at a very early period to a great reduction in the wages of workmen as it is vain to suppose that their Masters will give the same wages for ten hours labour, as they gave for twelve'.[72] There were various estimates of what such a reduction of wages would mean in monetary terms. Sir George Phillips declared wages would be reduced by 25 per cent, George Wood (Reformer: Kendal) calculated it at one-third, Sir James Graham estimated the amount from 20 to 25 per cent, and Peel maintained the loss would be equivalent to an income tax of 15 per cent on the labour of adults.[73] All of this was taken as an evil portent for the working class. The reduction of wages, Roebuck declared, would eliminate any chance for the moral improvement of the people. Both Mark Philips and Roebuck believed restriction of hours would make it necessary to regulate wages. In Roebuck's view, if the labourers' hours were reduced, they had a right to demand indemnities for the consequences of such an act, even to the extent of demanding the establishment of wage minimums.[74]

The critics of ten-hours legislation, as the previous discussion indicates, did not base their position on a simple theory of economic and social individualism. Taking a broad view of the complex and often ambiguous character of the factory question, they believed such matters could not be solved simply by legislation restricting working hours. Those opposing ten hours often took a political posture which this book has described as incrementalist in form and substance. They did not oppose factory legislation categorically, as the passage of the factory acts of 1833 and 1844 demonstrates. Appreciating the difficulties of ameliorating the condition of the working classes without threatening the strength and stability of the economic structure, they realised the factory question must be approached gradually and cautiously as well as from a wide and judicious perspective. Appreciating the way in which the plethora of economic considerations were intertwined and interrelated, the critics of the ten-hours measure believed it was inadequate for the improvement of working-class conditions, and that it, moreover, would lead to a further deterioration of those conditions. For example, Henry Labouchere believed the passage of a ten-hours bill would reduce production, creating a vacuum on the market and driving prices up. Speculators might attempt to fill the vacuum but would quickly fail in the face of foreign competition unrestrained by unfavourable legislation. This would, in turn, induce conflicts between the manufacturers and the working population as the former attempted to reduce wages in order to cover their increasing production costs.[75] Ten-hours legislation, as a consequence, spelled economic disaster not only for the manufacturer but for the worker as well. As Dennistoun put it:

. . . I venture to predict that not so many years will elapse till those very persons, on whose behalf you think you are now legislating, will demand of you, in a voice not to be misunderstood, to retrace your steps; and will call upon you to save them amidst the wreck, and anarchy, and confusion, which you yourselves, by your unwise and unjust legislation now, will have brought upon the country.[76]

The ten-hours bill was, for its critics, a legislative *cul de sac*, a nostrum, a foolish attempt to solve problems which could only be remedied by more sophisticated technical, fiscal, and economic governmental policies.

IV

The proponents of ten hours differed from their critics both in terms of the legislation they advocated as well as in political outlook. The critics of ten hours were content to recommend a complex series of educational, administrative, sanitary, and fiscal remedies in order to effect changes in the factory system. Ten-hours advocates, on the other hand, narrowly restricted their legislative concerns to the limitation of working hours. The political perspective of the critics of ten hours, as already noted, was marked by a cautious pragmatic concern for the piecemeal modification and amelioration of working-class conditions. In contrast, the proponents of ten-hours legislation, viewing the matter as a moral question, attacked the abuses in the factory system as detrimental to the morality and well-being of the factory workers as well as disruptive to the proper ordering of society. In so far as the movement for ten hours was informed by the views of Richard Oastler, Joseph Rayner Stephens, and the other 'Tory-Radicals', there is much about it which appears to be mere sentimentality and resembles political and social reaction. The lessons revealed by the division lists are clear: Conservatives like Oastler and Lord Ashley were joined by Liberals who supported the concept of the shorter day. Sir George Grey, Macaulay, and Lord John Russell, however, all recommended caution in the implementation of restrictive legislation and preferred an eleven-hour compromise bill.[77] As a consequence of these divided positions, the ten-hours movement was itself divided on a wide range of issues relating to economic and political policy.

The ten-hours movement began with Sadler's bill of 1832 and matured during the years of criticism of the royal commission and the factory act of 1833. *The Times*, on 18 May 1833, reprinted an article from the Leeds *Times* which criticised the royal commission for its secret proceedings. And, from Oastler's point of view, the commission was a 'mere instrument in the hands of the "bit of Parliament" of cotton manufacturers'.[78] Similarly, the proponents of a ten-hours measure were highly critical of the act of 1833. In their view, this legislation was supported by the friends of the manufacturers and the enemies of the people. Ashley denounced the measure and predicted it 'would produce ten-fold misery and ten-fold crime'. Oastler condemned the act as a failure and claimed it had been passed 'for the purpose of delusion': it was intended to soothe the popular agitation and then be repealed piecemeal.[79] On matters of detail, the act of 1833 was criticised on the ground that the relay system was ineffective, that it was difficult to detect offences, that millowners sat on the Bench adjudicating their own cases, that it was too complicated, and that it induced all manner of frauds.[80] An article in *Fraser's Magazine* showed no more pleasure with the act of 1844 because, from this author's

L

point of view, the act was intended to protect 'monied men and dead capital' and granted as little as could be conceded to the workers. There were many who agreed with Sir George Strickland (Reformer: Preston), who believed 'nothing short of a ten hour bill could satisfy the feelings of the public, or be productive of any advantage'.[81]

The supporters of legislation to restrict the hours of labour enjoyed an enormous rhetorical advantage over their opponents. They could draw on a long tradition of sentimental evangelical fervour, expressing their position in absolute moral terms. Lord Ashley described the issue as one of morality and religion and could sincerely assert that 'what was morally wrong could not be politically right'. As Hodder has suggested, Ashley took the factory question as an aspect of practical Christianity.[82] Many advocates of the ten-hours measure viewed the factory question in strict manichean terms. For them it was a simple question of right or wrong, justice or injustice, mammon or mercy.[83] Joseph Rayner Stephens was at his passionate best when he said:

> It is the question of law or no law—order or anarchy—religion or infidelity—heaven-sprung truth and peace and love; or hell-born, withering atheism. It is the working of the mystery mentioned in the Holy Scripture—the mystery of ungodliness—the battle directly, though not ostensibly—the struggle actually, though not openly avowed—the life and death struggle of Christ in his spirit, and through his spirit in his followers, against Belial in his spirit, and through his spirit in his children. It is the battle between God and Mammon—between Christ and Beelzebub, the prince of devils.[84]

There is an element of sentimentality about much of the rhetoric of the advocates of the ten-hours bill as the following petition from Bradford illustrates.

> We are poor factory children. We don't want to live without work—we are willing to work, but we will not be worked to death. The Doctors say 'ten hours is plenty'. We say so too. . . . The Bible does not tell our masters to work children at all. Jesus Christ would not deny us a Ten Hours Bill. We are sure he would not.[85]

Moreover, the ten-hours men were able to draw easy analogies between the factory question and the slave trade. Robert Southey, for example, regarded the factory system as 'more uniformly and incorrigibly evil' than the slave trade, and Oastler, John Fielden, Michael Sadler, Richard Monckton Milnes (Conservative: Ponte-fract) and Forster Alleyne M'Geachy (Conservative: Honiton) expanded and developed this parallel.[86]

At several points in the controversy over the factory question the advocates of ten hours attempted to disclaim any categorical condemnation of industrialism as a system. For the most part proponents of ten hours seemed content to attack the abuses of the factory system. His position, Sadler declared, was neither deter-mined by a hostility to the manufacturing interests nor by an adversity to the prosperity and extension of those interests. Oastler did not believe machinery itself was necessarily a curse but was converted into one by the extensive use of female and child labour. As Joseph Brotherton and Sir Robert Harry Inglis (Con-servative: Oxford) indicated, their objection was not aimed at individual millowners but at the corrupted factory system.[87] In spite of this moderate posture, the powerful rhetoric used by proponents of ten hours reveals a deep-rooted opposition, on the part of many, to the economic ethic which accompanied industrial development. The 'curse' of the factory system, Fielden believed, lay in the avarice and greed of the factory masters as they forced women and children to work hours of unnatural length. Andrew Garew O'Dwyer (Repealer: Drogheda) said that the factory masters did not destroy children 'wantonly or gratuitously' but did so in order to pocket an additional 10 or 15 per cent. The advocates of the shorter day, as a consequence, often attributed the miseries of the factory system to the unnatural greed which stimulated the unnatural competition of capitalist production. Lord Howick (Liberal: Sunderland), for example, saw no way to remedy the abuses of the factory system until the intensity of that competition which animated the factory system had been re-duced.[88]

One of the chief criticisms of the factory system was that extensive labour caused a deterioration of the physical condition of the workers. The deleterious results of overworking, Sadler stated, were evident in the fact that workers in the factories rarely lived to the age of forty. As George Bankes argued, to refuse to pass a ten-hours bill would result in the destruction of the 'physical energies' and the 'moral character' of the working classes. Similar statements relating extensive hours of labour to physical conditions were made by Macaulay, Ferrand, and the Bishop of London. The mortality rate, advocates of ten hours insisted, was higher in working-class districts than in rural regions. Charles Buller, while he did not believe that long hours were the sole causal factor, saw the mortality differential between such regions as Manchester and Wiltshire as a demonstration of the need for legislative action to reduce physical suffering and abuse. With the beginning of social investigations into the condition of the poor, promoters of ten-hours legislation had a ready supply of statistical ammunition to use in support of their cause. Thomas Wakley cited Chadwick's famous report of 1842 to show the results of the factory system and John Fielden cited the table of deaths compiled by the Registrar-General to relate the destruction of life to 'constant and unwholesome toil'.[89]

The factory system was also criticised because, as a consequence of its abuses, the natural order of society was disrupted. Because children and women took the place of men in the factory system, the children were prevented from enjoying a wholesome growth to maturity and the women were 'unsexed' and separated from their household duties. The two sexes were thus removed from their proper spheres of activity, eliminating the possibilities for a satisfying domestic life. Lord Ashley described the consequences.

> You are poisoning the very sources of order and happiness and virtue; you are tearing up root and branch, all the relations of families to each other; you are annulling, as it were, the institutions of domestic life, decreed by Providence himself, the wisest and kindest of earthly ordinances, the mainstay of social peace and virtue, and therein our national security.[90]

In addition, the system of excessive labour also poisoned the natural relations which should exist between master and worker, and, therefore, served as a perpetual grievance disturbing the 'order of nature' and causing perpetual discontent. Because of this disruption of the natural social order, the advocates of the ten-hours measure predicted political disaster if the House of Commons failed to pass an ameliorative measure. Frequently this prognosis was formulated in terms of class warfare. Lord Ashley warned against the separation of the rich from the poor, which would revive the 'ancient feud between the House of Want and the House of Have'. Lord John Manners and William Busfeild Ferrand forecast strikes, violence and combinations if the legislature refused to recognise the needs of the people. Lord John Russell predicted

> . . . if the Legislature were to neglect this subject, if it were to look for nothing but manufacturing wealth and commercial prosperity, and to say it mattered not what happened so long as the country possessed these, that they would some day or other awake from that pleasant dream to the sad reality of an immense mass of people estranged from those institutions, setting no value on that which was held to be sacred, and guided by the wildest demagogues, seeking to effect the worst and most mischievous desires.

As early as 1832, in a letter to Ashley, Southey had warned that until the working classes were improved morally, physically, and religiously, England would have more to fear from them than West Indian planters had to fear from their slaves.[91]

The ten-hours bill was the ameliorative measure which could, in the eyes of Oastler, Ashley, Fielden, Brotherton, Buller and Howick, best solve these physical, social and political problems. While some resorted exclusively to moral arguments, and others attempted to meet the economic arguments of their opponents, all believed the ten-hours measure to be an essential instrument for the improvement of the worker and English society. Oastler wrote from the Fleet Prison:

> The Premier may sneer at the Ten Hours' Factory Bill, but it is a fact, that very many of the wisest and most prudent factory masters have *now* come to the conclusion that *that* measure is the *only one* which *can* preserve our manufacturers from being devoured one of another. . . . if he would rescue hundreds of mill-owners from impending ruin, he must, *and that without delay*, pass a measure to controul [sic] their gigantic operation, and thus prevent that ruinous competition, which the wisest of mill-owners now forsee must result from their increasing stocks and the stagnation of demand.[92]

Moreover, one of the chief benefits of the ten-hours measure, or so its advocates believed, was the moral improvement of the working classes. Indeed, this was one of the great themes of the ten-hours movement. Lord John Russell, no easy sentimentalist, maintained that it was the duty of the state to ensure that the population was aware of religious doctrines, that they cultivate domestic affections and arts, and that they respect the laws and the government of the country. All this was impossible under the conditions of excessively prolonged labour. The previous factory acts, Sir George Grey noted in 1847, had produced an increase in the comfort and education of the people. The ten-hours measure was, therefore, no 'step in the dark' and would produce similar results.[93]

The opponents of the shorter day, it will be recalled, predicted that the condition of the working classes would be worsened because the reduction of hours would be followed by a reduction of wages. The ten-hours men answered this warning in several ways, all of which carried strong tones of upper-class paternalism. On the one hand, they regarded the reduction of wages as of little consequence compared with the benefits accruing from the diminution of working hours. Sadler believed the workers 'would prefer that reduced compensation, and readily submit to that loss, rather than their children should be over-worked and destroyed as at present'. The workers, John Stuart Wortley declared in 1844, would gladly risk such a loss and consider themselves repaid by the moral and physical benefits resulting from less hours. Lord Ashley considered that it would be better to have a 'sound and moral' working class with a smaller amount of wages than have an immoral and uneducated working class in better financial condition. Robert Vernon Smith (Liberal: Northampton), who had heard the working classes described as immoral and shiftless, suspected that high wages would produce profligacy rather than social improvement.[94] As these statements might be taken to indicate, the argument for ten-hours legislation was informed by more than sympathy for the plight of working children in the factory system. In addition to sympathy there are suggestions of an essential disdain for the working classes, which was coupled with the conviction that the upper orders of society were entitled and obligated to make paternalistic decisions regarding working-class wages and hours. The lower orders of society, the ten-hours men believed, were incapable of resolving their own difficulties unaided by upper-class leadership and action.

Yet, there was another approach to the question of wages. John

Fielden and the Marquis of Granby expected the reduction of hours to produce an increase rather than a reduction of wages. The effect of the shorter day, they believed, would reduce production. Assuming effective demand and the labour supply remained constant, new manufactories would be established, leading to an increase in the demand for labour which would, in turn, lead to the rise of wage levels. Indeed, in 1846, John Fielden attempted to show how the reduction of hours resulting from previous legislation had not produced lower wages.[95] The advocates of ten-hours legislation also maintained that the working classes would benefit in so far as the reduction of hours would equalise the labour market. Viscount Sandon viewed the ten-hours bill as a means for reducing periods of protracted unemployment. Since production carried on at the level of twelve hours labour per day produced gluts and frequent unemployment, William Francis Cowper (Whig: Hertford) believed the reduction of hours would eliminate these irregularities. In addition, Ferrand, Inglis and Russell also recommended the reduction of working hours as a means of distributing work more equally and uniformly throughout the labour force.[96] As these observations indicate, many members of parliament did not look on the economy as being driven by invariable laws of supply and demand: gluts, over-production, and unemployment were recognised facts of economic life.

The proponents of ten-hours legislation also attempted to answer their critics' 'commercial' objections to restrictive legislation. It has already been noted that the advocates of the shorter day rejected the appraisal of the Condition of England Question from the 'commercial' perspective. In their view, the industrial superiority of England should not depend on the suffering of women and children. Moreover, there was nothing to fear from foreign competition, 'the greatest bugbear that Englishmen were ever made to believe in'. Fielden believed England's geographical, technical and human resources would prevent her industry from falling into a competitive disadvantage.[97] The most telling piece of evidence brought to bear against the 'commercial' argument was the fact that England's competitive position had not suffered through previous factory legislation. This point was made frequently by Joseph Brotherton, John Stuart Wortley, Sir George Grey and Lord George Bentinck.[98] As Lord Ashley put it:

The commercial argument, in truth is really feeble; it has always been urged, and has never been verified, and yet experience should go for something in these considerations,—it was broached in 1816; repeated and enforced in evidence before committees, in speeches and pamphlets, in 1817, 1818, 1819, and utterly refuted by the whole subsequent history of the cotton trade from that day to the present—you had no diminution of produce, no fall in wages, no rise in price, no closing of markets, no irresistible rivalry from foreign competition, although you reduced your hours of working from 16, 14, 13, to 12 hours in the day.[99]

Rather than injuring British industry and commerce, the advocates of the ten-hours bill suggested that its passage would strengthen native industry because it would strengthen the working classes. As a resolution of the London Society for the Improvement of the Condition of the Factory Children on 23 February 1833 argued, the lasting strength and wealth of a nation are incompatible with an industrial system which is destructive of the physical, mental and moral powers of the working classes. If the labouring classes were given an opportunity to develop their intellectual and moral faculties, Benjamin Hawes suggested, their efficiency and, therefore, their value as labourers would increase.[100] An article in *The Times* on 2 April 1844 argued that England's position as a great power rested on the factory labourers. They, therefore, like the army and navy, should be considered 'an arm of the national service' and their health and security considered an aspect of national security and industrial prosperity. In addition to the moral and physical improvement of the working classes, the ten-hours bill was also conceived to be a means of accomplishing another beneficial object: the improvement of domestic and social harmony. With restricted labour, the 'natural state of things', as Charles Buller put it, would be restored: men performing heavy labour and women household tasks. Ashley said:

It is to *purify the social system*; to restore the woman to her domestic duties and the care of her family; to provide that the younger part may have time to learn what is necessary to fit them for their future stations in life; and that as wives and mothers, they may have leisure to practice those duties which they shall have learned as children.

The ten-hours bill was also conceived as a means of reconciling workers to their masters in a stable social order free of strikes and combinations. Buller and the Rev G. S. Bull maintained that social harmony could be produced by legislation for shorter hours, which would in its turn protect order and property. Bull stated: 'The firmer the foundation the better and broader, the more sure will be the stability and the prosperity of the superstructure'.[101]

The ten-hours movement had no extensive governmental theory with which to justify their legislative desideratum. It has been noted that the ten-hours bill contained no administrative machinery for enforcement. It has also been noted that the ten-hours movement, at the outset, opposed the royal commission and factory act of 1833, with its complex provisions for inspection and supervision. As a general rule, the ten-hours movement did not turn to government growth and creative administration for authority and the bonds of obligation. It found the bonds of obligation in the more 'natural' sphere of customary law and Christian humanitarianism. An article in *Fraser's Magazine*, in discussing the defeat of Peel's government in a division on the factory bill in March 1844, made this clear:

> The matter in dispute had much more connexion with benevolence than with the theory of government, with Christian philanthropy than with political theory.[102]

Such political theory as there was behind the ten-hours bill consisted in concepts of legislative paternalism emphasising the moral obligations of parliament to protect the defenceless. As the Bishop of Chester remarked in 1818, 'Parliament was the natural guardian of the unprotected'.[103] As a consequence, the proponents of the ten-hours bill looked on it as essentially a paternalistic measure. The purpose of the bill, *The Times* stated on 21 April 1847, was not to limit industry 'but only to exert a sort of parental control over useless labour and consuming toil'. Lord John Manners hailed the bill as a portent of 'good, paternal, patriarchal government for the future'.[104] Often the authority for measures restricting labour was derived from customary law and values. William Cobbett, in a letter to John Fielden published in the *Political Register*, wrote:

King Alfred, who was the real founder of English liberty and English law, laid it down as a rule, that the twenty-four hours should be divided thus: eight for labour, eight for rest, eight for recreation. And this was about the case in England for several hundreds of years.[105]

In a qualitative as well as a quantitative sense then, the intervention of the government required by the ten-hours movement differed from government intervention with regard to public health and the relief of the poor. In the latter cases, intervention was largely of an administrative character. Its emphasis, like that of the factory acts of 1833 and 1844, was on the establishment of a system of governmental machinery to supervise the administration of parliamentary enactments. The ten-hours movement, on the other hand, was concerned almost exclusively with legislative prohibition.

One of the most fascinating paradoxes of the ten-hours movement is that some of its strongest advocates were opposed to government growth, inspection, or any tendency towards 'centralisation'. In particular, men frequently known for their sympathies for the ten-hours bill were highly critical of the centralising and inspectorial aspects of the factory act of 1833. In 1835 Charles Hindley objected to the factory inspectors on the grounds that they had exceeded their authority. He pledged to oppose the bill of supply for their salaries until the inspectors' reports had been placed before parliament.[106] John Fielden raised the anti-centralisation bugbear in 1840 when he moved for a select committee to investigate the political activities of the factory inspectors after he was informed that they had been serving as spies for the Government:

> How did the House know either, seeing that they had been so employed, that Poor-law Commissioners, police, and all who were in direct communication with the Government, and the officers under them, had not been similarly employed? He believed they had; and he had no doubt that the Todmorden riots were caused by some such emissaries. The Government system of centralization naturally led to this, and to the establishment of a system of spying throughout the country. . . . The powers possessed by the inspectors under [the factory act] had been used for purposes of oppression, and their time, for anything that he knew, might have

been wholly taken up in this degrading occupation, instead of attending to their duties. . . .[107]

In this, Fielden was supported by such other ten-hours men as Henry Aglionby, H. G. Boldero, Thomas Slingsby Duncombe, Charles Hindley, Thomas Wakley, and Benjamin Disraeli.[108]

Richard Oastler was particularly opposed, as his position on the new poor law shows, to administrative intervention and government growth. Oastler disapproved of the factory inspectorate for several reasons. In the first place, Oastler disliked the inspectors because he believed they were the tools of the factory masters, who merely 'gloss over their death-warrants'. In the second place, he loathed the inspectorate because the government to which it was responsible had consumed the 'deadly draught' of 'Enlightened Liberalism'.[109] For Oastler, administrative intervention and inspection were unnecessary. He remarked to a group of his associates in Leeds in 1844:

> Well, then, my friends, we stand upon the same ground we ever did; and we offer to the country the Ten Hours' Bill—the simple, plain, efficient Ten Hours' Bill, unaccompanied by inspectors, superintendents, or any other government officers, who, let me tell you, are always the spies of the government. Let the stoppage of the moving power be enacted, or let the clauses for personal punishment to the millowners who shall wilfully break the law be adopted, and we can do without inspectors.[110]

Oastler's naïve confidence in the efficacy of simple prohibitive legislation made administrative intervention not only unnecessary but undesirable.[111] In the cases of the poor-law, public-health, and railway legislation, the proponents of those reforms, as we have observed, generally favoured and supported government growth. In contrast, many of the most vocal advocates of the ten-hours bill often opposed administrative intervention.

Since the ten-hours movement was supported by men of a variety of political attitudes, one would expect a division of opinion even within the ten-hours movement itself. Such a division of opinion can be found especially with regard to economic issues. Opinion was divided both on specific questions, such as the repeal of the corn laws, and also on the more general question of the focus and direction of economic activity and growth. Conservative Protectionists in the House of Commons and Richard Oastler outside the House opposed the repeal of the corn laws. Oastler viewed the Anti-Corn Law League as the enemy of landed society and the working classes. Free trade in corn, he maintained, was un-English, unsocial, and unnatural, since there was sufficient food for all in this 'nice little, right little, tight little island'. As free trade increased so also would world misery, wretchedness and destitution. He, furthermore, understood the free-trade programme as a threat to the established church, the throne and the aristocratic order:

> ... the Leaguers are marching upon the 'order' of the landlords, and are openly avowing, that your humiliation is necessary in the progression of their principles.

The free traders, according to Oastler, were the enemies of the working poor since they were the most obstinate opponents of the ten-hours bill. Oastler conceived of the corn laws as an instrument for the protection of the agricultural and handloom labourers, who would be driven into slavery in the factory system by the unholy alliance of the Anti-Corn Law League, factory owners, and the Poor Law Board.[112] Similarly, W. B. Ferrand maintained that the Anti-Corn Law League and the master manufacturers were engaged in a conspiracy against the working classes. Michael Sadler and Lord Ashley (before his conversion to free trade) saw no relationship between the tariff issue and the well-being of the working classes. Indeed, Sadler believed the 'grinding of the faces of the poor' would continue even if the corn laws were repealed.[113]

On the other hand, there were strong advocates of the ten-hours bill who also supported corn-law repeal. The corn laws, Colonel Robert Torrens held, were a violation of the principle of free labour since they prevented the workers from maximising their labour and using it to best advantage. He saw the dangers of foreign competition as stemming from foolish commercial policies and, in 1833, recommended the repeal of the corn laws and the limitation of the hours of labour.[114] Several other prominent members of parliament agreed with Torrens's essential position.[115] The most brilliant defence of the free-trade/ten-hours position is found in Lord Macaulay's speech of 22 May 1846. This speech does not, as it has sometimes been alleged, mark Macaulay's conversion from an extreme laissez-faire position, found in his review of Southey's *Colloquies on Society*. Although he recognised paternalistic government as more of a problem in the past than it was in 1846, both his review and his speech in 1846 rejected 'meddling patriarchal Government'.[116] Opposition to government paternalism, as Macaulay sought to show in his speech, was not necessarily inconsistent with his support for a ten-hours measure, and support for ten hours was not inconsistent with free trade. For Macaulay, free trade 'properly stated' meant it was inadvisable for government to interfere with persons of 'ripe age and sound mind' in merely commercial matters. However, it was an error to apply the principle of free trade to matters that were not 'purely commercial'. Non-interference was not applicable to matters of health, humanity and morality. Since the question of the hours of labour was one which concerned health and morality, the principle of free trade was not to be brought to bear against it. The government, Macaulay went so far as to state, might even interfere with the contracts of adults when 'such interference may appear advisable'.[117]

In addition to differing views on the corn laws, the advocates of a ten-hours bill were also divided on larger political, economic and social issues. Oastler was, as his biographer indicates, essentially a romantic whose views were shaped by his own dreams of the English past.[118] This reactionary outlook, with its reverence for institutional and social anachronisms, shaped his political, economic and social prescriptions for contemporary problems. Just as Oastler's political philosophy consisted in the kind of political arcadianism reflected in his views on the new poor law, so his economic views reflect a similar reverence for ancient institutions hedged in pristine purity and virtue. For Oastler, 'Enlightened Liberalism' was a force which acted in opposition to those economic elements he valued most: agricultural labour and the domestic system. From Oastler's point of view, the spirit of free trade/factory system/poor law struck a crippling blow to agricultural labour and the agricultural interest because the prospect of employment in the mills drew labourers and their families to the factory districts, where they were corrupted and ruined by excessive labour. He believed that once the labourers were useless to the factory owners they would be thrown back on the land for support.[119] In part, from Oastler's point of view, unemployment must have an agricultural and not an industrial solution if the country was to retain its prosperity.

> So long as we have a single acre of land uncultivated, and a single pair of hands unemployed, if we import the corn which those hands and that land might have created, whatever price we give for that corn, as a nation, we lose the whole amount.[120]

Oastler was opposed to any attempts to draw people from the 'plough to the spindle', maintaining that agricultural employment would provide the most 'healthy, rational, and pleasing occupation, and withal a more solid and secure foundation for national security'.[121]

Similarly, Oastler had a high regard for domestic manufacture. The system of domestic produce, as he saw it, had been a system in which the young could be trained in ancient skills and crafts. It was a productive arrangement where 'filial affection and parental feeling' were manifest. Refusing to recognise hand manufacture as inferior to power manufacture, he noted the existence of several improvements which might make the handloom superior to the power loom and which would, therefore, return manufacturing to the cottages. Since he was anxious to preserve domestic industry, Oastler felt that no new invention should be introduced until compensation had been paid to those workmen 'the value of whose labour would in consequence be reduced'.[122] The entire thrust of Oastler's economic views was to favour the older forms of production.

In addition, implicitly and explicitly, Oastler favoured a policy of restricting production to solve the problem of gluts and to relieve the labour of the factory workers.

> The universal cry now is, 'we are ruined because we produce too much'—my cry has been, for many years, 'Produce less.' Had my advice been taken ten years ago, the present losses of the factory masters would have been prevented.[123]

Refusing to regard England as an expanding 'workshop of the world', Oastler turned to restrictive measures as a means of limiting a competition which was ruinous to both manufacturer and worker. He was prepared, therefore, for the sake of domestic peace and the condition of the factory workers, to emphasise domestic trade at the expense of foreign trade.[124] Other advocates of the ten-hours bill, although they held no personal animosity towards the millowners, were willing to restrict industrial progress and sacrifice foreign trade in order to alleviate factory conditions through moral and humanitarian reform.[125] Generally speaking, they had little confidence in a policy of alleviating the conditions of the working classes through economic expansion. For them, economic expansion could only produce increased competition and greater misery.

Within the ten-hours movement, however, there were other men who did not share this archaic economic perspective. The appraisal of early Victorian economic problems of Viscount Howick, Charles Buller and Richard Monckton Milnes was far more progressive than that of Oastler. England, Charles Buller believed, had become an entirely new social state in the nineteenth century, and, as a consequence, required entirely new principles of legislation. For Buller the ten-hours bill was

. . . the first great step in a bold and new course of legislation, adopted with a view of alleviating great moral and physical suffering, and of averting national dangers which their old principles of legislation were not calculated to deal with, but which, if not dealt with, must imperil the peace, institutions, morality, and greatness of the country.[126]

For Viscount Howick, the machinery for dealing with factory problems was inadequate. After seeing the extent to which trade unions had flourished in England, Howick suggested a new mechanism consisting of organisations in which both workers and masters would be represented and which would bear the responsibility for formulating regulations for those branches of industry 'which Parliament was confessedly incapable of itself framing with advantage'.[127] This plan was in part suggested by the importance of the medieval guilds in stimulating the development of trade and civilisation. However, this was not an arcadian plan for a return to a set of medieval economic institutions. Howick was careful to specify the precautions which had to be taken to prevent these corporate bodies from 'degenerating into a mischievous monopoly'. He suggested that the power of revision over the acts of these corporations could be given to the Crown just as in the case of municipal corporations.[128] Howick, Buller, Monckton Milnes and Thomas Slingsby Duncombe, therefore, unlike Oastler and Stephens, emphasised the extent to which times had changed and in which new problems required new solutions.[129]

I have emphasised here the diverse character of the ten-hours movement as well as the extent to which it consisted in archaic, reactionary elements. The largest measure of the reactionary character of the ten-hours movement is evident in the extra-parliamentary agitation for the shorter day, which was led by Oastler, Stephens, and G. S. Bull. In the last analysis, this agitation should probably be considered a secondary factor in the passage of the ten-hours bill. Like the Anti-Corn Law League, the agitation of the short-time committees could, at best, raise the moral temperature out-of-doors.[130] The levers of power were located in the House of Commons where Oastler, Stephens, and Bull could not reach them. In the House, the cause was in the hands of Fielden and Ashley, who were unsuccessful in beating Peel's whips. It was only after the fall of Peel's government that Conservative MPs could join with Liberals and Radicals, having their own political perspective, to pass the ten-hours bill.[131]

V

From our vantage point, after fifty years' experience with the welfare state, there is much about the controversy over the factory question which appears facile and naïve. In the light of the extensive social legislation since the nineteenth century, the ten-hours measure does not seem particularly advanced or humane. Moreover, both the critics and proponents of the ten-hours bill were uncritical in their analysis of its economic effects because neither made an attempt to distinguish clearly between the long-run and the short-run effects of the limitation of hours. The simple reduction of hours was unlikely to meet the long-term problems of the working classes and a theory of economic growth could not do much to alleviate the immediate and short-term needs of the labourers in the factory districts. Yet, this controversy is enormously useful in an examination of attitudes towards the state in the early Victorian period.

The factory question, as much as any issue, raised the problem of economic orthodoxy.[132] To be sure, many participants in this controversy took refuge behind the opinions of the great authorities on economic matters in order to oppose state intervention. For example, Charles Wood and H. G. Ward referred to Adam Smith, and Joseph Hume cited Nassau Senior to show the dangers of legislative intervention.[133] Others, similarly, utilised dogmatic concepts of conventional economic wisdom. Brougham placed confidence in the 'mysterious decrees, the inscrutable dispensations of an All-wise and All-mighty Providence', Richard Cobden exhorted the labouring classes to 'look not to Parliament, look only to yourselves', and Hume vowed to sweep away every legislative restriction until 'one general and uniform principle of perfect liberty pervade our legislation'.[134] *The Economist*, however, was the most dogmatic spokesman for the non-interventionist position on the ten-hours question since it held the view that there could be no halfway house between 'perfect independent self-reliance and regulated socialism'.[135]

These unqualified, doctrinaire views, however, do not represent the whole story. Many, as I have tried to show in this chapter, saw the relationship between economic orthodoxy and the factory question in much more expediential terms. Political economy, Charles Hindley observed, was consistent with humane considerations. The Earl of Ellesmere and the Bishop of London, while opposing 'meddling government', believed the misery of the working classes justified legislative intervention.[136] Lord Macaulay, who saw no inconsistency in supporting both free trade in corn and the ten-hours bill, parodied the *Book of Common Prayer* saying:

We have regulated that which we ought to have left to regulate itself; we have left unregulated that which it was our especial business to have regulated.[137]

Sir George Grey, while rejecting direct interference with adult labour, appreciated the ten-hours issue as one of degree, not principle. Both he and Lord Wharncliffe viewed the whole question of factories as something of a special case which was removed from the normal area of orthodox economic concerns.[138] As much as Peel opposed the ten-hours bill and feared it would destroy the

M

wealth of the nation, even he felt that the general economic principles which should be brought to bear on legislative matters were
to be derived, not as mathematical formulae, 'but by observance
of facts, and from the conclusions of wisdom drawn from long
experience'. The principles of free trade, Peel acknowledged, did
not necessarily apply to legislation for the welfare of the working
classes.[139] These views are only a sample of many more which
could be cited here.

The factory acts of the early Victorian period were not, any
more than the new poor law, the Public Health Act, or the railway
acts of the 1840s, examples of collectivist legislation. To suggest
that they were would be to make the same mistake some have
made in considering Keynesianism or the New Deal in the United
States as socialistic. The function of the factory acts, as this
chapter has pointed out, was to provide machinery for the inspection of factories, to establish educational requirements for
child labourers, and to limit the hours of labour of young persons.
While the sphere of activity of the central government, to the
extent that it became involved in these activities, was enlarged,
the factory acts nationalised neither the means of production nor
distribution. The fundamental conflict at the heart of the controversy over this body of legislation was not one of non-interven-
tion versus state control of the factories. Those opposing the
ten-hours bill did not advocate absolute freedom from the government. Indeed, most favoured state intervention in forms which
would subject the factory system and child labour to the scrutiny
of inspection. The proponents of the ten-hours measure, for their
part, desired anything but a nationalised factory system. If anything, Oastler and others sharing his anachronistic views opposed
all forms of government growth and administrative intervention.
Consequently, the fundamental question at issue in the dispute
over the factories was concerned with the means by which the
working classes could be helped. The opponents of ten hours,
with their incrementalists' practical concern for gradual modification and consequent caution in tinkering with the economy,
favoured amelioration through an increasingly productive, expanding, industrial, economy. The proponents of ten hours, with
their moral and humanitarian criticism of factory abuses often
accompanied by reactionary economic and social views, believed

amelioration could come only through a restriction of working hours and restricted productivity. The fundamental point of controversy in the factory question was, to be brief, the limitation of labour as opposed to economic growth and development.

Notes to Chapter 5 will be found on pages 212–19.

Chapter 6 SOME CONCLUDING OBSERVATIONS

> All things are tending to a change. We are entering on a new political dispensation; and many of us probably will outlive the integrity of our aristocratic institutions. Men are talking, they know not why, and they do not reflect *how*, of *this* slight concession and *that*; of the 'enlargement of the franchise', and other vagaries.
>
> Lord Ashley (13 April 1848)

A MAJOR political question of the early Victorian period, an age in which traditional institutions were being undermined by the forces of change, was: what political forms shall bear legal responsibility for absorbing the conflicts and tensions generated by economic and social development? The answer which early Victorian politics provided to this question was, as we have seen, that the responsibility for governing the innovating forces of Victorian society should be divided between central and local, between public and private elements. If one considers the attitudes and opinions of Victorian politicians, rather than the ultimate consequences of their policies, state intervention and government growth in the 1830s and 1840s should be seen as part of the structure and assumptions of traditional political forms rather than as socialist attempts to create a welfare state. Certainly the governmental modifications of the second quarter of the nineteenth century do not meet Professor Briggs's definition of the welfare state, which would require them to alter the market forces in order to provide a guaranteed minimum income, and security against sickness, old age, and unemployment.[1] The new poor law, the Public Health Act, the railway acts, and factory legislation did none of these things. Limited in objective, and tempered by centuries of preference for limited government, government growth in early Victorian Britain was restrained in scope and modest in accomplishment.

Lord Macaulay, in his speech on the factory bill in 1847, provided an excellent contemporary definition of the parameters of state action. In his view, government should be characterised neither by the mercantilist flaw of continual intervention, nor by indifference to social problems and human suffering. It should be something less than 'meddling' government and something more than careless, indifferent, *pococurante* government.[2] The early Victorian administrative state, it is fair to say, with its blending of central and local, of public and private, authorities, was consistent with Macaulay's prescriptions. John Stuart Mill's statement of the scope of centralised authority is an almost classic summary of widespread attitudes towards this question.

The principal business of the central authority should be to give instruction, of the local authority to apply it. Power may be localized, but knowledge, to be most useful, must be centralized; there must be somewhere a focus at which all its scattered rays are collected, that the broken and coloured lights which exist elsewhere may find there what is necessary to complete and purify them.[3]

The creation of central departments during the second quarter of the nineteenth century represents an important qualitative attempt to redistribute legal responsibilities and to utilise the instruments of the national government in the effort to tame the potentially destructive powers of modern society. Conceived as these instruments were, however, in the contexts of traditional philanthropic ideals and local government, power continued to be diffused over a wide range of political authorities.

In accord with these general assumptions, the chief functions of the central agencies examined in this book were limited to the guidance and supervision of local administrative authorities. This, strictly speaking, was no system of checks and balances where one level of government existed to restrain or limit the power of others. Rather, it is more accurate to say, central and local authorities were instituted to complement the work of each other without violating each other's jurisdiction or function. As the cases of the Poor Law Amendment Act and the Public Health Act show, the central departments existed to aid in the organisation and reform of local authorities by providing those agencies with uniform procedures, information, and advice. The local authorities, on their part, existed to administer measures for pauper relief and urban sanitation. The central agencies, as constituted, did not usurp local responsibilities as their critics charged; still less could they be considered unconstitutional or despotic.

Similarly, railway legislation authorised an agency of the central government to supervise those railway matters which were conceived as being directly related to the public interest. While the railway legislation of the 1840s extended the authority of the central government, it applied strict limits to the range of government action. The act of 1844, for example, expressly forbade the inspectors from interfering in the day-to-day affairs of railway companies. Although Gladstone may have wished to go further, the act of 1844 was not an attempt to nationalise the railway system. It was an effort to provide legislative elbow-room so that, if necessary, at some time in the future, government might re-evaluate its relationship to the railways and establish provisions for the reduction of railway rates or the purchase of railway lines.

The factory acts represent a special case in so far as they show two separate manifestations of government intervention. The acts of 1833 and 1844, like the new poor law and the Public Health Act, called for supervision and inspection by a central department. As such they are examples of government growth and administrative intervention. The ten-hours act (1847), on the other hand, is less an example of government growth, because it merely contained provisions for legislative prohibition of extended hours and showed less concern for inspection and supervision. More accurately then, the ten-hours act was an expression of legislative rather than administrative intervention.

The attempt to determine which institutions and political mechanisms should hold legal responsibility for manipulating the forces of social change raised questions which generated intense political conflict. These questions were: what institutions are to be changed, what institutions are to be preserved, how is institutional change to take place, how will changes in some institutions affect the stability of others? While, generally speaking, interventionist measures passed through the House of Commons by large majorities, the discussion of these questions was full of vituperative controversy. With little emphasis upon matters of laissez-faire, individualism, or collectivism, these discussions consisted largely of a conflict between two political perspectives. These perspectives, which this book has taken pains to characterise, were based upon an historical vision of society and politics as opposed to an incrementalist view of social and political change.

The historical perspective on early Victorian state intervention and government growth stressed constitutional and legal concepts drawn from an appreciation of England's ancient institutions and practices. At points this idealisation of England's past became transformed into mythological form. Regarding state intervention in the form of the Poor Law Amendment Act and the Public Health Act as politically despotic, corrupting, and unconstitutional, the critics of government growth hoped to return to a system of political and social purity by the re-establishment of the forms of local government which they believed was enshrined in tradition, Common Law, and the 'ancient Saxon constitution'. This historical perspective often carried the flavour and tone of reverential admiration for paternalistic social arrangements with their ethic of *noblesse oblige*, social subordination, and deference. The opposition to 'centralisation' and the admiration for limited government was often a matter of passionate feeling rather than reasoned judgment. As John Stuart Mill put it, 'centralization was, and is, the subject not only of rational disapprobation, but of unreasoning prejudice'.[4]

The controversy over railway and factory legislation does not fit so neatly into the context of the historical perspective because so much of it was concerned with the practical questions of industrial growth and economic development. Nevertheless, these issues, in interesting if diverse ways, were seen through the perspective of historical insight and vision. Critics of the railway department of the Board of Trade, like the critics of the poor-law and public-health legislation, believed these agencies were contrary to the accepted traditions of English political practice. In the case of the factory acts, the historical vision of Oastler, Disraeli, Fielden, and others, supported the effort to obtain ten-hours legislation and, at the same time stood in opposition to the legislation of 1833 and 1844. The rights of factory children, like the concept of the rights of the poor, were conceived as historical rights having their theoretical basis in those ancient social relationships which provided social harmony and familial solidarity. This is a point which may be verified by division list analysis. The ten-hours measure was regarded by contemporaries as a completely different kind of state intervention than that found in the Public Health Act, or even the factory acts of 1833 and 1844, and as a consequence fits into quite a different attitude dimension.

In function, the historical perspective on nineteenth-century government growth was analogous to the use of the concept of the state of nature and the social contract in seventeenth- and eighteenth-century political thought. Like the social contract, the historical perspective was an alternative normative model against which contemporary institutions and practices could be evaluated and judged. To put the matter another way, both were intellectual devices, constructs if you will, for testing and measuring existing political and social forms and pointing towards improved arrangements. In form, the historical perspective also had seventeenth- and eighteenth-century precedents. Constitutional and legal arguments derived from the dim past were used as a defence for limited government in the seventeenth century in face of the increased use of royal prerogatives. In the eighteenth century, historical analogies were used to attack the power of the civil list, the standing army, and Walpole's financial policy.[5] In the nineteenth century, historical arguments were used again: this time as a criticism of 'centralisation', and 'government by commissions' in defence of limited, local self-government. Walter Bagehot caught this spirit when he observed:

> ... our freedom is the result of centuries of resistance, more or less legal, or more or less illegal, more or less audacious, or more or less timid, to the executive government. We have, accordingly, inherited the traditions of conflict, and preserve them in the fulness of victory. We look on State action, not as our own action, but as alien action; as an imposed tyranny from without, not as the consummated result of our own organized wishes.[6]

Considering the limited character of the measures discussed in this essay, it is difficult to understand fully the violent opposition of Toulmin Smith, Oastler, Disraeli, Sibthorp, Newdegate, and Urquhart. One is tempted, therefore, to draw analogies between the views of these men and Professor Daniel Bell's description of the 'radical right' in America. Whether these men feared the loss of their own social position, or the deterioration of their political power, their attitudes suggest a sense of confusion in the face of a world becoming ever more complex and artificial. Consequently, they evoked the image of the arcadian past as over against a life which was becoming increasingly industrialised, urbanised, modernised and effete.

In contrast to this political perspective based upon historical assumptions, another political viewpoint was at work, which found the guidelines for political action in political and administrative experience. Earlier studies of government growth and state intervention in the nineteenth century have implied that members of parliament, between 1833 and 1848, were captives of the politics of 'muddling through' who created a welfare state in spite of their laissez-faire convictions. The incrementalist perspective described in this book suggests greater purposefulness and forethought on the part of the proponents of government growth. Directed neither to the utopian goal of total social improvement nor guided by the theoretical principles of Benthamite utilitarianism or classical political economy, this incrementalist perspective pointed the way to cautious modifications in existing institutional arrangements. In this context, therefore, government growth in the early Victorian period consisted in an effort to effect change without violating accepted assumptions and traditions whether they be the conventional wisdoms of classical economics or the respect for local government. The primary instruments of this perspective were the Blue Books of parliamentary investigations and the reports of a small cadre of professional bureaucrats. These tools educated the political nation and through them the interest of government expanded until parliament became, as John Wilson Croker observed with some regret in 1844, 'a kind of national *proboscis*, as ready to pick up a pin as to root out an oak'.[7]

The incrementalist perspective was valuable in the poor-law and public-health controversies by indicating the means for reforming corrupt local institutions without eroding their power and authority. Incrementalism also proved to be a way by which parliament attempted to reduce the poor rates and the allowance system, and yet preserve the possibility for providing poor relief, depending upon local circumstances, where and when necessary.

In the case of the movement for public health the incrementalist perspective disavowed any attempt to eliminate the jurisdictions of local authorities. Rather, it was seen as a means for determining which functions were properly local and which were properly national. In the case of railway and factory legislation, incrementalism was a means for distinguishing between necessary government growth and forms of state intervention which might cripple and undermine the sources of national economic strength. It led, therefore, to the intrusion of government in the form of central supervision, but resisted government intervention which might lead to the nationalisation of railways. The incrementalist approach when applied to the factory system, similarly, led to the introduction of inspection and supervision, but stayed clear of ten-hours legislation. Viewing inspection as a modest modification in the existing system—there were, after all, analogies to these practices in the supervision of poor-law and railway administration —those holding the incrementalist perspective rejected the restriction of labour as a change which would affect the economy and prosperity of the country in a major way.

An appreciation of the historical and the incrementalist perspectives helps to show why early Victorian government growth took the limited forms it did. The historical perspective, with its reverence for traditional institutions and practices, was congenitally unable to adapt, with any ease at least, to novel political and social structures. The paternalism characteristic of the historical perspective which was present in the concern for local pauper relief, local health service, and legislative restriction of hours in the form of a ten-hours bill, conceived of social action in terms of traditional rather than new institutions. Similarly, the incrementalist perspective, while it may have been willing to accept certain new institutions or the adaptation of old institutions to new functions, stressed the importance of cautious piecemeal modification. Such views were hardly disposed to favour radical extensions of the state. In the light of what we now know, the ultimate consequence of incrementalist modification has been a vast extension of the power and authority of the central government. This is the view from hindsight, of course, and Victorian practitioners of the incrementalist's art would have disclaimed any such intention. The objective of incrementalist modification, as seen through the policy preferences of Gladstone, Morpeth, Althorp, Macaulay, Peel, Graham, and others, was to preserve the fundamental structures of the old order by accommodating them to the circumstances of a dynamic changing society. Such an accommodation often meant the utilisation of altered government structures, but it never meant the sacrifice of traditional institutions. These objectives and these intentions are a far cry from the objectives and intentions of men attempting to create a centralised welfare state.

Both the historical perspective and the incrementalist perspective could touch on and remain sympathetic to other Victorian attitudes. Government growth paralleled, as a consequence, a general antipathy to the state and state power. Lord John Russell, for example, who favoured all the interventionist measures considered here and many more besides, continued to fear that government action would limit individual activity. 'The interference of the state', Russell wrote to the Duke of Leinster on 17 October 1846, 'deadens private energy, prevents forethought and after superseding all other exertion finds itself at last unequal to the gigantic task it has undertaken'.[8] Just as there was no large group of opinion which dogmatically opposed state intervention and government growth, there was no wide body of opinion which favoured the monolithic application of state power. The problems generated by industrial and social change, most realised, could be solved only by the application of separate cures for separate problems and then only over a long period of time. As John Stuart Mill put it in 1842:

> The causes of existing evils, it seems to me, lie too deep, to be within reach of any one remedy, or set of remedies; nor would any remedial measure, which is at present practicable, amount to more than a slight palliative for those evils: their removal, I conceive, can only be accomplished by slow degrees, and through many successive efforts, each having its own particular end in view, and so various in their nature that a dissertation which attempted to embrace them all must be so general as to be very little available for the practical guidance of any.[9]

As a consequence government growth accompanied traditional values and traditional assumptions. State intervention in the early Victorian period did not preclude the elimination of contemporary slogans, be they 'local self-government', 'Anglo-Saxon liberties', or the slogans associated with the campaign for free trade. While the entire thrust of this book has been to show how early Victorian government growth occurred within the context of traditional institutions and traditional values, it is also important to suggest the ways in which these governmental modifications contributed to the character and shape of later political developments. First, as the cases of the Poor Law Amendment Act and the Public Health Act show, a new era was opened in the area of local government administration. Landed magnates, the vestiges of the old order, came to share political power and social authority with their less well-born neighbours, and reformed local institutions came to assume more power and authority for the care of economic and social problems. Second, governmental alterations in the early Victorian period were precedents for central inspection and delegated authority, which served as precursors for the shaping of central administration and government growth in the last decades of the nineteenth century. Taken together, the nineteenth-century revolution in government is a comforting paradigm of the way peaceful institutional change can occur in traditional political and social structures troubled and torn by massive economic and social dislocation.

Notes to Chapter 6 will be found on page 209.

NOTES

FOREWORD (pages 9–13)

1 See the Select Bibliography for a complete listing of the major contributions to the discussion of government growth in the nineteenth century. Let it suffice here to cite the most important summaries of these researches. O. O. G. M. MacDonagh, *A Pattern of Government Growth, 1800–1860: The Passenger Acts and their Enforcement* (London: 1961); Henry Parris, *Government and the Railways in Nineteenth-Century Britain* (London: 1965); David Roberts, *The Victorian Origins of the British Welfare State* (New Haven: 1960).
   In addition this subject has been widely debated in learned journals. See O. O. G. M. MacDonagh, 'The Nineteenth-Century Revolution in Government: A Reappraisal', *Historical Journal*, I, 1 (1958); Henry Parris, 'The Nineteenth-Century Revolution in Government: A Reappraisal Reappraised', *Historical Journal*, III, 1 (1960); David Roberts, 'Jeremy Bentham and the Victorian Administrative State', *Victorian Studies*, II (March 1959).

2 Great Britain, Parliament, *Parliamentary Papers* (House of Commons and Command), 'Second Report of the Select Committee on Railway Acts Enactments' (1846), XIV, 7–8. (Hereinafter Parliamentary Papers will be cited by the abbreviation *PP*. Whenever possible the pagination of the microcard edition of the Sessional Papers is used.)

Chapter 1   GOVERNMENT GROWTH IN EARLY VICTORIAN ENGLAND (pages 15–29)

1 David Roberts, *Victorian Origins of the British Welfare State* (New Haven: 1960), 327–33. (Hereinafter cited as Roberts.) This introductory discussion of government growth owes much to Professor Roberts's helpful study.

2 Ibid, 319.

3 See G. S. R. Kitson Clark, 'Statesmen in Disguise: Reflexions on the History of the Neutrality of the Civil Service', *Historical Journal*, II, 1 (1959), 35–6.

4 G. S. R. Kitson Clark, *The Making of Victorian England* (London:

1962), 97, 109. For a recent treatment of the growth of the modern bureaucracy see Henry Parris, 'The Origins of the Permanent Civil Service', *Public Administration* (1968).

5   For a more complete discussion of English local government see Roberts, chapter 1; and Sydney and Beatrice Webb, *English Local Government from the Revolution to the Municipal Corporations Act* (London: 1906–24).

6   Sydney and Beatrice Webb, *English Local Government: Statutory Authorities for Special Purposes* (London: 1922), 351–3. (Hereinafter cited as Webbs, *Statutory Authorities*.)

7   Ibid, 413.

8   Viscount Ebrington, *Unhealthiness of Towns, Its Causes and Remedies* (London: 1847), 39.

9   Webbs, *Statutory Authorities*, 428.

10 Ibid, 478. The expression 'local government' was not in use before the middle of the nineteenth century. The Webbs attribute the expression to the work and publications of Joshua Toulmin Smith, the arch-localist of the nineteenth century. Ibid, 335n. Sir Robert Ensor, on the other hand, attributes the expression to C. B. Adderley, the evangelical and Conservative MP, who was the president of the Board of Health in 1858 and the sponsor of the Local Government Act (1858). R. C. K. Ensor, *England, 1870–1914* (Oxford: 1966), 124–5.

11 Figures in this section can be found in Roberts, 14–16.

12 Quoted in Sir Ivor Jennings, *Parliament* (Cambridge: 1957), 1.

13 Roberts, 13–14.

14 Beatrice Webb, *My Apprenticeship* (London: 1926), 188n.

15 David Owen, *English Philanthropy, 1660–1960* (Cambridge, Mass: 1964), 4, 96.

16 Sir Robert Peel to the Queen, 7 May 1842. (Prime Minister's Correspondence at Windsor Castle.)

17 Sir James Graham to the Lord Lieutenant of Ireland, 6 February 1846. (Papers of Sir James Graham, Bart, Netherby, Cumberland.)

18 Report of the Select Committee on the Health of Towns, *PP* (1840), XI, 287.

19 Great Britain, Parliament, *Hansard's Parliamentary Debates*, 3rd series (1841), 56: 550–1. (Hereinafter cited as Hansard. All citations, save those noted to the contrary, are to the 3rd series.)

20 Sir John Simon, *Public Health Reports*, I (London: 1887), 45.

21 'The Sanitary Question', *Fraser's Magazine*, XXXVI (September 1847), 378.

22 John Stuart Mill to Henry S. Chapman, 8 November 1844, and John Stuart Mill to Sarah Austin, 18 January 1845, *The Earlier Letters of John Stuart Mill, 1812–1848*, ed Francis E. Mineka, vol II (Toronto: 1963), 640–3, 654–5.

23 'The Claims of Labour', *Westminster Review*, XLIII (June 1845), 449.

24 Mark Blaug, *Ricardian Economics, A Historical Study* (New Haven: 1958), 194; Edward Kittrell, ' "Laissez-faire" in English Classical Economics', *Journal of the History of Ideas*, XVII, 4 (1966).

25 Marian Bowley, *Nassau Senior and Classical Economics* (London: 1937), 244; *Edinburgh Review*, LXXIV (October 1841), 29; ibid, LXXXVIII (October 1848), 331–2.

26 John Earl Russell, *An Essay on the History of the English Government and Constitution, from the Reign of Henry VII to the Present Time*, 1st edition (London: 1821), 213; John Earl Russell, *An Essay on the History of the English Government and Constitution, from the Reign of Henry VII to the Present Time*, 2nd edition (London: 1823), 267.

27 Hansard (1834), 25: 224, 214, 225, 235–6.

28 Blaug, 193.

29 Ibid, 194.

30 John Stuart Mill, *Principles of Political Economy with Some of Their Applications to Social Philosophy*, Introduction by V. W. Bladen, textual editor, J. M. Robson (Toronto: 1965), Book V, 956.

31 McCulloch to Ashley, 28 March 1833. Edwin Hodder, *The Life and Work of the Seventh Earl of Shaftesbury, K. G.*, I (London: 1887), 157 (cited as Hodder); George Poulett Scrope, *Principles of Political Economy, deduced from the Natural Laws of Social Welfare, Applied to the Present State of Britain* (London: 1833), 357–8; Hansard (1833), 19: 900; Lionel Lord Robbins, *Robert Torrens and the Evolution of Classical Economics* (London: 1958), 323–4; Bowley, 255–6.

32 Norman Gash, *Reaction and Reconstruction in English Politics, 1832–1852* (Oxford: 1965), 129.

33 W. L. Burn, *The Age of Equipoise. A Study of the Mid-Victorian Generation* (London: 1964), 134.

34 *Edinburgh Review*, LXXXIII (January 1846), 70, 92.

35 Norman Gash, *Politics in the Age of Peel: A study in the Technique of Parliamentary Representation, 1830–1850* (London: 1953); H. J. Hanham, *Elections and Party Management: Politics in the Time of Disraeli and Gladstone* (London: 1959); D. C. Moore, 'Social Structure, Political Structure, and Public Opinion in Mid Victorian England', *Ideas and Institutions of Victorian Britain*, ed by Robert Robson (London: 1967); John Vincent, *The Formation of the Liberal Party, 1857–1868* (London: 1966); William O. Aydelotte, 'Voting Patterns in the House of Commons in the 1840's', *Comparative Studies in Society and History*, V, 2 (1963); 'The Conservative and Radical Interpretations of Early Victorian Social Legislation', *Victorian Studies*, XI, 2 (December 1967).

36 Sharon Turner, *The History of England During the Middle Ages*, 5 vols, 3rd ed (London: 1830); Henry Hallam, *The Constitutional History from the Accession of Henry VII to the Death of George III*, 2 vols (New York: 1882); John Lingard, *A History of England from the First Invasion by the Romans to the Revolution in 1688* (London: 1819–30); Thomas Babington Macaulay, *The History of England*

from the Accession of James the Second, 5 vols, 7th ed (London: 1850–61); Johannes M. Kemble, *Codex Diplomaticus Aevi Saxonici*, vols I–VI (Londini: 1839–48); John Mitchell Kemble, *The Saxons in England. A History of the English Commonwealth till the Period of the Norman Conquest*, 2 vols (London: 1849); Sharon Turner, *The History of the Anglo-Saxons from the Earliest Period to the Norman Conquest*, 3 vols, 5th ed (London: 1828); Benjamin Thorpe, *Ancient Laws and institutes of England; comprising laws enacted under the Anglo-Saxon Kings from Aethelbrith to Cnut, with an English translation of the Saxon; the Laws called Edward the Confessor's; the laws of William the Conqueror and those ascribed to Henry the First; also, Monumenta ecclesiastica anglicana, from the seventh to the tenth century; and the ancient Latin version of the Anglo-Saxon Laws. With a compendious glossary, & c . . .*, 2 vols (London: 1840); Sir Francis Palgrave, *The Rise and Progress of the English Commonwealth, Anglo-Saxon Period, Containing the Anglo-Saxon Policy, and the Institutes Arising Out of Laws and Usages which prevailed Before the Conquest*, 2 vols (London: 1832).

37   For a stimulating discussion of the concept of incrementalist decision-making see David Braybrooke and Charles E. Lindblom, *A Strategy of Decision: Policy Evaluation as a Social Process* (New York and London: 1963). While other explanations of decision-making are available, this incrementalist model seems most appropriate for the issues considered here.

38   Karl Popper, *The Open Society and Its Enemies*, I (London: 1945), 139–44 and 245n. Cited in Braybrooke and Lindblom, 82.

39   Joshua Toulmin Smith, *Government by Commissions Illegal and Pernicious. The Nature and Effects of All Commissions of Inquiry and other Crown Appointed Commissions, the Constitutional Principles of Taxation; and the Rights, Duties and Importance of Local Self-Government* (London: 1849), 367.

40   *Edinburgh Review*, LXXXIII (January 1846), 93–4.

41   Thomas Babington Macaulay, *The History of England from the Accession of James the Second*, III (New York: nd), 66–7.

42   *Edinburgh Review*, LXXXIII (January 1846), 72–84.

43   Hansard (1834), 25: 229, 246–7.

Chapter 2   CENTRAL AND LOCAL GOVERNMENT I (pages 30–68)

1   Samuel E. Finer, *The Life and Times of Sir Edwin Chadwick* (London: 1952), 40. (Hereinafter cited as Finer.)

2   Karl de Schweinitz, *England's Road to Social Security* (New York: 1961), 80. (Hereinafter cited as Schweinitz.)

3   Ibid.

4   Asa Briggs, *The Making of Modern England, 1783–1867: The Age of Improvement* (New York: 1965), 59. (Hereinafter cited as Briggs.)

The old poor law has, in the past decade, found its champion in the person of Professor Mark Blaug. As Mr Blaug argues, in a pair of closely reasoned articles, the old poor law was a mechanism for dealing with the problem of surplus labour in the rural sector of an underdeveloped economy. For a complete statement of these views see 'The Myth of the Old Poor Law and the Making of the New', *Journal of Economic History*, XXIII, 2 (1963), and 'The Old Poor Law Re-examined', *Journal of Economic History*, XXIV, 2 (1964).

5 Schweinitz, 114.

6 Finer, 42.

7 The Royal Commission consisted of C. J. London, J. F. Chester, W. Sturges Bourne, Nassau Senior, Henry Bishop, Henry Gawler, W. Coulson, James Traill, and Edwin Chadwick.

8 Finer, 42.

9 There has been some controversy with regard to the relative contributions of Senior and Chadwick to this report. See Sydney and Beatrice Webb, *English Poor Law History, Part II: The Last Hundred Years*, I (London: 1929), 56. (Hereinafter cited as Webb, *History*.); Schweinitz, 129; Finer, 48; and Marian Bowley, *Nassau Senior and Classical Economics* (London: 1937), 283ff. (Hereinafter cited as Bowley.)

10 Sir Denis Le Marchant, Bt, *Memoir of John Charles Viscount Althorp, Third Earl Spencer* (London: 1876), 483. Le Marchant had been a principal secretary to Lord Brougham and was an intimate of Althorp. See *DNB*, XXXIII, 22–3.

[Nassau Senior], *Remarks on the Opposition to the Poor Law Amendment Bill, By a Guardian* (London: 1841), 37. (Hereinafter cited as Senior, *Remarks*.)

11 Part of the controversy over the poor law in the 1830s and 1840s was directed to allegations of cruelty inflicted upon the poor by the administrators of the poor law. Cases of harshness both in deed and testimony can be found. Sir Francis Head wrote on 6 November 1835: 'It appears to me . . . that we have no discretion allowed to us to deliberate whether the system is good or bad. Our Poor Law Amendment Act is physic which the legislature in the character of physician, has prescribed to remedy an acknowledged evil. We are called upon to administer it, and it seems to me that the only discretion granted to us is to determine what period is to elapse *before all outdoor relief is stopped.*' Quoted in Sydney and Beatrice Webb, *English Poor Law Policy* (London: 1910), 86. Professor David Roberts, after a study of cruelty in the administration of the poor law, concludes that the truth of the matter must lie somewhere between the condemnation of G. R. W. Baxter, Frederick Engels, and Thomas Carlyle and the vindications of the poor-law policy found in the annual reports of the commissioners sitting on the central board. Mr Roberts argues that under the new poor law urgent cases were dealt with more efficiently than under the old, the

N

commissioners did not require the enforcement of the workhouse test too rigorously, and a judgment of the conduct of the administrators of the new poor law must take into account the cruel and harsh conditions of the time. See David Roberts, 'How Cruel was the Victorian Poor Law?', *Historical Journal*, VI, 1 (1963).

12 Webb, *History*, I, 178–9.

13 Ibid, 1.

14 Sir William O. Hart, *Introduction to the Law of Local Government and Administration*, 7th ed (London: 1962), 27.

15 Report from His Majesty's Commissioners for Inquiring into the Administration and Practical Operation of the Poor Laws, *PP* (1834), XXVII, 205.

16 *PP* (1834), XXVII, 169.

17 *PP* (1834), XXVII, 146 (author's italics).

18 *PP* (1834), XXVII, 170.

19 4 and 5 William IV, c 76, s 2; *PP* (1834), XXVII, 167; 4 and 5 William IV, c 76, s 15, 42, 46, and 52.

20 7 and 8 Victoria, c 101, s 12 and 85.

21 4 and 5 William IV, c 76, s 7, 9, and 12; 5 and 6 Victoria, c 57, s 2.

22 *PP* (1834), XXVII, 176–7, 183; 4 and 5 William IV, c 76, s 26 and 32. Parishes united for purposes of rating or settlement were not to be dissolved under the provisions included in clause 32.

    7 and 8 Victoria, c 101, s 32, 40 and 41. This act strengthened the authority of the central board, also provided the commissioners with the authority to add or separate parishes from unions without the consent of the union guardians. See s 61. On the other hand, the act established that parishes with populations exceeding 20,000 and governed by guardians under a local act and having adopted the provisions of 1 and 2 William IV, c 60 (An Act for the Better Regulation of Vestries, and for the Appointment of Auditors of Accounts) and parishes in the Metropolitan Police District united for purposes of settlement and rating, which had auditors, were not to be included in any district for the auditing of accounts. See s 65.

23 Ursula Henriques, 'How Cruel was the Victorian Poor Law?', *Historical Journal*, XI, 2 (1968), 366. (Cited as Henriques.)

24 *PP* (1834), XXVII, 186, 180.

25 4 and 5 William IV, c 76, s 46.

26 See, for example, Sir George Nicholls, *A History of the English Poor Law*, II (New York: 1898), 299. (Hereinafter cited as Nicholls.)

27 *PP* (1837–8), XVIII, pt 1, 39; 7 and 8 Victoria, c 101, s 49 and 37.

28 4 and 5 William IV, c 76, s 10, 16 and 17.

29 Ibid, s 21 and 22. According to Sir George Nicholls, Gilbert's act excluded the ordinary parochial authorities from taking part in the administration of poor relief. The justices of the peace and the visitors were 'vested with almost absolute power, the guardians being little more than the instruments for carrying the visitor's directions into effect'. Nicholls, II, 88–9.

30 *PP* (1834), XXVII, 166.
31 4 and 5 William IV, c 76, s 38, 54, 41 and 46.
32 *PP* (1834), XXVII, 185.
33 4 and 5 William IV, c 76, s 43, 61, 89, and 27.
34 Norman McCord, 'The Implementation of the 1834 Poor Law Amendment Act on Tyneside', *International Review of Social History*, XIV, Part 1 (1969), 97. (Hereinafter cited as McCord.)
35 4 and 5 William IV, c 76, s 32, 33, 34 and 23.
36 4 and 5 William IV, c 76, s 52; *PP* (1837–8), XVIII, pt 1, 40.
37 Sir Herbert Maxwell, *The Life and Letters of George William Frederick, Fourth Earl of Clarendon*, I (London: 1913), 86–7.
38 Hansard (1842), 64: 562.
39 Nicholls, II, 266; Hansard (1842), 64: 168–71; (1847), 92: 1,235–7.
40 Division on the second reading of the Poor Law bill 17 June 1842:

	+	%	–	%
Conservative (Protectionist)	82	83·7	16	16·3
Conservative (Peelite)	56	84·9	10	15·1
Conservative (Other)	23	82·1	5	17·9
Whig	27	87·1	4	12·9
Liberal	31	86·1	5	13·9
Reformer	19	79·2	5	20·8
Radical Reformer	4	33·3	8	66·7
Repealer	2	40·0	3	60·0
Liberal (Other)	3	60·0	2	40·0
All Conservatives	161	83·8	31	16·2
All Liberals	86	76·1	27	23·9

41 The outstanding exceptions to this general statement were the Radical Reformers. One would expect, with their presumed Benthamite bias, that they would support the new poor law in overwhelming numbers. Yet, as the division list shows, a full 66 per cent of the Radical Reformers opposed it. To be sure, some Radicals, such as George Grote (MP for London), John Arthur Roebuck (MP for Bath) and Harriet Martineau, continued to support it ardently. Yet others, such as Dr John Bowring (MP for Bolton) and Joseph Hume (MP for Montrose), came to oppose the measure. Their opposition was based on objections to the administration of the measure rather than objections to the principles of the Poor Law Amendment Act. Bowring felt the powers of the central board were exercised in his own constituency 'without any wisdom, discretion, or humanity'. By 1846 Hume believed the poor-law commissioners were unfit and incompetent and was prepared to bring forward a motion to remove them from office. Hume supported the legislation of 1847 because he believed the principles of the Poor Law Amendment Act could be best implemented by the new poor-law board with its president sitting in and responsible to parliament. For the views of the Radicals on the Victorian poor law see: Hansard (1834), 24: 545; (1842), 64: 592; Harriet Martineau, *Autobiography*, I

(Boston: 1879), 166, 168; Robert Kieffer Webb, *Harriet Martineau: Radical Victorian* (London: 1960), 129; Hansard (1842), 64: 556; (1846), 87: 1,104–5; (1847), 90: 535; 92: 350.

42 Samuel Roberts, *England's Glory: or, The Good Old Poor Laws, Addressed to the Working Classes of Sheffield* (London: 1836), cover. (Hereinafter cited as Roberts, *England's Glory*.)

43 See the speeches of the Earl of Malmesbury, Lord Alvanley, and Captain Pechell. Hansard (1834), 24: 1,066–7; 25: 442; (1842), 61: 1,086.

44 Henriques, 371.

45 Ibid, 370.

46 Ibid.

47 Hansard (1834), 22: 877 (author's italics); 24: 920–2.

48 Report of the Poor Law Commissioners to the Most Noble Marquis of Normanby, *PP* (1840), XVII, 191.

49 George Cornwall Lewis to E. W. Head, 31 July 1837. George Cornwall Lewis, *The Letters of George Cornwall Lewis* (London: 1870), 83. (Hereinafter cited as Lewis, *Letters*.)

50 Senior, *Remarks*, 55–69, 64.

51 See the speech of Mr Baring. Hansard (1834), 24: 924.

52 Hansard (1834), 22: 892; (1844), 76: 1,827.

53 *Quarterly Review*, LII (1834), 233; Hansard (1834), 23: 1,329. George Julius Duncombe Poulett Scrope (1796–1876), the brother of Charles Poulett Thomson, Lord Sydenham, was educated at Harrow, Pembroke College, Oxford, and St John's, Cambridge. He sat for Stroud from 1832 to 1867. His writings include works on the geology and extinct volcanoes of central France, a memoir of his brother, and an essay on the principles of political economy. See Boase, III, 465–6.

54 Hansard (1842), 64: 687, 262. Colonel Sibthorp (1783–1855), an ultra-conservative, ultra-protestant MP for Lincoln, was one of the most colourful members of the Victorian House of Commons. He served in the Peninsular War and succeeded to the family estates in 1822 upon the death of his elder brother Coningsby. Colonel Sibthorp was a deputy lieutenant and magistrate in the county of Lincoln and claimed to have originated the famous Chandos clause in the Reform Bill of 1832. *DNB*, LII, 188. For a fascinating discussion of Colonel Sibthorp's career see: Richard D. Altick, ' "Our Gallant Colonel" in *Punch* and Parliament', *Bulletin of the New York Public Library* (September 1965).

55 Roberts, *England's Glory*, 22.

56 Hansard (1847), 92: 1,175; (1842), 65: 498; 63: 446–7.

57 Hansard (1847), 92: 1,005.

58 See the speeches of Colonel Sibthorp, A. B. Cochrane, Thomas Wakley, John Fielden, General William Augustus Johnson, and Sir Samuel Whalley. Hansard (1844), 76: 325, 334; (1842), 64: 121, 654; (1843), 66: 1,184–5.

59 Rev Henry Johnson Marshall, BA, *On the Tendency of the New Poor Law Seriously to Impair the Morals and the Condition of the Working Class* (London: 1842), 46–7.
60 G. R. Wythen Baxter, *Book of the Bastilles* (London: 1841), 329–30, 332. The *Book of the Bastilles* is a rich and pithy digest of anti-poor law sentiment. (Hereinafter cited as Baxter, *Book of the Bastilles.*)
61 Hansard (1834), 24: 920, 325; (1842), 64: 234; 65: 76.
62 Hansard (1834), 24: 914. While Walter is often considered a Conservative, I list him as a Reformer in conformity with Dod's *Parliamentary Pocket Companion* (1833), 172.
63 Roberts, *England's Glory*, 23–4.
64 Hansard (1847), 92: 1,016; (1834), 23: 974–5; (1847), 93: 881.
65 See the speeches of Sir Samuel Whalley, Lord Alvanley, and George Frederick Young (Reformer: Tynemouth). Hansard (1834), 23: 1,277; 25: 265; 24: 918.
66 Hansard (1834), 24: 915, 345, 430; (1842), 64: 162–4; (1834), 25: 785.
67 Hansard (1834), 23: 963, 993–4, 959, 954; (1842), 64: 237.
68 Joshua Toulmin Smith (1816–69), a lawyer, phrenologist, Unitarian, American traveller, and antiquarian scholar, was born in Birmingham. Toulmin Smith first came to oppose government growth at the time the City of London was attempting to exclude itself from a general sanitary measure during the public-health controversy. While he directed the focus of his political activity against the General Board of Health (see Chapter 3), Smith's arguments were objections to all forms of government growth in the 1830s and 1840s. Smith, a Fellow of the Royal Society of Northern Antiquaries, wrote, in addition to several polemical volumes against 'centralization', a history of the parish system, a dialogue supporting the prior claim of the Norse for the discovery of America, and compiled a collection of documents on the medieval guilds.
69 *Fraser's Magazine*, XXIII (April 1841), 388.
70 Hansard (1834), 23: 1,331; (1847), 92: 1,173.
71 Hansard (1844), 76: 1,817.
72 Joshua Toulmin Smith, *Local Self-Government and Centralization: The Character of Each: And its Practical Tendencies as Affecting Social, Moral, and Political Welfare and Progress, Including Comprehensive Outlines of the English Constitution* (London: 1851), 360. (Hereinafter cited as Smith, *Local Self-Government.*)
73 See the speech of John Walter. Hansard (1834), 24: 913. Poulett Scrope observed: 'With all its defects, the Poor-law of England was a noble, a God-like institution—worthy of the age (the brightest in our national annals) in which it originated,—worthy of the great statesmen (Cecil, Burleigh, Bacon, and Walsingham) who enacted it. It amply deserved the title of the great charter of the English poor.' Hansard (1834), 23: 1,321–2.
74 Hansard (1834), 23: 1,323–4; Samuel Roberts, *Lessons for Statesmen*

with Anecdotes Respecting Them Calculated to Preserve the Aristocracy from Destruction and the Country from Ruin (London: 1846), 4. (Hereinafter cited as Roberts, *Lessons*.)

75 Robert Blake, *Disraeli* (London: 1966), 161.
76 Hansard (1841), 56: 377.
77 Disraeli said: 'Government did not institute the system of national education—did not institute the universities—did not create our colonial empire—it did not conquer India—it did not make our roads or build our bridges. It did not, even now that it was interfering with everything, make our railroads'. Hansard (1841), 56: 377.
78 Hansard (1841), 56: 377.
79 Hansard (1847), 92: 1,153; (1841), 56: 381, 379, 380 (author's italics).
80 Richard Oastler, *The Fleet Papers*, I (London: 1841), 178, 165. (Hereinafter cited as Oastler, *Fleet Papers*.)
81 Ibid, I, 39.
82 Ibid, I, 165–6.
83 An excerpt from Oastler's *Letter to Lord Normanby* is quoted in Baxter, *Book of the Bastilles*, 412; Hansard (1843), 66: 1,225.
84 *The People's Magazine* (February 1841), quoted in Baxter, *Book of the Bastilles*, 338.
85 Hansard (1842), 64: 141–2, 578.
86 Hansard (1847), 92: 1,129, 1,130; (1844), 76: 1,339; William Lutley Sclater, *A Letter to the Poor Law Commissioners for England and Wales on the Working of the New System by the Chairman of a Board of Guardians* (Basingstoke: 1836), 16; Hansard (1844), 76: 331.
87 Hansard (1834), 25: 606; 22: 877, 879; 24: 1,073; (1847), 92: 342.
88 See Lord Althorp's speech. Hansard (1834), 22: 879.
89 Hansard (1842), 65: 62.
90 Hansard (1834), 23: 971.
91 Hansard (1834), 23: 1,344; *PP* (1840), XVII, 183; Hansard (1847), 92: 341.
92 Hansard (1834), 24: 431; 23: 1,284; Senior, *Remarks*, 37–8, 42.
93 Hansard (1834), 22: 881; 23: 985, 1,285; (1847), 90: 530.
94 *PP* (1840), XVII, 185–6.
95 Hansard (1834), 23: 993.
96 *PP* (1840), XVII, 182–3, 186.
97 Hansard (1834), 25: 241, 635, 444; 24: 1,055; 23: 1,337.
98 *PP* (1840), XVII, 188–9.
99 *PP* (1834), XXIX, 458; Hansard (1834), 22: 883–5.
100 Hansard (1847), 92: 1,064; Edwin Chadwick, *An Article on the Principles and the Progress of the Poor Law Amendment Act and Also on the Nature of the Central Control and Improved Local Administration Introduced by that Statute* (London: 1837), 65. (Hereinafter cited as Chadwick, *Article on the Principles and Progress of the Poor Law Amendment Act*.); *PP* (1840), XVII, 182.

101 Chadwick, *Article on the Principles and Progress of the Poor Law Amendment Act*, 55.
102 *PP* (1834), XXVII, 163; *PP* (1834), XXIX, 376.
103 *PP* (1834), XXIX, 260; Chadwick, *Article on the Principles and Progress of the Poor Law Amendment Act*, 59.
104 Hansard (1834), 24: 350–1; 23: 1,340; *PP* (1840), XVII, 184.
105 Hansard (1834), 25: 241; 24: 1,059; (1842), 65: 508–9; (1844), 76: 348.
106 Hansard (1843), 66: 1,180; (1842), 64: 664.
107 See the article in the *Westminster Review*, XX (April 1834), 476.
108 Hansard (1847), 92: 1,224.
109 *Letters Addressed by the Poor Law Commissioners to the Secretary of State Respecting the Transactions of Business of the Commission* (London: 1847), 51–2.
110 10 and 11 Victoria, c 109, s 10.
111 Lewis to Grote, 26 January 1847; Lewis to Head, 6 August 1848. Lewis, *Letters*, 150, 183.
112 *PP* (1840), XVII, 192.
113 Hansard (1843), 66: 1,172.
114 Richard Hofstadter, *The Paranoid Style in American Politics and other Essays* (New York: 1965), 3–40; Daniel Bell, 'The Dispossessed', *The Radical Right*, ed Daniel Bell (New York: 1964).
115 For a discussion of the ambiguities of mid-Victorian radicalism see: Olive Anderson, 'The Janus Face of Mid-Nineteenth Century Radicalism: The Administrative Reform Association of 1855', *Victorian Studies*, VIII, 3 (1965).
116 John Riddoch Poynter, *Society and Pauperism: English Ideas on Poor Relief, 1795–1834* (London: 1969), 325–6.
117 Hansard (1844), 76: 1,347.
118 H. L. Beales, 'The New Poor Law' *History* (1931), 316.

Chapter 3 CENTRAL AND LOCAL GOVERNMENT II (pages 69–106)

1 Quoted in Sir John Simon's *English Sanitary Institutions, Reviewed in the Course of their Development, and in Some of their Political and Social Relations*, 2nd edition (London: 1897), 180. (Hereinafter cited as Simon, *English Sanitary Institutions*.)
2 This section is largely based on the excellent discussion of disease in the nineteenth century in Flinn's Introduction to Chadwick's *Report on the Sanitary Condition of the Labouring Population of Great Britain*, ed M. W. Flinn (Edinburgh: 1965), 8ff. (Hereinafter cited as Flinn. Chadwick's report is cited, Chadwick, *Sanitary* Report.)
3 Asa Briggs, 'Cholera and Society in the Nineteenth Century', *European Political History, 1815–1870: Aspects of Liberalism*, ed Eugene C. Black (New York: 1967), 58. (Hereinafter cited as Briggs, 'Cholera and Society'.)

4 Hansard (1848), 98: 779, 780.
5 Sir John Simon, *Public Health Reports*, I (London: 1887), 146. (Hereinafter cited as Simon, *Reports*.)
6 Briggs, 'Cholera and Society', 60.
7 Flinn, 21. Sir John Simon holds an ambiguous position in the history of the public-health movement. Simon was a member of the Health of Towns Association and deeply admired Chadwick's zeal for sanitary reform. Yet, as Royston Lambert argues, in 'diametrical opposition to Chadwick, Simon personified the claims of preventive medicine and science in sanitary affairs; and again, he symbolised and genuinely believed in the virtues of local sanitary government as against Chadwick's more "centralising" notions and ambitions'. Lambert indicates that the controversy over the General Board of Health, his appointment to the 'most jealously independent of local authorities', and his acceptance of the ideas of Toulmin Smith, the arch-localist in the public-health controversy, gave Simon an extreme and 'powerfully inhibiting deference towards the principle of local inviolability'. See Royston Lambert, *Sir John Simon, 1816–1904 and English Social Administration* (London: 1963), 110, 237–8. (Hereinafter cited as Lambert.)
   Some evidence suggests that Simon was just as concerned about the effective elimination of sanitary evils as he was the relative distribution of political authority between local and central governments. Simon clearly recognised that sanitary amelioration required more than 'petty reforms and patchwork legislation'. A complete cure demanded the attention and concern of 'the large mind of State-policy'. 'Comprehensive and scientific legislation', he realised, required action by a single agency of the executive authority. See Simon, *Reports*, I, 143, 154, 157–8.
8 Hansard (1845), 77: 4.
9 Hansard (1845), 79: 348; (1847), 93: 714; (1848), 99, 1,406.
10 *DNB*, LII, 367–8.
11 *The Lancet, A Journal of British and Foreign Medical and Chemical Science, Criticism, and News* (1846), II, 52.
12 *Abstract of the Proceedings of the Public Health Meeting Held at Exeter Hall, December 11, 1844* (London: nd), 3. See the discussion of the Health of Towns Association in Finer, 238–9.
13 Briggs, 334. There has been something of a controversy concerning the origin of sanitary reform and the public-health movement. B. Keith-Lucas has emphasised the importance of late eighteenth-century developments by citing the formation of the Manchester Board of Health in 1796 and the sanitary powers included in several of the early Local Improvements Acts. See B. Keith-Lucas, 'Some Influences Affecting the Development of Sanitary Legislation in England', *Economic History Review*, second series, VI (1953–4). More recently, E. P. Hennock has argued that 'the Manchester Board of Health failed, despite the best intentions to do the work

which would genuinely have made it an agency of sanitary reform' and that Keith-Lucas's 'suggestion ascribed a significance to the early Improvement Acts which in this context is hardly justified'. See E. P. Hennock, 'Urban Sanitary Reform a Generation Before Chadwick?', *Economic History Review*, second series, X (1957), 113.

14 Simon, *English Sanitary Institutions*, 178; Hansard (1847), 93: 750.

15 Even Royston Lambert in his excellent biography of Simon emphasises the 'Chadwickian', 'centralising' aspects of public-health legislation in the 1840s. See Lambert, 72. See also Sir William O. Hart, *Hart's Introduction to the Law of Local Government and Administration*, 7th edition (London: 1962), 461.

16 Flinn, 16–17.

17 Simon, *English Sanitary Institutions*, 201.

18 Hansard (1847), 91: 638; Lytton Strachey and Roger Fulford, eds, *The Greville Memoirs, 1814–1860*, V (London: 1938), 459. (Hereinafter cited as Greville.)

19 The Select Committee of 1840 consisted of Slaney, Lord James Stuart, Viscount Sandon, John Ponsonby, Camper, Greene, Richard Walker, Wilson Patten, Henry Verney, Baines, Oswald, Tufnell, Brotherton, Ingham, and William Smith O'Brien.

20 Report of the Select Committee on the Health of Towns, *PP* (1840), XI, 294–5.

21 Ibid.

22 Ibid, 295–6.

23 Ibid, 285, 291, 293, 295.

24 Ibid, 292.

25 Flinn, 51.

26 Lewis to Grote, 13 March 1842. Lewis, *Letters*, 119–20. Sir John Simon noted that the report 'was the work of Mr. Chadwick and was issued by the Commissioners as distinctively his: they, it was understood, not wishing to stand committed to the conclusions of their secretary in a field so unfamiliar to themselves'. Simon, *English Sanitary Institutions*, 191.

27 Elie Halévy, *The Growth of Philosophical Radicalism* (Boston: 1960), 430.

28 Finer, 475, 477, 478.

29 Chadwick, *Sanitary Report*, 423ff, 339. M. W. Flinn, however, assumes that, because of Chadwick's lack of faith in the efficiency of unaided local authorities, 'a central department with adequate supervisory powers, on the lines of the Poor Law Commission of 1834, had always been the central feature of his scheme'. See Flinn, 71. Professor Finer, on the other hand, has indicated that Chadwick's model for the General Board of Health was not the Poor Law Commission. At least by 1845 Chadwick had reacted against the concept of Board supervision and favoured an arrangement like that of the Education Committee which was attached to the Privy Council. See Finer, 304–5.

30 Chadwick, *Sanitary Report*, 423, 386.
31 Ibid, 379–80, 384–5, 397, 398, 403, 410, 424.
32 *On Unity: On the Evils of Disunity in Central and Local Administration* (1885), 2n.
33 Chadwick, *Sanitary Report*, 403.
34 Ibid, 149, 160, 162, 175, 183, 321, 161, 236, 238, 239, 250, 251; and Flinn, 51.
35 *PP* (1843), XII, 518.
36 Chadwick, *Sanitary Report*, 348–54.
37 Finer, 228.
38 The Commission consisted of Buccleuch, Lord Lincoln, Slaney, George Graham, H. T. De la Beche, Lyon Playfair, D. B. Reid, Richard Owen, W. Denison, Captain R. Eng, J. R. Martin, James Smith, Robert Stephenson, W. Cubitt.
39 Flinn, 67; Finer, 232; Simon, *English Sanitary Institutions*, 200.
40 Finer, 232.
41 First Report of the Commissioners for Inquiring into the State of the Large Towns and Populous Districts, *PP* (1844), XVII, xv; Second Report of the Commissioners for Inquiring into the State of the Large Towns and Populous Districts, *PP* (1845), XVIII, 6, 40.
42 *PP* (1845), XVIII, 6, 22, 67, 20, 13.
43 Ibid, 6. 'In the present system of local government, the administrative duties of local improvement Acts are frequently placed under the immediate direction of persons, who are seldom qualified by any professional education for the direction of scientific works. They are therefore dependent upon the acquirements of their officers for the necessary skills in the planning, and efficient execution of the works.' Ibid, 19.
44 Ibid, 28, 50–1, 54.
45 Ibid, 59, 45, 66.
46 A convenient comparison of these pieces of legislation can be found in an anonymous pamphlet entitled *Letter to Lord Morpeth on the Health of Towns Bill, by a Townsman* (London: nd), 3. (Hereinafter cited as *Letter to Lord Morpeth*.)
47 Elie Halévy, *A History of the English People, 1841–1852: The Age of Peel and Cobden*, Trans by E. I. Watkin (New York: 1948), 227.
48 Lewis to Head, 28 September 1848. Lewis, *Letters*, 185–6.
49 To appreciate the differences between the proposed legislation of 1847 and the Public Health Act compare The Bill for Improving the Health of Towns, *PP* (1847), I (especially pp 457, 458, 461–2, 463, 465, 466, 474, and 475); Hansard (1847), 91: 625; and A Bill for Promoting Public Health, *PP* (1847–8), V, 252, 254 with 11 and 12 Victoria, c 63.
50 *PP* (1847), I, 466; Hansard (1847), 91: 625 (author's italics).
51 11 and 12 Victoria, c 63, s 4, 5, 6, 8, 10, 40, 37, 119, and 83.
52 Ibid, s 12, 13, and 20. In the elections of members of local boards in non-corporate districts, there was provision for multiple voting

based on property. A person holding property with a rateable value of less than £50 had one vote. A person holding property with a rateable value in excess of £250 had six votes.

53 Ibid, s 1, 55, 68–9, 43, 45–6, 58, 44 and 73.

54 Ibid, s 75. There was one proviso: the local board could not construct waterworks if there was a water company within the district which was willing to supply water on terms judged reasonable by the general board. Ibid, s 86, 88, 109–10.

55 Ibid, s 122.

56 Ibid, s 49, 51, 60, 76.

57 Voting on the Health of Towns Bill (The division of 18 June 1847):

	+	%	−	%
Conservative Protectionists	34	43·6	44	56·4
Conservative Peelites	30	88·2	4	19·8
Conservative (Other)	5	71·4	2	28·6
Whigs	24	96·0	1	4·0
Liberals	43	100·0	0	0·0
Reformers	29	96·6	1	3·4
Radical Reformers	11	91·7	1	8·3
Repealers	5	100·0	0	0·0
Liberals (Other)	8	100·0	0	0·0
All Conservatives	69	57·0	50	43·0
All Liberals	118	97·6	3	2·4

58 I am grateful to Professor William O. Aydelotte for his wisdom on the subtleties of voting analysis. See his 'Voting Patterns in the British House of Commons in the 1840s', *Comparative Studies in Society and History*, V, 2 (1963), 155–6; 'The Conservative and Radical Interpretations of Early Victorian Social Legislation', *Victorian Studies*, XI, 2 (1967); and 'Laissez-Faire and State Intervention in Mid Nineteenth Century Britain' (to be published).

59 Flinn, 29–30; For a discussion of the limits of Evangelical social reform see Ford K. Brown, *Fathers of the Victorians* (Cambridge: 1961), 106–15.

60 *The Times*, 21 June 1847, 2 July 1847, and 8 May 1848.

61 'The Sanitary Question', *Fraser's Magazine*, XXXVI (1847), 371.

62 Richard Albert Lewis, *Edwin Chadwick and the Public Health Movement* (London: 1952), 320. (Hereinafter cited as Lewis.) Lambert, 66–7.

63 Simon, *English Sanitary Institutions*, 204.

64 Roberts, 79.

65 Hansard (1848), 98: 727; Joshua Toulmin Smith, *The Laws of England Relating to Public Health; including an epitome of the law of nuisances etc.* (London: 1848), viii. (Hereinafter cited as Smith, *Laws of England.*) *The Economist*, VI (13 May 1848), 536.

66 Hansard (1848), 98: 713. Like Toulmin Smith, Urquhart drew his material from English history. However, he also supported his views by drawing on his knowledge of the Orient. Urquhart maintained

that the concepts of government of the ancient Near East were identical to those of medieval England. He deplored, most of all, the loss of executive authority by the Crown and Privy Council as the Cabinet gradually assumed a larger role in the structure of government. This makes his protest against the General Board of Health somewhat incongruous since that body was attached to the Privy Council. Urquhart regarded the deterioration of the power of the Crown and Privy Council as the most significant violation of the ancient constitution. Urquhart called for his followers to resume the ancient rights of petitioning the Crown and impeachment. Palmerston and Sir James Graham were frequently the targets of these procedures. Thus, Urquhart's political ideal was responsible government. In all of this, Urquhart considered himself a Tory of Queen Anne's reign. See Olive Anderson, *A Liberal State at War* (London: 1967), 140–2. (Hereinafter cited as Anderson.) Urquhart also valued the institutions of local government and held that taxes should not be collected by the central government but by the municipalities 'according to ancient custom'. Charles Dod, *Parliamentary Pocket Companion*, 2nd ed (London: 1847), 248.

67 Hansard (1848), 98: 723.

68 Hansard (1847), 93: 1,103–4.

69 Joshua Toulmin Smith, *Government by Commissions, Illegal and Pernicious. The Nature and Effects of All Commissions of Inquiry and Other Crown-Appointed Commissions. The Constitutional Principles of Taxation; and the Rights, Duties, and Importance of Local Self-Government* (London: 1849), 152, 104. (Hereinafter cited as Smith, *Government by Commissions.*)

70 Hansard (1848), 98: 771; Smith, *Laws of England*, v–vi; Hansard (1848), 98: 714, 1,174; Smith, *Government by Commissions*, 297–8.

71 Smith, *Local Self-Government*, 24–5, 51, 59; *Government by Commissions*, 227.

72 Hansard (1847), 93: 750, 1,094.

73 'When the cholera last afflicted Europe, the deaths of disease in Paris were one in forty, while in London they were only one in 400. Paris lost upwards of 18,000, and the city of London less than 600 by disease.' Hansard (1848), 98: 779.

74 See the speech of Charles Newdigate Newdegate. Hansard (1847), 93: 1,105.

75 Smith, *Government by Commissions*, 298–9.

76 Hansard (1847), 93: 1,100; (1848), 98: 792–3.

77 *Letter to Lord Morpeth*, 5.

78 Hansard (1847), 93: 1,108.

79 Hansard (1847), 93: 727–8; (1848), 98: 710, 713.

80 Asa Briggs, *Victorian Cities* (London: 1963), 389.

81 Smith, *Government by Commissions*, 305; Hansard (1848), 98: 765, 774, 710, 713.

82 Hansard (1841), 57: 1,291; (1844), 76: 919; (1854), 135: 981.

83 *The Economist*, VI (13 May 1848), 537.
84 See note 68 in Chapter 2.
85 Anderson, 134-9.
86 Professor Aydelotte, using a very interesting argument, has been able to show that Toulmin Smith's categorical rejection of all forms of government growth was not a widely held view in the House of Commons. Professor Aydelotte argues that interventionist legislation falls into the two separate ideological dimensions characteristic of early Victorian politics. By comparing interventionist measures from each dimension it is possible to see how many MPs rejected both. In his comparison of voting on the ten-hours bill and public health, Professor Aydelotte has found that only two MPs followed Smith's extreme position and opposed both. William O. Aydelotte, 'Laissez-Faire and State Intervention in Mid-Nineteenth Century England', (to be published).
87 Smith, *Local Self-Government*, 191.
88 Peel to the Queen, 14 May 1846. (Prime Ministers' Correspondence at Windsor Castle.) Hansard (1846), 83: 539-53.
89 Smith, *Local Self-Government*, 11.
90 Ibid, 12. 'The question between centralization and Local Self-Government is a question between dogmatism on the one hand and discussion on the other; between the supremacy of an irresponsible oligarchy on the one hand, and the practical assertion of the rights and responsibilities of the freemen on the other.' Ibid, 397-8.
91 Ibid, 54; *Centralization or Representation? A Letter to the Metropolitan Sanatory Commissioners* (London: 1848), x. (Hereinafter cited as Smith, *Centralization or Representation*.) Smith, *Government by Commissions*, 175.
92 Smith, *Government by Commissions*, 93-4, 184; *Local Self-Government*, 294, 111.
93 Smith, *Local Self-Government*, 87, 192.
94 Ibid, 23.
95 Ibid, 123, 119, 122.
96 Smith, *Government by Commissions*, 341; *Laws of England*, 9; *Local Self-Government*, 165; As Smith put it: 'The merging of the Saxon octarchy and heptarchy into one kingdom, under Egbert, is justly considered as the true beginning of the greatness and dignity of the race which before, as since, occupied the land. That there cannot exist an *imperium in imperio* is considered a fundamental principle among all civilized nations. But these local Acts of Parliament do, both theoretically and practically, set at nought all such considerations and principles'. *Laws of England*, 10.
97 Smith, *Laws of England*, 10; *Local Self-Government*, 27.
98 Smith, *Local Self-Government*, 80.
99 Ibid, 46, 51, 53. 'Free institutions do not, then, exist, and national independence can never be ensured, nor individual independence

and forethought can characterize a people, unless true local self-government is fully and freely exercised in every district throughout the land; unshackled alike by cliqueism and by central inter-meddling.' Ibid, 31.

100 Smith, *Government by Commissions*, 316. 'It draws all classes nearer in kindliness and in daily life to one another, and teaches each man, practically, to do to others as he would be done by. It will not let the festering places of society lie hidden and unknown, concealed from view by the external glare and glitter of the favoured classes. Each wrong necessarily becomes promptly known: and the deep seated woes which, without it, ever and anon burst suddenly upon the sight, as from a till then still volcano, and seen and known ere they reach any height, and the needful remedy is at once applied. It makes each man feel that he has a stake in society; a stake which he must maintain both for his own sake and for the sake of all his fellows.' Smith, *Local Self-Government*, 47.

101 See, for example, Smith, *Government by Commissions*, 68–9.

102 Smith's explanation of the word 'sewer' is a good case in point. Smith, *Laws of England*, 67.

103 Smith, *Local Self-Government*, 400. The passage continues: 'It is the highest duty and privilege of Free Men to watch this Urda's spring, and to keep it ever pure and unbefouled. The Responsibility lies on all who reverence the memory of true-hearted fathers, who respect their own best interests, and who would hand down a Free Inheritance to their children, to draw continually from this Urda's spring, the waters by which only can the happy shelter of that Yggdrasil be kept still green and growing'.

104 *The Economist*, V (10 April 1847), 411–12; (11 December 1847), 1,421; VI (13 May 1848), 536; (20 May 1848), 564–6.

105 See the report of the Buccleuch Commission, *PP* (1845), XVIII, 3; and William Augustus Guy, *Unhealthiness of Towns, Its Causes and Remedies* (London: 1845), 43. (Hereinafter cited as Guy.)

106 Hansard (1847), 93: 1,103; (1848), 96: 389; 98: 737.

107 Hansard (1847), 93: 1,094; (1850), 111: 702.

108 See the article in *Fraser's Magazine*, XXXVI (September 1847), 369, 371.

109 Lewis, 279–80.

110 *The Times* (13 December 1847).

111 Hansard (1844), 76: 1,466.

112 Finer, 302–3.

113 Hansard (1848), 96: 389, 403.

114 Hansard (1848), 98: 1,181.

115 On 18 May 1848 *The Times* observed further: 'We would cherish to the utmost the principle of local administration. It has greatly contributed to that independence, to that feeling of responsibility, and to those political habits which distinguish the Englishman from the Frenchman and even the German. On that very account we must

rescue the principle from perversion. We will not have it made either the claptrap of a party, or a perpetual drag upon the wheel of legislation'.

116 Hansard (1847), 93: 1,102–3; (1848), 98: 735.
117 *The Lancet* (1848), I, 428–9.
118 Hansard (1848), 96: 387; 98: 768.
119 Hansard (1848), 98: 735–6, 738.
120 Tom Taylor, 'On Central and Local Action in Relation To Town Improvement', *Transactions of the National Association for the Promotion of Social Science, 1857* (London: 1858), 477. (Hereinafter cited as Taylor.) Taylor was a professor of English literature and language at the University of London from 1845 to 1847, and the art critic for *The Times* for many years. He became assistant secretary of the Board of Health in 1850 and secretary in 1854. In 1858 Taylor was named secretary of the sanitary department of the local government board. From 1872 to his death Taylor was editor of *Punch*.
121 Chadwick, *Sanitary Report*, 396; *PP* (1845), XVIII, 19, 71; *PP* (1847–8), XXXII, 55.
122 Hansard (1848), 99: 689; (1854), 135: 1,000; Benjamin Ward Richardson, *The Health of Towns, A Review of the Work of Edwin Chadwick*, I (London: 1887), 358; Taylor, 479.
123 *The Lancet* (1842–3), II, 901.
124 Hansard (1844), 76: 1,472; (1847), 93: 731.
125 Viscount Ebrington, *Unhealthiness of Towns, Its Causes and Remedies* (London: 1847), 3. (Hereinafter cited as Ebrington.)
126 *PP* (1840), XI, 285.
127 *Fraser's Magazine*, XXXVI (September 1847), 368.
128 Hansard (1848), 96: 413; (1845), 78: 335–6.
129 *PP* (1840), XI, 290, 293–4.
130 Chadwick, *Sanitary Report*, 423.
131 *PP* (1843), XII, 447, 599–600.
132 *PP* (1845), XVIII, 4–5.
133 Hansard (1848), 96: 413.
134 The Duke of Buccleuch stated in 1844: '. . . the great objection to the adaptation of measures for improving the sanatory condition of towns appeared to be a dread of the expense attending upon such measures'. Hansard (1844), 76: 1,485.
135 Finer, 300.
136 Simon, *Reports*, I, 486; Earl of Shaftesbury, 'On Public Health', *Transactions of the National Association for the Promotion of Social Science, 1858* (London: 1859), 94–5; Hansard (1854), 135: 971; Chadwick, *Sanitary Report*, 406, 408.
137 *PP* (1840), XI, 282, 283, 295.
138 Hansard (1847), 91: 634.
139 Hansard (1848), 98: 769–70; 96: 413.
140 Ebrington, 5–6.

141 Francis B. Head, 'Report on the Sanitary Condition of the Labour-
     ing Classes', *Quarterly Review*, LXXI (March 1843), 419.
142 Guy, 46.
143 Hansard (1845), 77: 23.
144 Sibthorp demanded to know why the Metropolis was excluded from
     the act while cleaner cities, such as Lincoln, were included. George
     Hudson accused the London MPs of making a political deal with
     the Government. Roebuck declared that Morpeth 'had spread his
     net wide; why was it cut, and this great fish let out? He (Mr.
     Roebuck), at least, would not act the part of the mouse, but would
     rather assist to reconstruct the net'. Hansard (1847), 92: 731; 93:
     1,093; (1848), 98: 710; (1847), 93: 1,097, 732–3.
145 Hansard (1847), 92: 669–70, 732; (1848), 96: 423; 98: 796.
146 Hansard (1841), 56: 538; (1847), 91: 644.
147 Guy, 44.
148 Lambert, 222–3.
149 Viscount Ebrington noted that a 'Committee of the House of
     Commons upon the water supply of the metropolis, reported that
     the supply of water was not subject to the operation of the usual
     laws which regulate supply, and that it indispensibly required
     legislative interference.
         'The same principle, as you will readily conceive, applied to other
     things besides water, such as gas, railways, . . .'. Ebrington, 38.
150 Hansard (1847), 93: 737. Ashley wrote on 26 September 1848: 'It
     will involve trouble, anxiety, reproach, abuse, unpopularity. I shall
     become a target for private assault and the public press; but how
     could I refuse?' Hodder, II, 253.
151 Lambert, 240.
152 Ibid, 223–4.
153 Ibid, 271, 606.

Chapter 4 PRIVATE OPPORTUNITIES AND PUBLIC RE-
SPONSIBILITIES (pages 107–36)

1 *A Second Letter to Sir Robert Peel, Bart., M.P. on Railway Legislation*, by Cautus (London: 1837), 20. (Hereinafter cited as *A Second
   Letter to Sir Robert Peel.*)
2 *A Letter to the Right Hon. W. E. Gladstone, M.P. President of the
   Board of Trade, on Railway Legislation* (London: 1844), 1–2. (Hereinafter cited as *A Letter to . . . Gladstone.*)
3 Henry Parris, *Government and the Railways in Nineteenth-Century
   Britain* (London: 1965), 229. (Hereinafter cited as Parris, *Government and the Railways.*)
4 Arthur W. Hart, *A Letter to the Right Hon. Lord John Russell, on the
   Assumption of the Railways by the Government* (London: 1849), 10.
5 Samuel Smiles, *Railway Property: Its Conditions and Prospects* (np:
   1849), 8. (Hereinafter cited as Smiles, *Railway Property.*)

6 *Westminster Review*, XLII (1844), 1.
7 Parris, *Government and the Railways*, 13–14; E. Cleveland-Stevens, *English Railways: Their Development and Relation to the State* (London: 1915), 61–2. (Hereinafter cited as Cleveland-Stevens.)
8 Parris, *Government and the Railways*, 208.
9 Ibid, ix.
10 Cleveland-Stevens, 72–3.
11 W. L. Burn, *The Age of Equipoise* (New York: 1965), 166. (Hereinafter cited as Burn.) See O. O. G. M. MacDonagh, *A Pattern of Government Growth, 1800–1860: The Passenger Acts and their Enforcement* (London: 1961). It is difficult to assess, in any absolute fashion, the relative degree of state control in two different spheres. There were more public acts regulating the passenger traffic, but the sea-lanes were far removed from the watchful eyes of inspecting officers. While there were fewer public railway acts in the early Victorian period, the railways were in constant view and subject to close and periodic examination.
12 Briggs, 340; Parris, *Government and the Railways*, viii; Henry Parris, 'Railway Policy in Peel's Administration', *Bulletin of the Institute of Historical Research*, XXXIII (1960), 180; Philip S. Bagwell, 'The Railway Interest: Its Organization and Influence, 1839–1914', *The Journal of Transport History*, VII, 2 (1965), 65–6.
13 Burn, 166.
14 Parris, *Government and the Railways*, 12.
15 The members of the Select Committee of 1839 were: Poulett Thomson, Sir Robert Peel, Shaw Lefevre, Lord Granville Somerset, Mr Thornely, Viscount Sandon, Mr Loch, Mr Freshfield, Sir John Guest, Lord Stanley, Mr Greene, Sir Harry Verney, Mr Bingham Baring, Sir James Graham, and Lord Seymour.
16 Second Report from the Select Committee on Railways, *PP* (1839), X, 139.
17 Parris, *Government and the Railways*, 29–31, 52–7, 103–5.
18 3 and 4 Victoria, c 97, s 1.
19 Parris, *Government and the Railways*, 31–3.
20 3 and 4 Victoria, c 97, s 11.
21 Ibid, s 5.
22 5 and 6 Victoria, c 55, s 6.
23 3 and 4 Victoria, c 97, s 10 and 18–19.
24 5 and 6 Victoria, c 55, s 11; 8 and 9 Victoria, c 20, s 12.
25 3 and 4 Victoria, c 97, s 1 and 3.
26 5 and 6 Victoria, c 55, s 7 and 8.
27 3 and 4 Victoria, c 97, s 7, 8, and 9.
28 8 and 9 Victoria, c 20, s 8, 36, 43, and 107.
29 John Morley, *The Life of William Ewart Gladstone*, I (London: 1903), 269. (Hereinafter cited as Morley.) Cleveland-Stevens, 115.
30 7 and 8 Victoria, c 85, s 1–2, 6, and 15.
31 *PP* (1844), XI, 34.

32 7 and 8 Victoria, c 85, s 15 (author's italics).

33 Hansard (1844), 76: 508, 484.

34 Hansard (1844), 76: 507. John Wilson Croker, who approved of the railway legislation of 1840 and had no reservations concerning the power of parliament in these matters but who also favoured restraint and caution with regard to government relationship to the railways, interpreted Conservative Government policy in 1844 to be a preparation for a 'transition' in that relationship. He read the third report of the Select Committee of 1844 as 'a lucid exposition of the present condition and future prospects of railways, and of the reasons which seem to render the intervention of the Government as trustees for the public indispensable, as far as it can be carried without infringing on existing rights . . .'. 'Railway Legislation', *Quarterly Review*, LXXIV (1844), 273–4.

35 James Morrison (1790–1857), who had acquired a fortune in the drapery trade, pressed for state intervention in railway affairs as early as 1836. In 1836 and 1845 he moved resolutions calling for the revision of railway tolls and charges at regular intervals and in 1846 obtained a select committee to inquire into the public interest in railway matters. Morrison entered parliament in 1830, sat for St Ives, Ipswich, and Inverness Burghs, and retired upon the dissolution of parliament in 1847.

36 Report from the Select Committee on Railway Acts Enactments, *PP* (1846), XIV, 3–4.

37 9 and 10 Victoria, c 105, s 1, 2, 9, and 11.

38 Ibid, s 7 and 8.

39 Roberts, 114–15.

40 The division on the second reading of Gladstone's railway bill on 11 July 1844:

	+	%	—	%
Conservative (Protectionist)	67	74·4	23	25·6
Conservative (Peelite)	47	92·2	4	7·8
Conservative (Other)	18	94·7	1	5·3
Whig	11	44·0	14	56·0
Liberal	13	32·5	27	67·5
Reformer	11	42·8	16	57·2
Radical Reformer	5	45·5	6	54·5
Repealer	1	50·0	1	50·0
Liberal (Other)	2	40·0	3	60·0
All Conservatives	132	82·5	28	17·5
All Liberals	44	39·0	67	61·0

41 Hansard (1836), 31: 686.

42 Hansard (1836), 33: 988; (1844), 76: 633, 524.

43 *PP* (1844), XI, 380; Hansard (1846), 85: 926, 1,325–8; Richard S. Lambert, *The Railway King, 1800–1871: A Study of George Hudson and the Business Morals of His Time* (London: 1934), 99–100.

44 *The Times* (2 and 18 April 1844).

45 Hansard (1840), 55: 931, 919.
46 Hansard (1840), 55: 921–2; (1844), 76: 647.
47 Hansard (1844), 76: 631–3.
48 Hansard (1844), 76: 655–6.
49 Hansard (1846), 85: 285.
50 Hansard (1837), 36: 1,162; (1844), 76: 523, 679–80.
51 Hansard (1847), 90: 403; 92: 847.
52 Samuel Shaen, jun, *A Review of Railway Legislation at Home and Abroad* (London: 1847), 1. (Hereinafter cited as Shaen, *A Review of Railway Legislation*.)
53 Hansard (1844), 76: 630–1, 635.
54 *PP* (1844), XI, 365; Hansard (1846), 83: 194.
55 Hansard (1840), 55: 906–7; (1842), 64: 181; 60: 173–4; (1847), 89: 1,203–4.
56 Shaen, *A Review of Railway Legislation*, 35; Hansard (1840), 55: 1,181–3.
57 *PP* (1841), XXV, 204; Hansard (1842), 60: 167 (author's italics); (1847), 89: 1,193.
58 *PP* (1841), XXV, 210; (1844), XI, 23.
59 Hansard (1844), 72: 236.
60 Hansard (1840), 55: 917.
61 Hansard (1842), 60: 176.
62 *PP* (1841), XXV, 204.
63 Parris, *Government and the Railways*, 81.
64 Hansard (1846), 88: 936.
65 *PP* (1846), XIV, 7.
66 Hansard (1836), 33: 979. Morrison was convinced that considerable intervention was possible before individual speculation was needlessly checked. Hansard (1836), 33: 978; (1846), 84: 1,233.
67 Hansard (1844), 76: 507, 1,187–8.
68 Hansard (1846), 83: 363.
69 *PP* (1846), XIV, 7–8. An anonymous pamphleteer put the case for the public character of railways in the following manner: 'The whole operation of railways is based on a specific contract, deliberately made between certain private individuals associated together and the nation; entered into by mutual agreement, after long deliberation, public investigation, and close examination, and solemnly ratified by the commons, the peers, and the sovereign of Great Britain'. *A Letter to . . . Gladstone*, 27.
70 Hansard (1836), 33: 979; James Morrison, *The Influence of English Railway Legislation on Trade and Industry* (London: 1848), 65. (Hereinafter cited as Morrison, *Influence of English Railway Legislation*.)
71 *PP* (1839), X, 133; (1846), XIV, 8.
72 Hansard (1844), 76: 517; (1846), 84: 1,246.
73 Hansard (1844), 76: 500; 72: 236.
74 Hansard (1847), 92: 853–4. In 1846, it is fascinating to note,

Newdegate himself favoured legislation to check speculation. See Hansard (1846), 85: 929–30.

75 Hansard (1844), 76: 528; (1846), 85: 932–3; (1847), 92: 822.
76 Hansard (1846), 85: 868, 923–4.
77 Hansard (1846), 85: 662, 881; Morrison, *Influence of English Railway Legislation*, 63.
78 Hansard (1836), 33: 981–2; 31: 685; *PP* (1846), XIV, 13–14.
79 Smiles, *Railway Property*, 10; Hansard (1836), 31: 672.
80 *PP* (1844), XI, 22.
81 Hansard (1836), 31: 1,114–15.
82 *What Will Parliament Do With the Railways?* (London: 1836), 16.
83 *PP* (1844), XI, 26; Hansard (1844), 72: 239; (1847), 93: 783.
84 *A Second Letter to Sir Robert Peel*, 6, 8.
85 *A Letter to . . . Gladstone*, 11, 12, 16, 2, 53, 3.
86 Ibid, 53, 15, 16, 42.
87 Ibid, 22.
88 Hansard (1836), 31: 682.
89 *Railways and the Board of Trade* (London: 1845), 18–20.
90 Hansard (1842), 60: 169. Sibthorp's vehement opposition to the railways was paralleled, perhaps, by a wider prejudice against the railways in early Victorian Britain. See John Wilson Croker, 'Railway Legislation', *Quarterly Review*, LXXIV (1844), 240–1.
91 Hansard (1844), 76: 515–16. Sibthorp's position was not entirely lacking in consistency. He opposed the Railway Commission on the grounds that it would contribute to increased patronage and expense. In 1847, Sibthorp voted against the bill of supply for the Railway Commission. On that occasion he said: 'If these Commissioners must have 17,000£ a year, let it come out of the pockets of the Railway Companies. Heaven knew they made money enough'. Hansard (1846), 88: 929, 935; (1847), 92: 1,270.
92 *Some Words on Railway Legislation in a Letter Addressed to Sir Robert Peel, Bart.*, by Cautus (London: 1837), 3–4.
93 Burn, 166.

Chapter 5   THE RESTRICTION OF LABOUR AND ECONOMIC GROWTH (pages 137–79)

1 Hansard (1833), 19: 900; (1844), 73: 1,256; Karl Marx, *Selected Works*, II, Prepared at the Marx-Engels-Lenin Institute, under the editorship of V. Adoratsky (New York: nd), 439; John Morley, *The Life of Richard Cobden*, I (London: 1881), 302–3.
2 G. M. Young, *Portrait of an Age*, 2nd edition (Oxford: 1953), 47; Roberts, 38.
3 Alfred [Samuel Kydd], *The History of the Factory Movement from the Year 1802 to the Enactment of the Ten Hours Bill in 1847*, II (London: 1857), 56–7. This work is of some importance because

Kydd used the private papers of Richard Oastler in its compilation. (Hereinafter cited as Alfred.)

4 Geoffrey Francis Andrew Best, *Shaftesbury* (New York: 1964), 82.

5 The members of the Royal Commission were Francis Bisset Hawkins, Sir David Barry Knight, Leonard Horner, John Elliot Drinkwater, Robert Mackintosh, James Stuart, John Welsford Cawell, Edward Carkton Tufnell, Alfred Power, Stephen Woolriche, John Spencer, Charles Loudon, Thomas Tooke, Southwood Smith, and Edwin Chadwick.

6 First Report of the Central Board of His Majesty's Commissioners appointed to collect Information in the Manufacturing Districts as to the Employment of Children in Factories, and as to the Propriety and Means of Curtailing the Hours of their Labour, *PP* (1833), XX, 51.

7 Ibid, 33–7.

8 Ibid, 52–3.

9 Ibid, 68–9.

10 Ibid, 71–2.

11 Ibid, 73.

12 M. W. Thomas, *Early Factory Legislation* (Leigh-on-Sea: 1948), 62.

13 3 and 4 William 4, c 103, s 1, 2. Children between the ages of eleven and eighteen, without a certificate of age, could be employed for only nine hours. See s 14.

14 Ibid, s 7, 8, 11.

15 Ibid, s 17. This clause superseded the clause in 42 George 3, c 73, which provided that the justices of the peace were to appoint non-interested factory visitors.

16 Ibid, s 18, 33, 34, 45.

17 Ibid, s 20, 21, 1.

18 Report of the Commission for Inquiring into the Employment and Condition of Children in Mines and Manufactories, *PP* (1843), XIII, 424.

19 Ibid, 519–21, 523.

20 Ibid, 518, 523.

21 7 and 8 Victoria, c 15, s 29, 32.

22 Ibid, s 2, 3.

23 Ibid, s 6, 5, 8, 13, 14, 24, 27.

24 Ibid, s 38, 39.

25 *PP* (1831–2), II, 1.

26 Ibid, 2–3.

27 J. T. Ward, *The Factory Movement* (London: 1962), 289, 412, 415–17. (Hereinafter cited as Ward.)

28 Greville, V, 169.

29 Aydelotte, 'The Conservative and Radical Interpretations of Early Victorian Social Reform', 233–4.

30 William O. Aydelotte, 'The House of Commons in the 1840's', *History*, XXXIX (October 1954), 260. As this study also shows,

social position had almost no bearing on voting on the ten-hours question. In 1844, by insignificant majorities, the Peerage-Baronet-age-Gentry slightly supported it and the non-PBG slightly opposed it. In 1847 each group favoured the measure by a proportion of two to one. Ibid, 260–1.

31   Voting on the Ten-hours Question:

	1844				1846				1847			
	+	%	−	%	+	%	−	%	+	%	−	%
Cons (Prot)	59	57	44	43	105	70	45	30	92	94	6	6
Cons (Peel)	26	36	46	64	8	10	69	90	16	37	27	63
Cons (other)	10	33	20	67	9	56	7	44	11	100	0	0
Whig	22	59	15	41	15	50	15	50	14	58	10	42
Lib	24	63	14	37	25	48	27	52	24	54	20	46
Ref	16	49	17	51	16	36	28	64	16	50	16	50
Rad Ref	6	43	8	57	6	46	7	54	9	56	7	44
Repealer	3	75	1	25	4	100	0	0	7	100	0	0
Lib (other)	5	63	3	37	4	57	3	43	4	80	1	20
All Cons	95	46	110	54	122	50	121	50	119	78	33	22
All Libs	76	57	58	43	70	47	80	53	74	58	54	42

32   Hansard (1846), 86: 1,080.

33   Graham to the Attorney General, 8 May 1844. (Graham Papers at Netherby Hall, Cumberland.)

34   Hansard (1847), 90: 791; 91: 1,132.

35   Hansard (1847), 91: 1,133, 1,138.

36   Ward, 412–14.

37   Geoffrey Crabtree's *The Factory Commission, the Legality of its Appointment Questioned and the Illegality of its Proceedings Proved* (London: 1833) was not directed against the administrative machinery established by the act of 1833 but against the Royal Commission appointed by the Crown to investigate the factory system in 1833. The Crown, Crabtree asserted, did not have the proper authority to appoint the Commission. 'I am nearly certain that the Factory Commission is an appointment against law, and I am quite certain that if the law of England is to prevail, the proceedings must be quashed for their illegality.'

38   Hansard (1833), 20: 583–5.

39   Hansard (1839), 48: 1,065; (1844), 74: 136.

40   *DNB*, LXIX, 318; Hansard (1844), 74: 635.

41   *The Economist*, VI (12 February 1848), 173.

42   Hansard (1846), 86: 1,062.

43   Hansard (1819), 1st Series, 40: 1,131.

44   Hansard (1833), 15: 1,295.

45   Hansard (1844), 75: 151; *The Economist*, I (8 June 1844), 869.

46 Hansard (1839), 48: 1,071–2; (1833), 19: 246; Robert Eadon Leader, *Life and Letters of John Arthur Roebuck* (New York: 1897), 285; Hansard (1847), 90: 161; (1844), 73: 1,372.

47 Hansard (1818), 1st Series, 37: 1,260; (1833), 19: 893.

48 Hansard (1818), 1st Series, 38: 359; (1846), 83: 409; (1833), 19: 238.

49 Hansard (1833), 17: 92; (1844), 73: 1,390.

50 Hansard (1844), 74: 615–16, 667; (1833), 19: 910; (1844), 73: 1,183.

51 Hansard (1846), 86: 1,052; (1847), 90: 797; (1846), 86: 1,024; (1844), 74: 1,076–7; (1847), 90: 815.

52 Graham Wallas, *The Life of Francis Place, 1774–1854* (New York: 1919), 173–4.

53 Hansard (1844), 73: 1,669–70; (1846), 85: 1,237–8.

54 Hansard (1844), 74: 683; (1847), 92: 916; (1847), 89: 1,075; 90: 164.

55 Hansard (1832), 9: 1,096–7; (1833), 19: 904; (1838), 44: 439; (1833), 15: 1,162.

56 Hansard (1836), 33: 766; (1839), 48: 1,076, 1,081; 45: 891; (1844), 73: 1,148–9, 1,151; (1846), 86: 1,076–7. The corn-law issue was sometimes used as a weapon against Conservative Protectionists who favoured a ten-hours bill. H. G. Ward returned Ashley's taunt of inhumanity by declaring that that was a suspicious charge from one who had voted for a measure which increased the price of food. Hansard (1844), 73: 1,427.

57 I have found two exceptions to this. In 1844 Joseph Hume opposed the factory bill because it was a 'new attempt to put shackles upon commerce'. Hansard (1844), 74: 336. The same year *The Economist* spoke of inconsistent legislation in which the principles of some acts were at variance with the principles of others. Acts emphasising commercial freedom passed in one session would be joined the next by acts based on 'antiquated and exploded a-century-ago notions'. *The Economist*, I (6 July 1844), 962.

58 Hansard (1846), 86: 1,019; (1847), 90: 780; 89: 1,136–7, 1,147–8; 91: 126.

59 See, for example, the remarks of the Earl of Grosvenor, Thomas Gisborne, and Henry Labouchere. Hansard (1819), 1st Series, 39: 344; (1833), 19: 912; (1846), 86: 480.

60 Hansard (1844), 73: 1,215.

61 Hansard (1833), 19: 892; Peel to the Queen, 19 March 1844. (Prime Ministers' Correspondence, Windsor Castle.)

62 Hansard (1844), 73: 1,103, 1,186–7.

63 Hansard (1833), 19: 239; (1844), 73: 1,187; (1847), 90: 158, 166; *The Economist*, I (23 March 1844), 609.

64 Hansard (1833), 19: 886, 911; (1846), 86: 1,005–6; (1847), 90: 137.

65 *Westminster Review*, XVIII (April 1833), 383.

66 Hansard (1844), 73: 1,457; (1846), 86: 1,014.

67 Hansard (1833), 19: 221; (1844), 73: 1,520–1.

68 Hansard (1832), 9: 1,095; (1844), 74: 1,069; (1847), 89: 1,076.
69 Hansard (1846), 83: 401; (1847), 90: 806.
70 Hansard (1844), 74: 923–4.
71 Hansard (1844), 73: 1,245, 1,111; 75: 150; (1847), 92: 906.
72 Peel to the Queen, 19 March 1844. (Prime Ministers' Correspondence, Windsor Castle.)
73 Hansard (1833), 19: 892, 896; (1844), 73: 1,457; (1846), 86: 1,064–5.
74 Hansard (1844), 74: 967, 136, 969.
75 Hansard (1846), 86: 479–80.
76 Hansard (1847), 90: 140.
77 Hansard (1846), 86: 521, 523; (1847), 89: 1,094; 90: 783–4; (1846), 86: 1,043–4; (1847), 91: 1,128.
78 Oastler, *Fleet Papers*, I, 275.
79 Ashley to Oastler (19 July 1833), quoted in Ward, 106; Oastler, *Fleet Papers*, I, 71.
80 Copy of a Memorial from the Short-time Committee of Manchester, addressed to His Majesty's Secretary of State for the Home Department, *PP* (1837), I, 207; Hansard (1838), 44: 390–1; 48: 1,066, 1,069. The Report from the Select Committee on the Act for the Regulation of Mills and Factories, *PP* (1841), IX, 563, congratulated the House of Commons and the country on the 'partial success' of the act of 1833, but indicated that various defects in the legislation had become apparent and much remained to be done.
81 *Fraser's Magazine*, XXIX (May 1844), 621; Hansard (1833), 16: 879.
82 Alfred, II, 20; Hansard (1844), 74: 900; Hodder, I, 407.
83 See the views of John Fielden as found in *The Curse of the Factory System* (London: 1836), 48. See also the parliamentary speeches of William Cobbett, Richard Lalor Sheil, Joseph Brotherton, and Thomas Slingsby Duncombe. Hansard (1833), 19: 249, 251, 894–5; (1844), 73: 1,450.
84 Alfred, II, 99.
85 *The Times* (10 June 1833).
86 Hodder, I, 146; Alfred, I, 99; Fielden, *The Curse of the Factory System*, 14; Hansard (1832), 11: 380; 13: 502; (1844), 74: 1,021–2, 1,041.
87 Michael Thomas Sadler, *Protest Against the Secret Proceedings of the Factory Commission in Leeds* (Leeds: 1833), 16; Hansard (1832), 11: 341; Oastler to Peel, printed in *The Times* of 6 May 1844; Hansard (1833), 16: 642; 19: 229.
88 Fielden, *The Curse of the Factory System*, 34; Hansard (1833), 15: 1,165; (1832), 10: 22; (1844), 73: 1,128–9.
89 Hansard (1832), 11: 372; (1846), 86: 999, 1,040; (1847), 90: 140; 92: 927; (1844), 73: 1,435; (1846), 86: 1,048; (1847), 89: 489.
90 Hansard (1844), 73: 1,118; (1818), 1st Series, 38: 344; (1846), 83: 392; (1844), 74: 959; 73: 1,092–3, 1,100. See also Oastler's testimony before Sadler's Select Committee, *PP* (1831–2), XV, 455.

91 Hansard (1844), 73: 1,099; (1846), 83: 393; 86: 503; (1847), 89:
    495; (1844), 74: 1,102–3; Southey to Ashley, 15 January 1832,
    Hodder, I, 129.
92 Oastler, *Fleet Papers*, II, 115–16.
93 Hansard (1847), 89: 1,149; 91: 134–5, 141; (1847), 89: 1,087–8.
94 Hansard (1832), 10: 192; (1844), 73: 1,118–19, 1,380; 74: 912–13;
    73: 1,405–6.
95 Hansard (1844), 73: 1,234; (1847), 89: 1,126; (1846), 85: 1,226.
96 Hansard (1844), 73: 1,131; (1846), 86: 489; (1847), 90: 145, 168;
    91: 139.
97 Fielden, *The Curse of the Factory System*, 61, 56.
98 Hansard (1833), 16: 1,002; (1844), 73: 1,118, 1,199; (1846), 85:
    1,227–8; 86: 1,020. At times the analogy to slave-trade abolition was
    also used in this context. As a letter to *The Times* noted on 10 May
    1844, the city of Liverpool had not declined after the slave trade was
    abolished. See also, Brotherton's speech in Hansard (1833), 19: 895.
99 Hansard (1844), 74: 912.
100 Alfred, II, 5.
101 Hansard (1844), 73: 1,438; Earl of Shaftesbury, *Speeches upon
    Subjects having relation chiefly to the Claims and Interests of the
    Labouring Class* (London: 1868), 150; Hansard (1844), 73: 1,436;
    Alfred, II, 30. See also the speeches of W. Smith, Sir George
    Strickland, Lord John Manners and Joseph Brotherton in Hansard
    (1818), 1st Series, 38: 366–7; (1832), 10: 191; (1846), 83: 399; 86:
    527.
102 *Fraser's Magazine*, XXIX (May 1844), 617.
103 Hansard (1818), 1st Series, 38: 794.
104 Hansard (1846), 86: 504.
105 *Cobbett's Political Register*, LXXXII (14 December 1833), 641.
106 Hansard (1835), 28: 895–6.
107 Hansard (1840), 55: 785–6, 789–90.
108 Hansard (1840), 55: 808–9. Interestingly, on this occasion Fielden
    was opposed by Lord Ashley, Joseph Brotherton, and G. F. Muntz.
109 Oastler, *Fleet Papers*, I, 365. See ibid, II, 421 for Oastler's suspicions
    of Peel's government.
110 Alfred, II, 210.
111 Oastler related his opposition to the new poor law to his support for
    the ten-hours bill. In a letter dated July 1856 he wrote: 'The two
    questions were, are, and ever must be inseparately connected. It was
    in evidence that the new poor law was intended to be used to
    perpetuate slavery in factories. The Ten Hours' Bill was intended
    to destroy that slavery. It was in evidence that the new poor law was
    intended to decrease the wages of the factory operatives. The Ten
    Hours' Bill was, as I always believed, and maintained, calculated to
    increase those wages. It was in evidence that the new poor law was,
    by the introduction of the families of agricultural labourers into the
    factory districts, intended to increase the competition for labour in

factories. The Ten Hours' Bill was intended and calculated to decrease that competition. For those and for other very weighty reasons, we resolved, as I think, most wisely, and I am sure, as Ten Hours' men, most consistently, to resist the passing of the New Poor Law Bill'. Alfred, II, 79. Samuel Kydd agreed that the ten-hours agitation, while separate from the anti-poor law movement, 'was analogous in spirit'. Ibid, II, 76.

112 Oastler, *Fleet Papers*, II, 15, 40, 70; I, 162; II, 41–2.
113 Hansard (1847), 90: 152; (1832), 11: 382; (1839), 48: 1,079.
114 Hansard (1833), 19: 901–2.
115 See the speeches of Brotherton, Muntz, Lord John Russell, Grey, Hawes, Buller, and Howick. Hansard (1839), 48: 1,083; (1844), 74: 977; 73: 1,260; 74: 664; 73: 1,201, 1,670; 74: 1,047, 1,048–9, 1,051; 73: 1,441, 1,443, 1,446–7; 74: 935, 937, 939, 940. As Benjamin Hawes argued, 'the operatives might be safely left to go into the labour-market unfettered' after the removal of commercial restrictions. Hansard (1844), 73: 1,670–1.
116 *Edinburgh Review*, L (January 1830), 550; Hansard (1846), 86: 1,029–30.
117 Hansard (1846), 86: 1,031, 1,033, 1,034, 1,035.
118 Cecil Driver, *Tory Radical: The Life of Richard Oastler* (Oxford: 1946), 4.
119 See Oastler's testimony before Sadler's Select Committee, *PP* (1831–2), XV, 455.
120 Oastler, *Fleet Papers*, I, 165.
121 Ibid, II, 14.
122 *PP* (1831–2), XV, 455, 459; Alfred, I, 92.
123 Oastler, *Fleet Papers*, I, 325.
124 Ibid, II, 115–16, 8.
125 See the speeches of John Hardy, George Richard Robinson, and Lord Ashley in Hansard (1833), 17: 105, 102; 19: 889 as well as John Fielden's *The Curse of the Factory System*, iv.
126 Hansard (1844), 73: 1,433–4.
127 Hansard (1844), 73: 1,129–30.
128 Hansard (1844), 73: 1,129–30, 1,191.
129 Hansard (1844), 74: 1,025–6; 73: 1,623.
130 Norman McCord has argued that the League did not have sufficient independent political strength to force repeal in the face of the power of a united landed interest. See Norman McCord, *The Anti-Corn Law League, 1838–1846* (London: 1958), 208; and McCord, 'Cobden and Bright in Politics', *Ideas and Institutions of Victorian Britain*, ed R. Robson (London: 1967), 94. Just as Peel, and not the League, was responsible for corn-law repeal, so too politicians inside the House of Commons, not outside agitation, were largely responsible for ten-hours legislation.
131 David Roberts, 'Tory Paternalism and Social Reform in Early Victorian England', *American Historical Review*, LXIII, 2 (1958),

329; W. O. Aydelotte, 'The House of Commons in the 1840's', 258–60.

132 See above, pp 22–4.

133 Hansard (1844), 74: 682; (1846), 86: 1,013; (1847), 89: 1,077.

134 Hansard (1844), 73: 1,465; Morley, *The Life of Richard Cobden*, I, 467; Hansard (1847), 89: 1,074, 1,080.

135 William D. Grampp, *The Manchester School of Economics* (Stanford: 1960), 13–14; *The Economist*, I (10 March 1844), 625.

136 Hansard (1844), 74: 135; (1847), 92: 893–4, 930.

137 Hansard (1846), 86: 1,044.

138 Hansard (1844), 73: 1,200–1; (1847), 89: 1,084; 92: 943.

139 Hansard (1844), 74: 650–1; (1846), 86: 1,062.

Chapter 6 SOME CONCLUDING OBSERVATIONS (pages 180–8)

1 Asa Briggs, 'The Welfare State in Historical Perspective', *Archives Européens de Sociologie*, II, 2 (1961), 228.

2 Hansard (1846), 86: 1,029–30.

3 John Stuart Mill, *Considerations on Representative Government* (Gateway edition, Chicago: 1962), 302–3.

4 John Stuart Mill, *Autobiography* (New York: nd), 146.

5 See J. G. A. Pocock's *The Ancient Constitution and the Feudal Law: English Historical Thought in the Seventeenth-Century* (Cambridge: 1957), and Isaac Kramnick, 'Augustan Politics and English Historiography: The Debate on the English Past, 1730–35', *History and Theory*, VI, 1 (1967).

6 Walter Bagehot, *The English Constitution* (Ithaca, New York: 1966), 262.

7 *Quarterly Review*, LXXIV (1844), 271.

8 G. P. Gooch, ed, *Later Correspondence of Lord John Russell*, I (London: 1925), 157.

9 J. S. Mill to J. Whiting, 15 October 1842, *The Earlier Letters of John Stuart Mill, 1812–1848*, II, 550.

Select Bibliography

MANUSCRIPT SOURCES

The Letters of Sir Robert Peel to Queen Victoria, Prime Ministers' Correspondence at Windsor Castle (microfilm positive located in the Library of the University of Iowa, Iowa City, Iowa).

The Papers of Sir James Graham, Netherby Hall, Cumberland (microfilm positive located in the Newberry Library, Chicago, Illinois).

PARLIAMENTARY SOURCES

Great Britain, Parliament, *Hansard's Parliamentary Debates*, 1st, 2nd, and 3rd series (1818-54).

The Statutes of the United Kingdom of Great Britain and Ireland.

Parliamentary Papers

Report of the Minutes of Evidence taken before the Select Committee on the State of Children employed in the manufactories of the United Kingdom (1816), III.

Report from the Committee on the 'Bill to regulate the Labour of Children in the Mills and Factories of the United Kingdom' (1831-2), XV.

First Report of the Central Board of His Majesty's Commissioners appointed to collect Information in the Manufacturing Districts, as to the Employment of Children in Factories, and as to the Propriety and Means of Curtailing the Hours of their Labour (1833), XX.

The Select Committee of the House of Lords Appointed to Consider the Poor Laws (1833), XXXII.

Report from His Majesty's Commissioners for Inquiring into

the Administration and Practical Operation of the Poor Laws (1834), XXVII.

Report of His Majesty's Commissioners for Inquiring into the Administration and Practical Operation of the Poor Laws, Appendix A, Part III (1834), XXIX.

Regulations Lately Issued by Leonard Horner Inspector of Factories (1836), XLV.

Copy of a Memorial from the Short-time Committee of Manchester, addressed to His Majesty's Secretary of State for the Home Department (1837), L.

Report from the Select Committee on the Poor Law Amendment Act (1837), XVII.

Report from the Select Committee of the House of Lords appointed to examine into the several cases alluded to in certain papers respecting the operation of the Poor Law Amendment Act (1837-8), XI.

Report from the Select Committee on the Poor Law Amendment Act (1837-8), XVIII.

First Report from the Select Committee on Railways (1839), X.

Second Report from the Select Committee on Railways (1839), X.

Report of the Select Committee on the Act for the Regulation of Mills and Factories (1840), X.

Report of the Select Committee on the Health of Towns (1840), XI.

Report of the Poor Law Commissioners to the Most Noble the Marquis of Normanby, Her Majesty's Principal Secretary of State for the Home Department, on the Continuance of the Poor Law Commission and on some further amendment of the Laws relating to the Relief of the Poor (1840), XVII.

Report from the Select Committee on the Act for the Regulation of Mills and Factories (1841), IX.

Report of the Officers of the Railway Department to the Right Honorable The President of the Board of Trade (1841), XXV.

Report on the Sanitary Condition of the Labouring Population of Great Britain (1842), ed by M. W. Flinn (Edinburgh: 1965).

Report on the Sanitary Condition of the Labouring Population of Great Britain: A Supplementary Report on the Result of a special Inquiry into the Practice of Interment in Towns (1843), XXI.

Second Report of the Commission for Inquiring into the Employment and Condition of Children in Mines and Manufactories (1843), XIII.

Third Report from the Select Committee on Railways (1844), XI.

Fifth Report from the Select Committee on Railways (1844), XI.

First Report of the Commissioners for Inquiring into the State of Large Towns and Populous Districts (1844), XVII.

Second Report of the Commissioners for Inquiring into the State of the Large Towns and Populous Districts (1845), XVIII.

Report from the Select Committee on the Andover Union (1846), V.

Report from the Select Committee on Railway Acts Enactments (1846), XIV.

Second Report from the Select Committee on Railway Acts Enactments, together with minutes of evidence (1846), XIV.

Report of the Metropolitan Sanitary Commission (1847–8), XXXII.

CONTEMPORARY SOURCES

Abstract of the Proceedings of the Public Health Meeting Held at Exeter Hall December 11, 1844 (London: nd).

Answers to certain Objections made to Sir Robert Peel's Bill for Ameliorating the Condition of Children Employed in Cotton Manufactories (Manchester: 1819).

The Health and Sickness of Town Populations Considered with Reference to Proposed Sanatory Legislation and to the Establishment of a Comprehensive System of Medical Police and District Dispensaries (London: 1846).

Letters Addressed by the Poor Law Commissioners to the Secretary of State Respecting the Transaction of the Business of the Commission (London: 1847).

Letter to Lord Morpeth on the Health of Towns Bill, by a Towns-man (London: nd).

Observations Upon the Present Railway Mania (1845).

Railways and the Board of Trade (1845).

What Will Parliament Do With the Railways? (London: 1836).

Alfred [Samuel Kydd]. *The History of the Factory Movement from the Year 1802 to the Enactment of the Ten Hours Bill in 1847*, 2 vols (London: 1857).

Baxter, G. R. Wythen. *Book of the Bastilles* (London: 1841).

[Chadwick, Edwin]. *Article on the Principles and Progress of the Poor Law Amendment Act; and also on the value of the Central Control and improved local administration introduced by that statute* (London: 1837).

Crabtree, Geoffrey. *Factory Commission, The Legality of its Appointment Questioned and the Illegality of its Proceedings Proved* (London: 1833).

Ebrington, Viscount. *Unhealthiness of Towns, Its Causes and Remedies* (London: 1847).

Fielden, John. *The Curse of the Factory System; or, A Short Account of the Origin of Factory Cruelties; of the Attempts to Protect the Children by Law; of Their Present Sufferings; Our Duty Towards Them; Injustice of Mr. Thomson's Bill; the Folly of the Political Economists; a Warning Against Sending the Children of the South into the Factories of the North* (London: 1836).

[Galt, William]. *Railway Reform; Its Expediency and Practicability Considered. With a Copious Appendix Containing a Description of all the Railways in Great Britain and Ireland; Fluctuations in the Prices of Shares; Statistical and Parliamentary Returns* (1843).

Gurney, J. H. *The New Poor Law the Poor Man's Friend. A Plain Address to the Labouring Classes Among his Parishioners* (Leicester: 1836).

Guy, William Augustus. *Unhealthiness of Towns, Its Causes and Remedies* (London: 1845).

Hart, Arthur W. *A Letter to the Right Hon. Lord John Russell on the Assumption of Railways by Government* (1849).

Horner, Leonard. *The Factory Act, Explained, with Some Remarks on its Origin, Nature, and Tendency* (Glasgow: 1834).

Kay-Shuttleworth, James. *Moral and Physical Condition of the Working Classes Employed in the Cotton Manufacture in Manchester* (London: 1832).

Laing, Samuel. *Observations on Mr. Strutt's Amended Railway Regulation Bill Now Before Parliament* (Westminster: 1847).

Lardner, Dionysius. *Railway Economy; a Treatise on the New Art of Transport, Its Management, Prospects, and Relations, Commercial, Financial, Social, With an Exposition of the Practical Results of Railways in Operation in the United Kingdom, on the Continent, and in America* (1850).

Leslie, John. *A Letter to the Industrious Classes, on the Operation of the Poor Laws as Affecting their Independence and Comfort* (1835).

Liddle, John. *On the Moral and Physical Evils Resulting from the Neglect of Sanitary Measures* (London: 1847).

Marshall, Rev Henry Johnson, BA. *On the Tendency of the New Poor Law Seriously to Impair the Morals and the Condition of the Working Class* (London: 1842).

Morrison, James. *The Influence of English Railway Legislation on Trade and Industry* (London: 1848).

Martineau, Harriet. *The Factory Controversy: A Warning Against Meddling Legislation* (Manchester: 1855).

—— *Poor Laws and Paupers Illustrated*, 2 vols (London: 1833-4).

Mill, John Stuart. *Principles of Political Economy*, 7th ed (London: 1871).

—— *On Liberty and Considerations on Representative Government*, ed R. B. McCallum (Oxford: 1948).

Nicholls, George, and Mackay, T. *History of the English Poor Law*, 3 vols (London: 1854 and 1899).

Oastler, Richard. *Brougham versus Brougham on the New Poor Law with an Appendix Consisting of a Letter to Lord John Russell* (London: 1847).

—— *The Factory Question: The Law or the Needle* (London: 1836).

Parker, Henry Slater. *Letters to the Right Hon. Sir James Graham, Bart., on the Subject of Recent Proceedings Connected with the Andover Union* (London: 1845).

Richardson, Benjamin Ward. *The Health of Towns: A Review of the Works of Edwin Chadwick*, 2 vols (London: 1887).

Roberts, Samuel. *England's Glory; or, The Good Old Poor Laws, Addressed to the Working Classes of Sheffield* (London: 1836).
—— *Lessons for Statesmen with Anecdotes Respecting Them Calculated to Preserve the Aristocracy from Destruction and the Country from Ruin* (London: 1846).
Russell, John Earl. *An Essay on the History of the English Government and Constitution* (London: 1865).
Sadler, Michael Thomas. *Protest Against the Secret Proceeding of the Factory Commission in Leeds* (Leeds: 1833).
[Sclater, William Lutley]. *A Letter to the Poor Law Commissioners for England and Wales on the Working of the New System by the Chairman of a Board of Guardians* (Basingstoke: 1836).
Scrope, George Poulett. *Political Economy versus the Handloom Weavers* (Bradford: 1835).
—— *Principles of Political Economy, deduced from the Natural Laws of Social Welfare, Applied to the Present State of Britain* (London: 1833).
[Senior, Nassau William]. *Outline of the Poor Law Amendment Act* (1834).
—— *Remarks on the Opposition to the Poor Law Amendment Bill, by a Guardian* (London: 1841).
Shaen, Samuel, jun. *A Review of Railways and Railway Legislation at Home and Abroad* (London: 1847).
Shaftesbury, Earl of. *Speeches upon Subjects Having Relation Chiefly to the Claims and Interests of the Labouring Class* (London: 1868).
Simon, Sir John. *English Sanitary Institutions, Reviewed in the Course of their Development, and in Some of their Political and Social Relations* (London: 1897).
—— *Public Health Reports*, 2 vols (London: 1887).
Smiles, Samuel. *Railway Property: its Condition and Prospect* (1849).
Smith, Joshua Toulmin. *Centralization or Representation? A Letter to the Metropolitan Sanatory Commissioners* (London: 1848).
—— *Government by Commissions Illegal and Pernicious, The Nature and Effects of All Commissions of Inquiry and Other*

P

Crown Appointed Commissions, The Constitutional Principles of Taxation; and the Rights, Duties, and Importance of Local Self-Government (London: 1849).

—— *The Laws of England Relating to Public Health; Including an Epitome of the Law of Nuisances etc.* (London: 1848).

—— *Local Self-Government and Centralization: the Characteristics of Each; and its Practical Tendencies as Affecting Social, Moral, and Political Welfare and Progress, Including Comprehensive Outlines of the English Constitution* (London: 1851).

[Stephen, George]. *A Letter to the Rt. Hon. Lord Russell . . . on the Probable Increase of Rural Crime, in Consequence of the Introduction of the New Poor Law and the Railroad Systems* (1836).

Torrens, Robert. *A Letter to Lord Ashley on the Principles which Regulate Wages* (London: 1844).

Whitmore, William Wolryche. *Letter to Lord John Russell, on Railways* (1847).

Willoughby, Sir Henry, Bart. *A Few Remarks on the Poor Law Commission and on the Necessity of Providing an Adequate Protection for the Poor* (London: 1847).

MEMOIRS, BIOGRAPHY AND MISCELLANEOUS LETTERS

Hodder, Edwin. *The Life and Work of the Seventh Earl of Shaftesbury, K. G.,* 3 vols (London: 1887).

Holyoake, George Jacob. *Life of Joseph Rayner Stephens; Preacher and Political Orator* (London: nd).

Jennings, Louis J. *The Correspondence and Diaries of the Late Right Honourable John Wilson Croker, LL.D., F.R.S.,* 3 vols (London: 1885).

Leader, Robert Eadon. *Life and Letters of John Arthur Roebuck* (New York: 1897).

Leech, H. J., ed. *The Public Letters of the Rt. Hon. John Bright* (London: 1895).

LeMarchant, Sir Denis, Bart. *Memoir of John Charles Viscount Althorp, Third Earl Spencer* (London: 1876).

Lewis, George Cornwall. *Letters of George Cornwall Lewis* (London: 1870).

Martineau, Harriet. *Autobiography,* 2 vols (Boston: 1879).

Maxwell, Sir Herbert, ed. *The Creevey Papers: A Selection from the Correspondence and Diaries of the Late Thomas Creevey M.P.* (London: 1912).
—— *Life and Letters of George William Frederick, Fourth Earl of Clarendon* (London: 1913).
Maxwell, William Hamilton. *Memoirs of the Right Honourable Sir Robert Peel, Bart.*, 2 vols (London: 1842).
Mill, John Stuart. *Autobiography* (Garden City, New York, nd).
—— *Letters*, ed Hugh S. R. Eliot (London: 1910).
—— *Earlier Letters of John Stuart Mill, 1812-1848*, 2 vols, ed [Francis E. Mineka] (Toronto: 1963).
Morley, John. *The Life of Richard Cobden*, 2 vols (London: 1881).
—— *The Life of William Ewart Gladstone*, 3 vols (London: 1903).
Parker, Charles Stuart. *Life and Letters of Sir James Graham, Second Baronet of Netherby, P. C., G. C. B., 1792-1861*, 2 vols (London: 1907).
—— ed. *Sir Robert Peel, From his Private Papers*, 3 vols (London: 1899).
Simon, Sir John. *Personal Recollections* (London: 1894).
Strachey, Lytton and Roger Fulford, eds. *The Greville Memoirs, 1814-1860*, 8 vols (London: 1938).
Trevelyan, George Otto. *The Life and Letters of Lord Macaulay*, 2 vols (New York: 1875).

NEWSPAPERS AND PERIODICALS
The Times
Blackwood's Magazine
Cobbett's Political Register
The Economist
Edinburgh Review
Fraser's Magazine
The Lancet, A Journal of British and Foreign Medical and Chemical Science, Criticism and News
Oastler, Richard. *The Fleet Papers.*
Quarterly Review
Ten Hours Advocate and Journal of Literature and Art
Westminster Review

CRITICAL WORKS

BOOKS

Ausubel, Herman. *John Bright, Victorian Reformer* (London: 1966).

Bagehot, Walter. *The English Constitution* (London: 1867).

Best, G. F. A. *Shaftesbury* (New York: 1964).

Blaug, Mark. *Ricardian Economics: A Historical Study* (New Haven: 1958).

Bowley, Marian. *Nassau Senior and Classical Economics* (London: 1937).

Briggs, Asa. *The Making of Modern England, 1783–1867: The Age of Improvement* (New York: 1965).

—— *Victorian Cities* (London: 1963).

Burn, W. L. *The Age of Equipoise* (London: 1964).

Clark, G. S. R. Kitson. *The Making of Victorian England* (Cambridge, Mass: 1962).

Cleveland-Stevens, E. *English Railways: Their Development and their Relationship to the State* (London: 1915).

Driver, Cecil. *Tory Radical: The Life of Richard Oastler* (Oxford: 1946).

Erickson, Arvel B. *The Public Career of Sir James Graham* (Oxford: 1952).

Finer, Samuel E. *The Life and Times of Sir Edwin Chadwick* (London: 1952).

Gash, Norman. *Reaction and Reconstruction in English Politics, 1832–1852* (Oxford: 1965).

Grampp, William. *The Manchester School of Economics* (Stanford: 1960).

Lambert, Richard S. *The Railway King, 1800–1871: A Study of George Hudson and the Business Morals of His Time* (London: 1934).

Lambert, Royston. *Sir John Simon and English Social Administration* (London: 1963).

Lewis, R. A. *Edwin Chadwick and the Public Health Movement* (London: 1952).

MacDonagh, O. O. G. M. *A Pattern of Government Growth, 1800–1860: The Passenger Acts and their Enforcement* (London: 1961).

Parris, Henry. *Government and the Railways in 19th Century Britain* (London: 1965).

Prouty, R. *The Transformation of the Board of Trade, 1830–1855* (London: 1957).

Robbins, Lionel. *Robert Torrens and the Evolution of Classical Economics* (London: 1958).

—— *The Theory of Economic Policy in English Classical Political Economy* (London: 1952).

Roberts, David. *The Victorian Origins of the British Welfare State* (New Haven: 1960).

Samuels, Warren J. *The Classical Theory of Economic Policy* (New York: 1966).

Schweinitz, Karl de. *England's Road to Social Security* (New York: 1961).

Thomas, M. W. *Early Factory Legislation* (London: 1948).

Trevelyan, George Macaulay. *The Life of John Bright* (Boston and New York: 1925).

Wallas, Graham. *The Life of Francis Place, 1771–1854* (New York: 1919).

Ward, John Trevor. *The Factory Movement* (London: 1962).

—— *Sir James Graham* (London: 1967).

Webb, R. K. *Harriet Martineau, A Victorian Radical* (London: 1960).

—— *The British Working Class Reader, 1790–1848: Literacy and Social Tension* (London: 1955).

Webb, Sydney and Beatrice. *English Poor Law History*, 3 vols (London: 1927–9).

—— *English Poor Law Policy* (London: 1910).

ARTICLES

Anderson, Olive. 'The Janus Face of Mid-Nineteenth Century Radicalism: The Administrative Reform Association of 1855', *Victorian Studies*, VIII, 3 (1965).

Aydelotte, William O. 'The Conservative and Radical Interpretations of Early Victorian Social Legislation', *Victorian Studies*, XI, 2 (1967).

—— 'The House of Commons in the 1840's', *History*, 137 (1954).

—— 'Nineteenth Century British Pamphlets', *Newberry Library Bulletin*, second series, II, 6 (1951).

—— 'Parties and Issues in Early Victorian England', *Journal of British Studies*, V, 2 (1966).

—— 'Voting Patterns in the House of Commons in the 1840's', *Comparative Studies in Society and History*, V, 2 (1963).

Bagwell, Philip S. 'The Railway Interest: Its Organization and Influence, 1839–1914', *The Journal of Transport History*, VII, 2 (1965).

Blaug, Mark. 'The Classical Economists and the Factory Acts: A Re-examination', *Quarterly Journal of Economics*, LXXII, 2 (1958).

—— 'The Myth of the Old Poor Law and the Making of the New', *Journal of Economic History*, XXIII, 2 (1963).

—— 'The Poor Law Re-examined', *Journal of Economic History*, XXIV, 2 (1964).

Brebner, J. Bartlet. 'Laissez-faire and State Intervention in Nineteenth Century Britain', *The Making of English History*, ed Schuyler and Ausubel (New York: 1952).

Briggs, Asa. 'Cholera and Society in the Nineteenth Century', *European Political History, 1815–1870: Aspects of Liberalism*, ed Eugene C. Black (New York, 1967).

Cromwell, Valerie. 'Interpretations of Nineteenth Century Administration: An Analysis', *Victorian Studies*, IX, 3 (1966).

Gutchen, Robert M. 'Local Government and Centralization in Nineteenth Century England', *Historical Journal*, IV, 1 (1961).

Hart, Jenifer. 'Nineteenth Century Social Reform: A Tory Interpretation of History', *Past and Present*, 31 (1965).

Hume, L. J. 'Jeremy Bentham and the Nineteenth-Century Revolution in Government', *Historical Journal*, X, 4 (1967).

Kittrell, Edward. ' "Laissez-faire" in English Classical Economics', *Journal of the History of Ideas*, XXVII, 4 (1966).

MacDonagh, O. O. G. M. 'Coal Mines Regulation: The First Decade, 1842–1852', *Ideas and Institutions of Victorian Britain*, ed Robert Robson (London: 1967).

—— 'The Nineteenth Century Revolution in Government: A Reappraisal', *Historical Journal*, I, 1 (1958).

Parris, Henry. 'The Nineteenth Century Revolution in Government: A Reappraisal Reappraised', *Historical Journal*, III, 1 (1960).

—— 'Railway Policy in Peel's Administration', *Bulletin of the Institute of Historical Research*, XXXIII (1960).

Roberts, David. 'How Cruel was the Victorian Poor Law?', *Historical Journal*, VI (1963).

—— 'Jeremy Bentham and the Victorian Administrative State', *Victorian Studies*, II, 3 (1959).

—— 'Tory Paternalism and Social Reform in Early Victorian England', *American Historical Review*, LXIII, 2 (1958).

Thomas, M. W. 'The Origins of Administrative Centralization', *Current Legal Problems*, ed G. W. Keeton and G. Schwartzenberger, III (1950).

WORKS OF REFERENCE

Boase, Frederic. *Modern English Biography* (London: 1965).

Dictionary of National Biography.

Dod, Charles. *The Parliamentary Pocket Companion* (London: 1833, 1839, 1844, 1847).

Hart, W. O. *Hart's Introduction to the Law of Local Government and Administration*, 7th ed (London: 1962).

Williams, Judith Blow. *A Guide to the Printed Materials for English Social and Economic History, 1750–1850*, 2 vols (New York: 1926).

Index